THE DYNAMIC HORSE

A BIOMECHANICAL GUIDE TO EQUINE MOVEMENT AND PERFORMANCE

Hilary M. Clayton, BVMS, PhD, MRCVS

Mary Anne McPhail Dressage Chair in Equine Sports Medicine
Department of Large Animal Clinical Sciences
College of Veterinary Medicine
Michigan State University
East Lansing, MI 48824-1314

Sport Horse Publications

3145 Sandhill Road
Mason, MI 48854-1925
Phone/fax: (517) 333-3833

Book Design: **Hilary M. Clayton**

Illustrations: **Susan E. Harris**

Graphics: **Joel L. Lanovaz and David R. Mullineaux**

Cover Photograph: **Roberta Wells**

Cover Design: **Sharp Des!gns, Inc., Lansing, Michigan**

ISBN: 097476700X

LCCN: 2003099081

© **Sport Horse Publications 2004**

Attention corporations, universities, colleges, and professional organizations: Quantity discounts are available on bulk purchases of this book for educational or gift purposes. Special books or excerpts can be created to fit specific needs. For information, please contact Sport Horse Publications, 3145 Sandhill Road, Mason, MI 48854-1925. Phone/fax: (517) 333-3833.

DEDICATION

To Flora E. F. Lindsay, colleague, mentor, and friend in the early years of my career in academia, who encouraged me to pursue my interest in equine locomotion and biomechanics.

ABOUT THE AUTHOR

Dr. Hilary M. Clayton has trained horses of many breeds in various sporting disciplines. Her interest in equestrian sports led her to study veterinary medicine and to pursue a career in academia. Her research is directed toward understanding the mechanics of equine performance and lameness. She is the first incumbent of the Mary Anne McPhail Dressage Chair in Equine Sports Medicine at Michigan State University.

Dr. Clayton has a talent for making a complex subject understandable, without diluting the scientific content. *The Dynamic Horse* is written with characteristic clarity and will be an excellent companion for her popular text *Conditioning Sport Horses*.

Other books by Hilary M. Clayton:

Conditioning Sport Horses

Hilary M. Clayton, Sport Horse Publications, Mason, MI

Colour Atlas of Large Animal Clinical Anatomy

Hilary M. Clayton & Peter F. Flood, Mosby-Wolfe, London

Equine Locomotion

Willem Back and Hilary Clayton, WB Saunders, London

Clinical Anatomy of the Horse

Hilary M. Clayton, Peter F. Flood and Diana S. Rosenstein, Mosby, London

Activate Your Horse's Core

Narelle C. Stubbs & Hilary M. Clayton, Sport Horse Publications, Mason, MI

CONTENTS

PREFACE

Biomechanical principles can be applied in understanding many aspects of equine movement and performance. This book describes the laws and principles of biomechanics, and illustrates their effects using examples that will be familiar to those who are accustomed to working around horses.

Biomechanics describes and measures mechanical events in living bodies. It involves elements of the biological and physical sciences. Indeed, the word biomechanics is derived from Latin words that reflect this duality: *bio* refers to the biological aspect, while *mechanics* refers to the physical aspect. In this book, the focus is on biological principles and practical applications, rather than physics and mathematics. Some formulae and calculations are included, but these can be skipped over by the mathematically-challenged without detracting from the content.

Biomechanical analysis offers a useful perspective on equine anatomy, physiology, and locomotion. It takes some time and effort to become familiar with the concepts and to learn to assess the horse in mechanical terms, but the new insights and understanding are well worth the effort. Movement is an essential part of the horse's lifestyle and is an important component of all equestrian sports. Movement results from internal and external forces acting on the horse's body. Biomechanics encompasses the study of movements and the forces responsible for the movements. Biomechanical analysis measures the qualities that are observed by a judge or trainer. It is the ability to measure or quantify movement that distinguishes scientific studies from simple observations.

As the reader progresses through this book, the terminology of equine biomechanics will be explained. A glossary is included at the front of the book for easy reference. The appendices provide additional information: Appendix A describes the International System of units in which biomechanical variables are measured and Appendix B lists the abbreviations for biomechanical terms that are used throughout the book. For the more mathematically inclined, vector calculations are described in Appendix C.

GLOSSARY

Abduction: Movement of a body part away from the midsagittal plane.

Acceleration: The rate of change of velocity, a vector quantity.

Angular Acceleration: Rate at which angular velocity changes.

Linear Acceleration: Rate at which linear velocity changes.

Adduction: Movement of a body part toward the midsagittal plane.

Advanced placement: Time elapsing between footfalls of a pair of limbs.

Advanced completion: Time elapsing between lift-offs of a pair of limbs.

Aerial phase: Period of time during which none of the limbs is in contact with the ground. Also called suspension.

Aerial time: Time during which a projectile is airborne. Sum of ascent time and descent time.

Angular displacement: Amount of rotation in a specified direction, a vector quantity.

Angular distance: Length of the angular path through which a body rotates, regardless of the direction of rotation, a scalar quantity.

Angular speed: Rate of rotation determined as angular distance divided by time, a scalar quantity.

Angular velocity: Rate of rotation determined as angular displacement divided by time, a vector quantity.

Base of support: Area circumscribed by a body's contacts with the ground.

Biomechanics: Scientific study of living systems using physical principles.

Body: A distinct mass, animate or inanimate.

Breakover: Terminal part of stance phase during which the heels of the hoof rotate around the toe, which is still in contact with the ground.

Center of mass: Point through which the weight of a body acts.

Centrifugal: Directed away from the center.

Centripetal: Directed toward the center.

Components: Elements into which a vector quantity can be resolved.

Couple: Two equal, opposite, and parallel forces acting concurrently that tend to cause rotation of a body without translation.

Couplet: Footfalls of a pair of limbs that are separated by a short time interval.

Cursorial: Adapted for running.

Data: Numbers generated by making measurements.

Diagonal dissociation at contact: Time elapsing between footfalls of a diagonal pair of limbs. Also called diagonal advanced placement.

Diagonal dissociation at lift-off: Time elapsing between lift-offs of a diagonal pair of limbs. Also called diagonal advanced completion.

Displacement: Length of a straight line joining the initial and final positions of a body, and taking account of the direction the line takes, a vector quantity.

Distal: Away from the center of the body; the opposite of proximal.

Distance: Length of the path followed by a body in any direction, a scalar quantity.

Duration: time elapsing between two events.

> *Stance Duration*: Time between ground contact and lift off.
>
> *Swing Duration*: Time between lift-off and the next ground contact.
>
> *Step Duration*: Time between successive footfalls of the front limbs or the hind limbs.
>
> *Stride Duration*: Period of time occupied by a complete stride.

Dynamics: Branch of kinetics that studies bodies in motion. Relates forces with motion.

Elasticity: Ability of a body or material to resist deformation and to restore the original shape and size after it has been deformed.

Energetics: Describes work done during locomotion.

Energy: The capacity for doing work.

> *Kinetic energy*: Energy due to movement.
>
>> *Rotational kinetic energy*: Kinetic energy associated with rotation of a body around its center of mass.
>>
>> *Translational kinetic energy*: Kinetic energy associated with movement of the center of mass of a body.
>
> *Mechanical energy*: Sum of kinetic energy and potential energy of a body.
>
> *Potential energy*: Energy stored in the system in latent form.
>
>> *Elastic potential energy*: Potential energy due to deformation. Also known as strain energy.
>>
>> *Gravitational potential energy*: Potential energy due to location in a gravitational field.

Equilibrium: State that exists when all parts of a body are at rest or moving with the same constant velocity.

> *Dynamic equilibrium*: State of equilibrium in which all parts of the body are moving with the same constant velocity.
>
> *Stable equilibrium*: Equilibrium position from which a small displacement generates forces that tend to return the system to its original position.
>
> *Static equilibrium*: State of equilibrium in which the body is at rest.
>
> *Unstable equilibrium*: Equilibrium position from which a small displacement generates forces that tend to move the system away from its original position.
>
> *Neutral equilibrium*: Equilibrium position from which a small displacement does not cause forces acting either toward or away from the original position.

Footfall diagram: Diagram showing sequence of footfalls in a gait.

Footfall sequence: Order of footfalls in a gait.

Footfall timing diagram: Diagram showing sequence and timing of footfalls in a gait.

Force: A measure of the action of one body on another that tends to change a body's state of rest or uniform motion in a straight line. A vector quantity defined by its magnitude, direction, and point of application.

Centrifugal force: Outward force created by a body moving along a curved path.

Centripetal force: Inwardly directed force acting toward the center of rotation that prevents a body that is moving on a curved path from flying off at a tangent.

Eccentric force: Force exerted on a body that does not pass through its center of mass. Tends to cause translation and rotation of the body.

External force: Force acting between a body and the environment.

Internal force: Force acting between body parts.

Force platform: Device for measuring ground reaction forces.

Free body diagram: Diagram of a body completely free of its environment, with all the forces acting on it shown as vectors.

Friction: Force that opposes movement of one body over the surface of another body. Tangential component of a contact force between two bodies.

Limiting friction: Force that opposes initiation of movement of one body over another.

Rolling friction: Force that opposes the rolling of one body over the surface of another body.

Sliding friction: Force that opposes sliding movement of one body over the surface of another body.

Fulcrum: Axis about which a lever turns.

Gait: Characteristic limb coordination pattern recognized by the sequence and timing of the footfalls and other kinematic characteristics.

Asymmetrical gait: Gait in which movements of the front limb pair and/or the hind limb pair are not symmetrical on the left and right sides.

Leaping gait: Gait that has one or more aerial phases in each stride. Also known as a running gait.

Stepping gait: Gait in which there is always at least one limb in contact with the ground throughout the stride. There is no aerial phase. Also known as a walking gait.

Symmetrical gait: Gait in which movements of the front limb pair and the hind limb pair show left-right symmetry.

Gait analysis: Study of gaits and movements.

Gait diagram: Diagrammatic representation of the temporal relationships between the limbs in a gait.

General motion: Movement involving a combination of translation and rotation.

Gravity: Force that attracts bodies toward the center of the earth. For practical purposes the value of the gravitational force is 9.81 N.

Ground reaction force: External force exerted by the ground against the hoof.

> *Longitudinal force*: Component of ground reaction force acting horizontally along the longitudinal axis of the horse's body.
>
>> *Braking force*: Longitudinal force acting opposite to the direction of progression.
>>
>> *Propulsive force*: Longitudinal force acting in the direction of progression.
>
> *Normal reaction force*: Ground reaction force component acting perpendicular to the surface.
>
> *Transverse force*: Ground reaction force component acting horizontally across the horse's body.
>
> *Vertical force*: Ground reaction force component acting vertically.

Impact: Collision of two bodies during a very short interval of time.

Impact phase: Early part of stance phase, immediately after a hoof contacts the ground, during which the hoof is rapidly decelerated.

Impulse: Sum of the forces acting over a period of time.

Inertia: Reluctance of a body to change its state of rest or motion.

Kinematics: Branch of biomechanics describing the motion of bodies.

Kinesiology: Science of movement.

Kinetics: Branch of biomechanics describing the forces involved in creating and changing motion.

Lateral: Away from or further from the midsagittal plane. Opposite of medial.

Lateral dissociation at contact: Time elapsing between placement of a lateral pair of limbs. Also called lateral advanced placement.

Lateral dissociation at lift-off: Time elapsing between lift-offs of a lateral pair of limbs. Also called lateral advanced completion.

Length: Distance between two points.

> *Diagonal length*: Separation of diagonal pair of hooves during stance phase.

> *Lateral length*: Separation of lateral pair of hooves during stance phase.

> *Step length*: Distance between successive footfalls of the left and right hind limbs or the left and right front limbs.

> *Stride length*: Displacement of center of mass during a complete stride.

> *Tracking length*: Displacement in the direction of motion between a front hoof print and the succeeding hoof print of the lateral hind limb.

Lever: A rigid body rotating around a fulcrum that increases the effect produced when a force is exerted on a body.

> *First-class lever*: A lever that has the fulcrum positioned between the force and the resistance.

> *Second-class lever*: Lever in which the resistance is located between the force and the fulcrum.

> *Third-class lever*: Lever in which the force acts between the resistance and the fulcrum.

Ligament: Fibrous band of connective tissue connecting bone to bone.

Limb-support sequence: Sequence of limb combinations that support the body during a stride.

Line of gravity: Vertical line projected through the center of mass.

Locomotion: Act of moving from place to place.

Mass: Quantity of matter of which a body is composed. Resists change in velocity and creates gravitational attraction between bodies.

Mechanical energy: Capacity to do work or the amount of work a body contains at an instant in time.

Medial: Toward or closer to the midsagittal (medial) plane, opposite of lateral.

Midstance: Time in stance phase when cannon segment is vertical.

Moment or moment of force: Turning effect produced by a couple. Also called torque.

Moment arm: Perpendicular distance from the center of rotation to the line of action of a force.

Moment of inertia: Resistance of a body to angular motion. Depends on the mass of the body and the distribution of the mass relative to the axis of rotation.

Momentum: Quantity of motion possessed by a body. Product of mass and velocity.

Angular momentum: Quantity of rotational motion possessed by a body. Calculated as the product of moment of inertia and angular velocity.

Muscular action: Production of force by a muscle.

Concentric muscular action: Muscular action in which the muscle shortens as it generates tension.

Eccentric muscular action: Muscular action in which the muscle lengthens as it generates tension.

Isometric muscular action: Muscular action in which muscle length is unchanged as tension is generated.

Plane: Anatomically-based division of the body.

Dorsal plane: Divides the body into dorsal and ventral parts. Runs perpendicular to the median and transverse planes.

Median plane: Divides the head, body or limb longitudinally into equal right and left halves.

Sagittal plane: Passes through the head, body or limb parallel to the median plane.

Transverse plane: Cuts across the head, body or limb perpendicular to its long axis.

Power: Rate of working.

Pressure: Force per unit area.

Proximal: Toward the center of the body; the opposite of distal.

Radial: Acting perpendicular to a line or surface.

Rhythm: Timing of the footfalls during a stride.

Rotation: Type of motion in which the body follows a circular path with all parts of the body traveling through the same angle, in the same direction, in the same time.

Scalar: Quantity that is defined by its magnitude only – it has no direction.

Speed: Rate of movement determined as the distance covered divided by the time taken, a scalar quantity.

Stance phase: Part of the stride when the hoof is in contact with the ground.

Statics: Study of bodies in equilibrium.

Strain: Deformation expressed as a fraction of the original dimensions.

Stress: Load per unit of cross-sectional area.

Stride: Complete cycle of limb movements during a gait.

Stride rate: Rate of repetition of the strides. Also known as tempo.

Support diagram: Diagram showing the sequence of supporting limbs during the stride.

Suspension: Period when none of the limbs is in contact with the ground. Also called aerial phase.

Swing phase: Part of the stride when the hoof has no contact with the ground.

System: Unit of study in biomechanics.

Tangential: Acting along a line or surface.

Tempo: Rate of repetition of the strides.

Temporal kinematics: Measurements that describe the timing and coordination of movements.

Tendon: Fibrous band connecting muscle to bone.

Torque: Turning effect produced by a couple. Also called moment of force.

Trajectory: Path of a projectile.

Translation: Type of motion in which all parts of the body travel the same distance, in the same direction, in the same time. Also known as linear motion.

Vector: Quantity defined by its magnitude and direction.

Velocity: Rate of movement determined as the displacement divided by the time taken, a vector quantity.

Weight: Force exerted on a body due to gravity.

Work: Work is done when a force moves a body. Time must elapse and movement must occur for work to be done.

> *Negative work*: Work done by a force directed opposite to the direction of displacement. A muscle does negative work when it acts eccentrically to resist elongation.

> *Positive work*: Work done by a force directed toward the direction of displacement. A muscle does positive work when it acts concentrically.

INTRODUCTION

The Language of Biomechanics

*Biomechanics is the study of the structure and function of
biological systems using the methods of mechanics.*

In its broadest sense, biomechanics encompasses a wide spectrum of biological
activities as diverse as the mechanics of blood flow through the circulatory
system, the physical properties of the skin, and the behavior of bone in
response to loading during locomotion. This book describes the principles
underlying the science of biomechanics, then illustrates how these principles
apply to horsemanship and equine locomotion. Through knowledge of
biomechanics, the reader will develop a better understanding of how horses
move and perform.

An important aspect of any scientific discipline is to establish a terminology
that is clear and unambiguous. Definitions of biomechanical terms are given
in the glossary. Some of the general terms used in this book and their meanings
are as follows:

Kinesiology is the science of movement.

Kinematics describes motion without considering the forces that cause motion
to occur.

Kinetics describes the forces responsible for producing motion.

Statics is the study of bodies in equilibrium.

Dynamics is the study of bodies in motion.

Energetics explores the work done during locomotion. It links biomechanics
with physiology.

Gait analysis studies all aspects (kinematics, kinetics, statics, dynamics, and
energetics) of gaits and movements.

Observations and Measurements

A system of measurement is required to describe the movements and forces that are of interest. When we watch a horse, our observations about the movement patterns are subjective in nature. With practice, our powers of observation improve, but even the most astute observer's eye has limited accuracy. Scientific analysis makes precise, numerical measurements that describe the event of interest quantitatively.

Example: Observation of a horse gives an impression of the size of the horse, from which its height and weight can be estimated. If a measuring stick and a weighing scale are available, the horse's height and weight can be measured more accurately. The visual estimates are subjective or qualitative, the readings on the measuring stick and weighing scale are objective or quantitative.

Measurements are made relative to a standard that is used to define the units of measure. It is convenient to measure the height of a horse relative to a 1 meter standard. If a horse is 1.5 meters tall, we know that the horse's height (the quantity measured) is 50 per cent greater (the relationship) than 1 meter (the standard unit of measurement). The measurement process depends on having a consistent standard.

In the Middle Ages, the English system of measurement was developed, based on biological standards that were not consistent. Force measurements were based on pounds, with one pound being the weight of 7,000 grains of wheat. Since the grains of wheat were plumper in rainy years than in times of drought, the standard changed from year to year. Distance measurements included the cubit (distance from the elbow to the fingertips – about 1.5 feet), the yard (typical stride length of a person), and the foot. The standard distance of a foot was based on the length of the king's foot. Each time a new king ascended the throne, his foot size was measured, and the lengths of all the objects in the kingdom were redetermined. Horses were measured in hands, with a hand being the spread of the hand from the tip of the little finger to the tip of the thumb.

Eventually the English units were standardized and, as a result, the measurements became consistent. However, the origin of the system in biological measurements resulted in there being no common denominator in the units: There are twelve inches in a foot, three feet in a yard, and 1,760 yards in a mile. This problem was overcome by the metric system, which is now used in all scientific studies and has been adopted for general usage by most countries (a notable exception being the United States).

Scientific measurements are now standardized by the International System of Units or SI system. It is a metric system, in which measurements are based on constant geophysical values. For example, the unit of length is the meter, which is 1/10,000,000 of the distance on the earth's surface from the equator to the North or South Pole.

The units of measurement for distance, force, and volume are based on multiples of ten, which are indicated by prefixes:

Milli: 1/1,000	Deca = 10	Mega = 1,000,000
Centi: 1/100	Hecto = 100	Giga = 1,000,000,000
Deci = 1/10	Kilo = 1,000	

The SI units have standard abbreviations, such as 'km' for kilometer (a unit of distance), 'N' for newton (a unit of force), or 'J' for joule (a unit of work or energy). The names and abbreviations of the SI units used in biomechanics are listed in Appendix A, and the symbols used to represent biomechanical terms are shown in Appendix B at the end of the book.

The SI system is used throughout this book. However, in some equestrian sports, it is customary to use other units. Where appropriate, these more familiar units are also given for comparison. For example, the SI units for distance are kilometers, meters, centimeters, and millimeters, but in horse racing parlance, distances are usually measured in miles and furlongs.

Data

Data (singular datum) are the numbers that result from making measurements. Data must be measured with precision and consistency using a suitable technique. The first requirement in selecting an appropriate measuring technique is validity, which means that the test should be appropriate for measuring what it is designed to measure. Another requirement is reliability, which describes the consistency of the data and tells us whether the data are repeatable over time under identical conditions. If a test is unreliable, the data vary from test to test or from day to day, even though the quantity being measured has not changed. Objectivity means that the data are collected without bias by the investigator. This is particularly important when the investigator has a certain expectation or preconceived idea about the outcome. To overcome this bias, research studies are sometimes designed so that the investigator is 'blinded' to the condition being studied. A 'double blind' study is one in which neither the investigator nor the subject is aware of which condition or treatment is being studied at a particular time.

After data have been collected, they are organized by a process called statistics. This is a mathematical technique that organizes, analyzes, and presents the information for interpretation and evaluation. Interpretation is the final stage of a research study. It is a philosophical process based on the knowledge and experience of the researcher.

Scalars and Vectors

Measurements made during biomechanical analysis are classified into two types: scalars and vectors. A scalar quantity is one that is completely described in terms of its size or magnitude. For example, mass is a scalar quantity; a horse has the same mass in different locations on the surface of the earth, regardless of whether the horse is standing up, lying down, or jumping a fence. Other examples of scalar quantities include distance and speed. Scalar quantities do not act in a specific direction, and they are easily added or subtracted by summation of their magnitudes.

Example: A horse with a mass of 500 kg, is ridden by a rider with a mass of 50 kg, using tack with mass 10 kg. The total mass of horse, rider, and tack is:

$500 + 50 + 10 = 560$ kg.

A vector quantity is characterized not only by its magnitude, but also by the direction in which it acts. Force is an example of a vector quantity; the effect of a compressive (pushing) force is quite different from the effect of a tensile (pulling) force, even though the two forces have the same magnitude. To predict the effect of a force of a certain magnitude, we need to know its direction and the location at which it acts. Other vector quantities include displacement, velocity, and acceleration.

The effect of vectors can be depicted by a vector diagram in which each vector is represented by an arrow. A convenient scale is chosen, with the length of the arrow representing the magnitude of the vector. The arrow points in the direction in which the vector acts. Summation or resolution of vectors can be accomplished graphically or mathematically (Appendix C).

Types of Movement

Locomotion is the act of moving from one location to another. Movement of the entire horse involves independent motion of many body parts, primarily the limbs, but also the trunk, head, and neck. At any moment, different parts of the horse's body may be moving at different speeds and in different directions. The term *translation* describes movement that occurs in a straight line, whereas *rotation* involves angular (turning) motion. Every movement a horse performs, from flicking an ear to jumping a fence, can be categorized as translational motion, rotational motion or, more commonly, some combination of both.

Translation

Translation occurs when all parts of the body travel the same distance, in the same direction, in the same time.

Translation is also known as linear motion. Translational movement implies that all the body parts retain the same relationship to each other over a period of time. If one part of the body moves relative to another, it does not fulfill the conditions for translational motion. For example, when a horse flicks an ear, the ear moves independently of the rest of the body, so the movement is not translational. During equine locomotion, it is difficult to find examples of purely translational motion except for very brief periods of time.

Example: A horse standing motionless in a trailer as it is transported along the freeway (figure 1.1) undergoes translational motion in that all parts of the horse's body are moving in the same direction at the same speed. The trailer, however, does not show translational motion, because the wheels are rotating relative to the body of the trailer, which means that different parts of the trailer are moving at different speeds and in different directions.

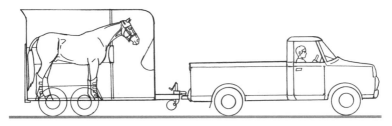

Figure 1.1: A horse traveling along the freeway in a trailer undergoes translational motion.

One way of establishing whether a body is undergoing translation is to examine a series of pictures and to draw straight lines connecting the same anatomical points in sequential pictures. If the movement is translational, the connecting lines are equal in length and parallel to each other.

The use of connecting lines to determine whether motion is translational is not infallible. In figure 1.2, for example, if the first and last diagrams are compared, the horse appears to be undergoing translational motion. The intervening diagram, however, clearly shows that motion is not translational, since the limbs are rotating relative to the trunk.

Rotation

> *Rotation occurs when the body follows a circular path with all parts of the body traveling through the same angle, in the same direction, in the same time.*

A wheel spinning around a stationary axle undergoes rotation. All parts of the rim and spokes move through the same angle, in the same direction, during

Figure 1.2: Sequential diagrams of a galloping horse. Lines connecting the toe of the right hind hoof and the toe of the right front hoof in the left and right diagrams are equal in length and parallel, but they do not pass through the same points on the intermediate diagram, indicating that the motion is not translational.

the same period of time (figure 1.3). Although a point on the rim moves further than a point on the axle, they rotate through equal angles as the wheel spins.

A freely moveable body rotates around its center of mass when an eccentric (off center) force is applied (chapter 8). The farther from the center of mass the force is applied, the faster the body will rotate. If a body is constrained to move around an axis or fulcrum, however, a force applied to any part of the body will cause rotation.

Example: A gate with hinges is constrained to rotate around its hinges (axis of rotation) regardless of where a force is applied to it. Depending on its direction, a force swings the gate open or closed, but it cannot cause translation.

Example: When a jumping horse is airborne over a fence, its body rotates forward around the center of mass. This rotation allows the horse to take off from the hind limbs and land on the front limbs. If the horse hits a solid fence with its chest, the point of contact between the horse's chest and the top of the fence acts as a fulcrum; the horse's body continues to rotate as it somersaults forward around this fulcrum.

Descriptions of equine motion may refer to the entire body of the horse, or they may describe the movements of individual body segments, such as the head, neck, trunk, and limbs. The limb segments, which are shown in figure 1.4, rotate relative to each other around axes located at the joints, which are

Figure 1.3: A wheel spinning on its axle undergoes rotational motion.

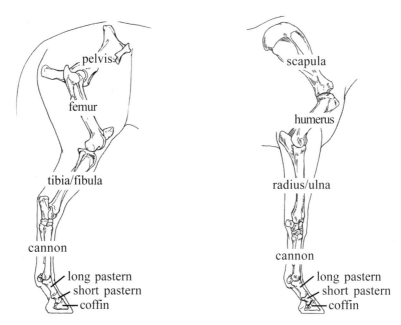

Figure 1.4: Bones forming the main segments of hind limb (left) and front limb (right).

named in figure 1.5. By convention, a limb segment is described as rotating around the joint above it. The movements are usually expressed in terms of the motion of the distal (lower) segment relative to the proximal (upper) segment.

Example: Movements of the stifle joint are described in terms of rotation of the tibia, which is the bone below the stifle, relative to the position of the femur, which is the bone above the stifle.

Angular motions of the joints are described in three directions: flexion/extension, abduction/adduction, and internal/external rotation. Flexion and extension are seen when the horse is viewed from the side. Each joint has a flexor surface and an extensor surface, which are determined by anatomical convention as shown in figure 1.5. Flexion involves a decrease in the angle on the flexor side, extension involves an increase in the angle on the flexor side, which can also be expressed as a decrease in the angle on the extensor side.

Changes in the angle on the outside (lateral aspect) or inside (medial aspect) of a joint, as seen when the limbs are viewed from in front or behind. The movements are described by the terms abduction and adduction. Abduction is a decrease in the angle between the segments on the lateral (outer) aspect of the limb. Adduction is a decrease in the angle between the segments on the medial (inner) aspect of the limbs. Most of the joints in the horses' limbs, except the shoulder and hip, show only small amounts of adduction or abduction.

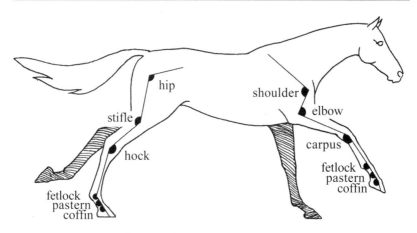

Figure 1.5: Joints of the hind and front limbs. Each joint is labeled and marked by an arc on its flexor side.

When the limb is viewed along its long axis (from above or below), rotations of the joints around that axis are described as internal and external rotation or circumduction of the distal segment. Internal rotation is also called pronation; external rotation is also called supination. The horses' limbs have evolved in a manner that allows only a small amount of pronation and supination. Other species have considerably more rotational motion, as shown, for example, by a cat supinating its front limb to lick its paw.

General Motion

Purely translational or purely rotational motion seldom occurs in horses, except for rather brief periods of time. Locomotion involves a combination of translation and rotation, which is known as general motion.

> *General motion involves a combination of translation and rotation.*

Example: As the wheels of a cart roll over the ground, each wheel rotates around its axle and, at the same time, the wheel as a whole is translated across the ground. Therefore, the wheel undergoes general motion.

We might consider equine locomotion to consist of translational movement of the horse's head, neck, and trunk, combined with rotational movements of the limbs. Even this is an oversimplification; the head and neck are rotating relative to the trunk, and the trunk shows some rotation during each stride. Furthermore, different segments of the limbs rotate at different speeds and in different directions, while the limb as a whole shows translational movement over the ground. Overall, the movements of the horse's body parts during locomotion are best described as complex general motion.

KINEMATICS

THE STUDY OF MOVEMENT

TEMPORAL KINEMATICS

CHAPTER 2

Abbreviations used in this chapter:

LH: Left hind limb

RH: Right hind limb

LF: Left front limb

RF: Right front limb

Temporal kinematics describe the timing and coordination of limb movements. Time is a scalar quantity, which implies that it has magnitude but does not act in any particular direction. The SI units of measurement are hours (h), minutes (min), seconds (s), and milliseconds (ms).

When a horse moves at a constant speed, temporal measurements are quite consistent from stride to stride. Greater variations are found between different horses than between consecutive strides of the same horse. Many research studies involve comparisons between different horses under similar circumstances or sequential evaluations of the same horse at different times or under different conditions. Since speed affects the temporal measurements, it is important to control and measure the horse's speed.

$$\text{Speed} = \frac{\text{Distance}}{\text{Time}}$$

This chapter describes measurement of time. Distance measurements are covered in chapter 3.

Measurement of Time

Stopwatch

Events are timed using a variety of techniques. One of the simplest is to use a stopwatch to record the elapsed time. This is not a very accurate technique, since it relies on the reaction time of the individual who operates the watch.

The longer the duration of an event, however, the less the influence of small inaccuracies in the start and stop times.

Timing Lights

Timing lights offer a more accurate method of starting and stopping the recording. When the horse breaks a beam between a transmitter and receiver, it triggers the clock to start or stop. This method is used to time some types of equestrian competitions, including show jumping and barrel racing. Timing lights are sometimes used in research laboratories to record the time taken by the horse to cover a measured distance, from which the average speed over that distance is calculated. This is useful information in studies that require a number of trials to be recorded at similar speeds.

Slow Motion Replay

Many of the events in the equine locomotor cycle occur too rapidly to be measured, or even seen, by the human eye. Slow motion replay facilitates visualization of these events, and their duration can be measured accurately from knowledge of the sampling rate of the recording equipment and the number of samples (frames) occupied by the event of interest (Clayton 1991b; Clayton 1996).

Example: A video recording was made at a sampling rate of 30 frames/s. If the stance phase (time during which the hoof is in contact with the ground) occupies 6 video frames, the duration of the stance phase in seconds (s) is calculated as:

$$\text{Time} = \frac{\text{Number of Frames}}{\text{Frame Rate (frames/s)}} = \frac{6}{30} = 0.2 \text{ s}$$

Sampling Theorem

The appropriate sampling rate for measuring the duration of an event is determined according to the sampling theorem. This states that the sampling rate should be at least double, and preferably four to five times higher than the frequency of the event of interest.

If stance duration is 0.2 s or 1/5 s, this is equivalent to a frequency of 5 times/s or 5 Hz. Accurate measurement of this event would require a sampling rate of at least 10 Hz and preferably 20 to 25 Hz. Video cameras have a sampling (recording) rate of 30 Hz (25 Hz in Europe), which is adequate for measuring stance duration at the trot. When horses move at faster speeds, their stance duration decreases, so higher frame rates are needed. For example, at the gallop, accurate measurement of a stance duration of 0.1 s (frequency 10 Hz) requires a sampling rate of at least 40-50 Hz.

Gaits

Horses perform a wide repertoire of gaits that vary in the coordination of the movements of the four limbs. Specific gaits are recognized and differentiated primarily by differences in the sequence and timing of the footfalls (chapter 14). Gaits with similar temporal characteristics may be distinguished by stylistic differences related to animation of the limbs and nodding movements of the head and neck.

> *A gait is a characteristic limb coordination pattern recognized*
> *by the sequence and timing of the footfalls.*

The gait chosen by a horse depends on the speed of movement, the genetically determined gait repertoire of the individual horse, and the type of training the horse has received.

The Horse's Stride

A gait is defined by the limb coordination pattern, with the same pattern of limb movements being performed repeatedly, stride after stride. A single stride comprises a complete cycle of limb movements, and a series of similar strides is performed during locomotion at any particular gait. Thus, a single stride can be regarded as the representative 'unit' of a gait.

> *A stride is a complete cycle of limb movements.*

Phases of the Stride

During a complete stride, each limb has a stance phase and a swing phase. The stance phase is the period of hoof contact with the ground (figure 2.1). During stance, the limb pushes against the ground to support the horse's weight and provide propulsion. The terminal part of the stance phase, called breakover, occupies the time from heel off to toe off. During breakover, the heels rotate around the toe, which is still in contact with the ground.

The swing phase is the period when the hoof has no contact with the ground as it swings forward in preparation for the next stance phase (figure 2.1). When watching a horse in motion, it is easy to focus on the swing phase, because this stage of the stride shows the expressiveness of the horse's movement.

The forces on the limb during the swing phase are relatively small, especially in the distal limb, so deviations in the movement pattern as the limb swings forward are unlikely to affect soundness. This is in contrast to the large weight-bearing forces that are present in the stance phase. Repetitive loading during stance is the cause of the majority of injuries to the horse's bones, joints, ligaments, and tendons.

Figure 2.1: Phases of the stride. In the diagram on the left, the right hind and left front limbs are in the stance phase, and the left hind and right front limbs are in the swing phase. In the diagram on the right, all limbs are in the swing phase, and the horse is in an aerial phase.

Some gaits have one or more aerial phases in each stride, when none of the limbs is in contact with the ground (figure 2.1).

Footfall Sequence

Each gait has a characteristic sequence of footfalls that describes the order of hoof contacts with the ground during a stride, and the coordination between the left hind (LH), right hind (RH), left front (LF), and right front (RF) limbs.

In a four-beat gait, each hoof contacts the ground separately; the footfall sequence may be lateral, diagonal, transverse, or rotary (figure 2.2). The lateral and diagonal sequences alternate between footfalls of a hind limb and a front limb. In a lateral sequence, contact of a hind limb is followed by contact of the front limb on the same side of the body. In a diagonal sequence, contact of a hind limb is followed by contact of the diagonal front limb. In the transverse and rotary sequences, the order of footfalls is hind, hind, front, front. In a transverse sequence, the footfalls alternate between left and right limbs, whereas in a rotary sequence, the footfalls follow a circular pattern.

Two-beat gaits have a lateral, diagonal, or transverse coordination pattern. In a lateral two-beat gait, contact of the lateral limb pairs (LH and LF, RH and RF) are synchronized. In a diagonal, two-beat gait, contacts of the diagonal limb pairs (LH and RF, RH and LF) are synchronized. In a transverse, two-beat gait, contact of the two hind limbs is synchronized and contact of the two front limbs is synchronized.

In a three-beat gait, movements of one pair of limbs, diagonal, lateral or transverse, are synchronized.

The point in the cycle at which a stride starts and ends is arbitrary; the start can be defined as any point in the cyclic pattern of limb movements, and the stride ends at the same point in the next cycle. In this book, LH contact indicates the start of the stride. This does not imply that the LH has any special functional significance, it is merely a convenient and repeatable point in the stride pattern.

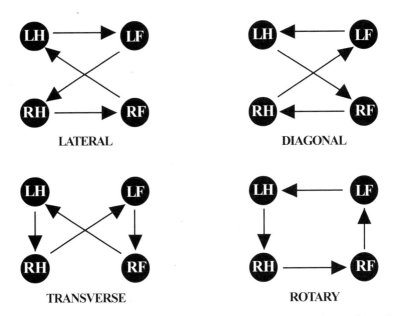

Figure 2.2: Footfall sequences in four-beat gaits. Arrows indicate the order of footfalls. LH: left hind; RH: right hind; LF: left front; RF: right front.

Rhythm

Rhythm describes the timing of the footfalls within a stride.

Each gait has a characteristic rhythm determined by the time elapsing between successive footfalls. Different gaits are easily recognized visually, by watching the limb movements, or audibly, by listening to the sound of the footfalls.

When a gait has a four-beat rhythm, each hoof contacts the ground separately, as in the walk and the gallop. In a two-beat rhythm, the limbs contact the ground in pairs. The diagonal pairs move synchronously in the trot; the lateral pairs move synchronously in the pace. The three-beat rhythm of the canter has one diagonal pair of limbs contacting the ground together. The rhythm of a gait is described as regular when there are equal intervals of time between successive footfalls. This is in contrast to an irregular rhythm in which the time intervals between successive footfalls are unequal.

Although the walk and the gallop are both four-beat gaits, they are easily distinguished by the rhythm of the footfalls. The walk has a regular rhythm in which the footfalls are separated by equal intervals of time. The gallop has an irregular rhythm with three short intervals and one long interval. Short intervals separate footfalls of the trailing hind, leading hind, trailing front, and leading front limbs. A long interval separates footfalls of the leading front and trailing hind limbs. In addition to differences in rhythm, the lateral footfall sequence of the walk is different from the transverse footfall sequence of the gallop.

23

Temporal Gait Variables

A number of temporal gait variables are measured that describe and differentiate the limb coordination patterns of the gaits and characterize the movements of individual horses. Temporal characteristics have been described for dressage horses (Clayton 1994a; Clayton 1994b; Clayton 1995; Clayton 1997; Deuel and Park 1990), show jumpers (Clayton and Barlow 1989; Clayton and Barlow 1991; Clayton et al. 1995; Deuel and Park 1991), eventers (Leach and Ormrod 1984 ; Deuel and Park 1993), race horses (Drevemo et al. 1980a; Drevemo et al. 1980b; Ratzlaff et al. 1985; Deuel and Lawrence 1986; Seder and Vickery 1993; Wilson et al. 1988a; Wilson et al. 1988b; Yamanobe et al. 1992), and gaited horses (Clayton and Bradbury 1995; Zips et al. 2001; Nicodemus and Clayton 2003).

The common temporal gait variables are defined in the following sections.

Stride Duration

The stride starts at any point in the cycle of limb movements and ends at the same point in the next cycle. The time elapsing between the same event in successive strides is the stride duration.

Stride duration is the period of time occupied by a complete stride.

The units of stride duration are seconds (s) or milliseconds (ms).

Stride Rate or Tempo

Stride rate or tempo describes the rate of repetition of the strides or the number of strides performed during a certain period of time (usually one minute). The unit of measurement is strides per minute (strides/min).

Stride rate or tempo is the rate of repetition of the strides.

Stride rate and stride duration have an inverse relationship: an increase in stride rate implies a decrease in stride duration and vice versa.

$$\text{Stride Rate} = \frac{1}{\text{Stride Duration}}$$

Typical stride durations and stride rates for a variety of equine gaits are shown in table 2.1. Within each gait, stride duration tends to decrease as speed increases.

Gait	Stride Duration (s)	Stride Rate (strides/min)
Medium walk	1.09	55
Passage	1.09	55
Piaffe	1.09	55
Jog	0.95	63
Marcha picada	0.93	65
Rack	0.82	73
Working trot	0.76	79
Lope	0.72	83
Running walk	0.68	88
Fox trot	0.63	95
Paso llano	0.63	95
Sobreandando	0.62	97
Marcha batida	0.61	99
Working canter	0.59	101
Tölt	0.57	105
Paso corto	0.48	124
Paso largo	0.46	130
Racing pace	0.46	130
Racing gallop	0.42	142
Racing trot	0.40	151
Classic fino	0.36	166

Table 2.1: Stride duration and stride rate of equine gaits performed at speeds typical of the gait. The gaits are listed in order of increasing stride rate. Stride durations are in seconds (s).

Stance Phase

The stance phase is the time during which the hoof is in contact with the ground.

Each limb has a stance phase in every stride.

Swing Phase

The swing phase of a limb is the time during which there is no contact between the hoof and ground.

Each limb has a swing phase in every stride.

Stance and Swing Durations

Stance duration is the time elapsing between hoof placement on the ground and lift-off.

Swing duration is the time elapsing between lift-off and the subsequent hoof placement.

When the overall stride duration decreases, swing duration tends to show relatively less reduction than stance duration.

Aerial Phase (Suspension)

An aerial phase is a period of time during which none of the limbs is in contact with the ground.

The aerial phase is also referred to as a period of suspension. However, the word *suspension* has several definitions and can be interpreted in different ways. To avoid confusion, the term aerial phase is used in preference to suspension in this book. Aerial duration is defined as the time elapsing between lift-off of the last limb to leave the ground at the start of the aerial phase until the next hoof placement on the ground. When a horse is airborne, all the limbs are in the swing phase simultaneously.

Some gaits usually have one aerial phase per stride (canter, gallop), others have two aerial phases per stride (trot, pace). The walk does not have an aerial phase. The presence of one or more aerial phases differentiates a leaping gait from a stepping gait (chapter 14).

Time between Footfalls

The time intervals between successive footfalls determines the rhythm and regularity of a gait and the temporal symmetry between left and right sides.

Example: In a regular walk, the four footfalls are equally spaced in time. Therefore, the time elapsing between successive footfalls is one-fourth (25 percent) of stride duration. If the walk has a stride duration of 1.2 s (1,200 ms), the time between successive footfalls is 0.3 s (300 ms).

Step Duration

*Front step duration is the time elapsing between successive
footfalls of the two front limbs.*

Left front step duration: time from LF footfall to RF footfall.

Right front step duration: time from RF footfall to LF footfall.

*Hind step duration is the time elapsing between successive
footfalls of the two hind limbs.*

Left hind step duration: time from LH footfall to RH footfall.

Right hind step duration: time from RH footfall to LH footfall.

Diagonal Dissociation at Contact

Gaits in which the diagonal limbs appear to move synchronously often show a slight asynchrony between movements of the diagonal pair when viewed in slow motion, which is called diagonal dissociation (figure 2.3).

Diagonal dissociation at contact, also known as diagonal advanced placement (DAP), is the time elapsing between successive footfalls of a diagonal (LH-RF or RH-LF) pair of limbs in gaits such as the trot or foxtrot. Diagonal dissociation is assigned a positive value if the hind footfall precedes the front footfall, dissociation is zero if the footfalls occur synchronously, and the value is negative if the front footfall precedes the hind footfall.

In the racing trot, the front footfall usually precedes that of the diagonal hind limb (negative diagonal dissociation at contact) and the duration of the diagonal dissociation tends to increase with speed (Drevemo et al. 1980b).

In dressage horses, positive diagonal dissociation at contact is regarded as an indicator of quality in the trot (Holmström et al. 1994). Positive diagonal dissociation (figure 2.3) occurs naturally in well-balanced, young horses and the amount of positive dissociation tends to increase with training as the horse moves with more collection and elevation of the forehand. However, about 20 per cent of dressage competitors at the Seoul Olympic Games had a negative diagonal dissociation at contact in the trot (Deuel and Park 1990), which shows that this characteristic does not preclude a horse from being successful in dressage, though it may make training more difficult.

Lateral Dissociation at Contact

Lateral dissociation at contact, also known as lateral advanced placement, is the time elapsing between successive footfalls of a lateral (LH-LF or RH-RF) pair of limbs. It is used to describe gaits in which the lateral limbs move almost

Figure 2.3: Positive diagonal dissociation at contact, in which the hind footfall precedes the diagonal front footfall (left), and negative diagonal dissociation at contact, in which the front footfall precedes the diagonal hind footfall (right) at the trot.

synchronously, such as the pace or stepping pace. Lateral dissociation is positive if contact of the hind footfall precedes the front footfall, zero if the footfalls occur synchronously, and negative if the front footfall precedes that of the hind limb.

At the racing pace, the lateral pairs of limbs move almost synchronously, but the hind limb contacts the ground slightly before the lateral front limb (positive lateral dissociation at contact) (Wilson et al. 1988a). In the stepping pace, the dissociation at contact is long enough to be visible to an observer.

Time between Lift-offs

The lift-off sequence of the limbs is often, though not always, the same as their placement sequence. The time between lift-offs, and even the lift-off sequence, is affected by both the time between footfalls and the stance durations of the individual limbs. In the walk, for example, stance durations tend to be longer in the hind limbs than the front limbs, especially when the horse moves with a degree of collection or animation. Consequently, time between footfalls is longer than the time between lift-offs of the hind limb and lateral front limb.

Diagonal Dissociation at Lift-off

Diagonal dissociation at lift-off (or diagonal advanced completion) is the time elapsing between lift-offs of a diagonal (LH-RF or RH-LF) pair of limbs in gaits that have the diagonal limb pairs moving almost synchronously, such as the trot or foxtrot. The value is positive if the hind limb lifts off before the front limb, zero if they lift-off synchronously, and negative if the front limb precedes the hind limb.

Lateral Dissociation at Lift-off

Lateral dissociation at lift-off (or lateral advanced completion) is the time elapsing between lift-offs of a lateral (LH-LF or RH-RF) pair of limbs. It is used to describe gaits in which a lateral pair of limbs move almost synchronously, such as the pace or stepping pace. The value is positive if the hind limb lifts off before the front limb, zero if they lift-off synchronously, and negative if the front limb lifts off before the hind limb.

Standardization of Temporal Variables

Variations in stride duration between different horses or within one horse at different speeds make it difficult to compare temporal variables. Comparisons are facilitated by removing the effect of stride duration in a process called standardizing or normalizing. This process regards a complete stride as the unit for comparison, and it expresses the temporal variables as a percentage of stride duration. Standardization to stance duration facilitates comparisons between temporal variables in strides with different durations.

Example: As speed increases at the gallop, there are reductions in stride duration, stance duration, and swing duration. Standardization of the temporal variables to stride duration shows that there is a relatively larger reduction in stance duration than in swing duration, which has the effect of preserving swing duration as speed increases.

Limb Support Sequence

At any moment in the stride, the horse may be supported by a single limb (unipedal support), two limbs (bipedal support), three limbs (tripedal support), four limbs (quadripedal support), or it may be in an aerial phase when none of the limbs is in contact with the ground (Leach et al. 1984). Each gait has a typical sequence of supports, which is described by the limb support sequence.

> *The limb support sequence describes the limb combinations that support the body sequentially during a stride.*

As a general rule, an increase in speed within a gait is associated with shorter stance durations, which results in fewer limbs supporting the body. Consequently, the limb support sequence for a gait may vary with speed. Typical limb support sequences for the common gaits performed at moderate speeds are shown in table 2.2, but it should be noted that other support sequences occur, especially at speeds in the upper and lower ranges for each gait.

Gait	Limb Support Sequence
Medium Walk	RH-RF-LH : RF-LH : RF-LH-LF : LH-LF : LH-LF-RH : LF-RH : LF-RH-RF : RH-RF
Running Walk	RH-RF-LH : RF-LH : LH : LH-LF : LH-LF-RH : LF-RH : RH : RH-RF
Racing Pace	LH : LH-LF : LF : AIRBORNE : RH : RH-RF : RF : AIRBORNE
Working Trot	LH-RF : AIRBORNE : RH-LF : AIRBORNE
Racing Trot	RF-LH : LH : AIRBORNE : LF : LF-RH : RH : AIRBORNE : RF
Canter (right lead)	LH : LH-RH-LF : RH-LF : RH-LF-RF : RF: AIRBORNE
Gallop (right lead)	LH : LH-RH : RH : RH-LF : LF : LF-RF : RF : AIRBORNE

Table 2.2: Typical limb support sequences for common equine gaits. For each gait the stride is considered to begin with the left hind footfall.

Temporal Stride Diagrams

To facilitate descriptions of gaits and comparisons between different gaits, the temporal characteristics may be represented diagrammatically. Different types of temporal stride diagrams exist that vary in their complexity and in the amount of information portrayed. In this chapter, the walk will be used to illustrate the different types of temporal stride diagrams. The diagrams can easily be extended to show a larger number strides, which gives a more realistic impression of the relationships between the limbs in successive strides.

Footfall Diagram

The footfall diagram shows the order of limb placements in a stride by listing the limbs in the order in which the footfalls occur (figure 2.4).

LH : LF : RH : RF : LH

Figure 2.4: Footfall diagram for the walk.

Footfall Timing Diagram

The footfall timing diagram (figure 2.5) plots the footfall sequence against a time scale. It contains more temporal information than the footfall diagram.

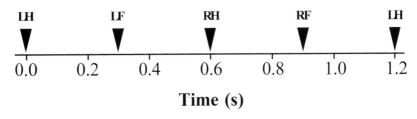

Figure 2.5: Footfall timing diagram for the walk. The arrows indicate the footfalls of the left hind (LH), left front (LF), right hind (RH), and right front (RF) limbs.

The addition of a time scale makes it possible to calculate stride duration, tempo of the strides, and time between footfalls. The times between successive footfalls indicate whether the rhythm of the gait is regular (equal time intervals between footfalls) or irregular (unequal time intervals between footfalls). In figure 2.5, successive footfalls are separated by 0.3 s and the walk has a regular rhythm. The stride duration is 1.2 s, and the stride rate (tempo) is calculated as follows:

$$\text{Stride Rate} = \frac{1}{\text{Stride Duration}} = \frac{1}{1.2} = 0.83 \text{ strides/s}$$

A stride rate of 0.83 strides/s is equivalent to 50 strides/min.

$$0.83 \text{ strides/s} * 60 \text{ seconds} = 50 \text{ strides/min}$$

The asterisk indicates multiplication.

Although the footfall timing diagram describes the stride duration, and the tempo and rhythm of the footfalls, it does not give any information about stance durations, time between lift-offs, or limb support sequences.

Support Diagram

The support diagram is a diagrammatic representation of the limb support sequences during a complete stride (figure 2.6). The order of footfalls and lift-offs are also obvious from the support diagram, but since there is no time scale, it does not indicate the durations of the different support phases.

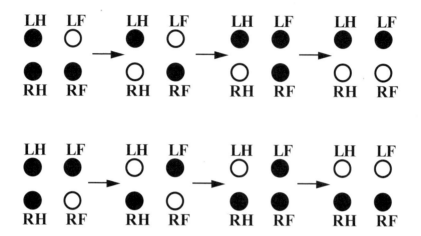

Figure 2.6: Support diagram for the walk. The hooves are represented as circles: filled circles indicate hooves in the stance phase, open circles represent hooves in the swing phase. The sequence progresses from left to right, with a new diagram being shown after each footfall or lift-off.

Gait Diagram

A gait diagram is a graphical method of depicting the temporal relationships between the limbs during a gait (figure 2.7). It includes a time scale, and it shows the stance and swing durations of each limb and the coordination of these phases between different limbs. A gait diagram provides complete temporal information about the stride, including the sequence and timing of limb contacts and lift-offs, stance durations, the sequence and duration of support and aerial phases, stride duration, and tempo.

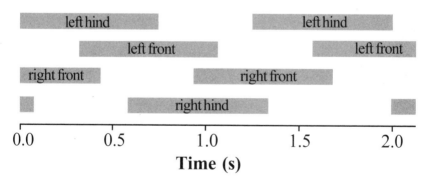

Figure 2.7: Gait diagram recorded over a period of 2 seconds at the walk. Filled bars represent stance phases, open areas between bars represent swing phases.

CHAPTER 3

LINEAR KINEMATICS

Linear kinematics is the study of translational movement.

Locomotion is the result of a complex and intricate coordination of the movements of the limbs and the body that includes both translational and rotational motion of various body segments (chapter 1). This chapter looks at the overall translational motion of the entire body without considering the rotations of the individual body parts.

Linear Distance and Linear Displacement

Linear distance and linear displacement describe how far a body moves over a period of time. Although the two terms are often used interchangeably in everyday language, in biomechanics they are not the same. Distance is a scalar quantity that measures the total distance traveled regardless of the direction of movement.

The distance through which a body moves is the length of the path it follows, regardless of the direction of the path.

Displacement is a vector quantity, which means that it takes account of both the distance traveled and direction in which the movement occurs. It is measured as a straight line from the starting point to the finishing point, with the direction of the line being specified. The direction can be determined from a compass reading.

The displacement of a body is measured by the length and direction of a straight line joining its initial and final positions.

Linear distance and linear displacement are measured using the SI units of kilometers (km), meters (m), and centimeters (cm). However, in equestrian sports, some distances are traditionally measured in other units such as miles, furlongs (f), and yards (yd).

Conversions:

1 mile = 1,760 yd = 1,624 m

1 furlong = 1/8 mile = 203 m

1 yd = 92.3 cm

The shortest distance between two points is a straight line between them; any deviation of the path from a straight line increases the distance covered. For motion in a straight line, distance and displacement are equal, but for motion that deviates from a straight line, distance is always further than displacement.

Some examples from equestrian sports will be used to illustrate the differences between distance and displacement.

Example: In a 20 x 40 m dressage arena, the diagonal from M to K is 34.4 m long. During a free walk on the diagonal, a horse that follows a straight line from marker to marker covers a distance of 34.4 m and undergoes a displacement of 34.4 m, whereas a horse that wanders off the line covers a longer distance, say 36.0 m but still has a displacement of 34.4 m (figure 3.1). It is not possible to cover a shorter distance than 34.4 m in getting from M to K. Regardless of the line the horse takes during the free walk, the displacement during this movement is always 34.4 m, with the direction depending on the orientation of the arena.

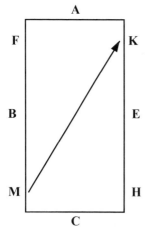 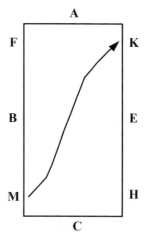

Figure 3.1: Distance and displacement of a horse crossing a 20 m x 40 m dressage arena on a diagonal line from M to K. The horse's displacement in walking from M to K is 34.4 m (left), with the direction depending on the orientation of the arena. A horse that wanders off the diagonal line covers a longer distance (right), though the displacement is still 34.4 m.

Example: A Quarter Horse racing over a straight track may cover a distance that is a little longer than the displacement from start to finish if the horse moves across the track or around other horses during the race. A horse that undergoes a displacement of 406 m (440 yd), East (figure 3.2), may cover a distance slightly greater than 406 m during the course of the race.

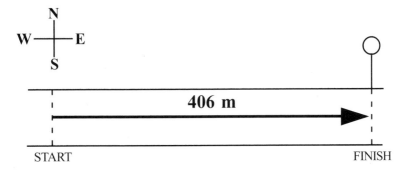

Figure 3.2: A horse racing on a straight track undergoes a displacement of 406 m (440 yd), East, but the distance covered may be longer than 406 m.

Example: When Thoroughbreds race around turns, the distance covered is usually quite different from the displacement. In figure 3.3, a race over a distance of 1,827 m (9 furlongs) counterclockwise around a 1,624 m (1 mile) track covers slightly more than one complete circuit of the track from start to finish. The distance of the race is approximately 1,827 m (9 furlongs) but the displacement in this example is only 203 m (1 furlong), East.

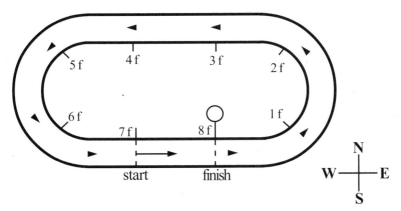

Figure 3.3: Oval racetrack with circumference of 1,624 m (1 mile) showing location of furlong posts. A horse racing counterclockwise around two turns (arrows) over a distance of 1,827 m (9 furlongs) from start to finish has a displacement of only 203 m (1 furlong), East.

Example: In endurance racing, the path taken during a race is much more complicated than that followed around an oval race track; the direction changes frequently, and there are often loops that have their start and finish in close proximity, but between them the trail covers a long distance. In a 160 km (100 mile) race, the horse travels a distance of approximately 160 km, but the displacement is usually a small fraction of that distance.

Example: A show-jumping course designer estimates the distance of a jumping course by walking the course with a measuring wheel. The wheel is set to zero at the start and is pushed around the course from fence to fence, following the path that the average competitor is likely to take (figure 3.4). The measurement ends as the wheel crosses the finish line. The reading on the wheel is the distance of the course, and this is used to calculate the time allowed based on the speed for the class, which is specified in the rules.

$$\text{Time Allowed} = \frac{\text{Distance}}{\text{Speed}}$$

The horse's displacement during the round is measured as the length of a straight line between the start and finish. If the same timing lights are used to record the start and finish, the displacement during the round is zero.

From the examples above, it is apparent that distance is usually a more relevant measurement than displacement in equestrian sports.

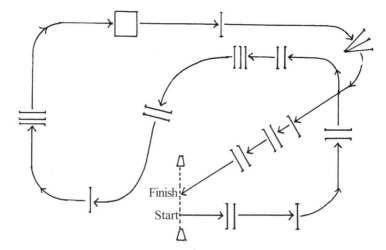

Figure 3.4: Distance of a show-jumping course is measured from fence to fence as the path followed by a typical competitor (arrows). Displacement is measured between start and finish lines. In this case, displacement is zero.

Stride Length

Stride length measures the displacement of the horse's center of mass in the direction of movement during a complete stride, but since it is quite difficult to determine the location of the center of mass, stride length is often approximated by measuring the separation of successive ground contacts (hoof prints) of the same hoof (figure 3.5). A slightly more accurate approximation is achieved by averaging the stride lengths measured by separation of successive hoof prints of all four hooves.

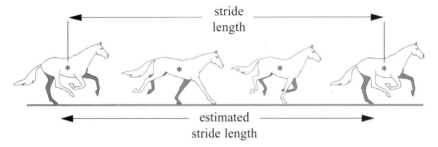

Figure 3.5: Measurement of stride length. Displacement of the horse's center of mass (*) during a complete stride is approximated by measuring the length between successive hoof prints of one limb, in this case the left hind.

Step Length

Front and hind step lengths (figure 3.6) measure the separations in the direction of motion between successive front limb contacts and between successive hind limb contacts, respectively.

Front step length is measured between successive hoof prints of the two front limbs.

LF step length: length from LF hoof print to RF hoof print.

RF step length: length from RF hoof print to LF hoof print.

LF STEP LENGTH + RF STEP LENGTH = STRIDE LENGTH

Hind step length is measured between successive hoof prints of the two hind limbs

LH step length: length from LH hoof print to RH hoof print.

RH step length: length from RH hoof print to LH hoof print.

LH STEP LENGTH + RH STEP LENGTH = STRIDE LENGTH

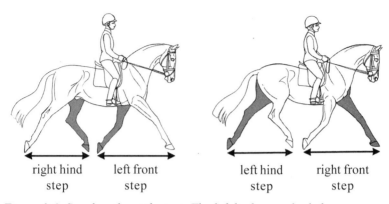

| right hind | left front | left hind | right front |
| step | step | step | step |

Figure 3.6: Step lengths at the trot. The left limbs are shaded.

Diagonal Length

The term diagonal length is used in the description of gaits that have one or both diagonal pairs of limbs (RF-LH, LF-RH) moving synchronously, such as trot and canter. Diagonal length is the separation in the direction of motion between hoof prints of a diagonal limb pair during the diagonal stance phase (figure 3.7). The diagonal is named according to the front limb: the left diagonal comprises LF and RH limbs; the right diagonal comprises RF and LH limbs.

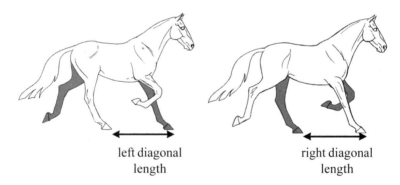

| left diagonal | right diagonal |
| length | length |

Figure 3.7: Left and right diagonal lengths at the trot. The left limbs are shaded.

Lateral Length

The term lateral length is used in the description of gaits that have one or both lateral pairs (LF-LH, RF-RH) moving more-or-less synchronously, such as the pace. Lateral length is defined as the separation in the direction of motion

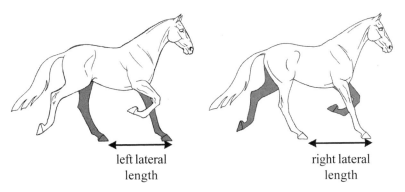

left lateral
length

right lateral
length

Figure 3.8: Left and right lateral lengths at the pace. The left limbs are shaded.

between hoof prints of a lateral limb pair during the lateral stance phase (figure 3.8). The left lateral pair comprises LF and LH limbs. The right lateral pair comprises RF and RH limbs.

Tracking Length

Tracking length is the separation in the direction of motion between a front hoof print and the succeeding hoof print of the lateral hind hoof. If the hind hoof steps into the print of the front hoof, the tracking length is zero, and the horse is said to be tracking up. If the hind hoof steps behind the front hoof, the tracking length has a negative value, and the horse is said to be under-tracking or not tracking up. If the hind hoof steps ahead of the front hoof, the tracking length has a positive value, and the horse is said to be over-tracking.

The main mechanism for changing stride length at all gaits is to adjust the tracking length (Clayton 1994a, Clayton 1994b, Clayton 1995). This is particularly relevant in dressage horses that are required to maintain the same tempo, while making transitions between the collected, working, medium, and extended gaits. For example, in the collected trot, horses tend not to track up (tracking length is negative). In the working trot, they show a small amount of over-tracking (tracking length is positive), and during the medium and extended trots there are progressive increases in over-tracking (table 3.1). In addition to the increase in tracking length, the medium and extended trots have a small increase in diagonal length due to the lengthening of the horse's frame, which accounts for the remainder of the increase in stride length. Since increases in tracking length and diagonal length are present on both the left and right diagonals, the effect of the increases on stride length is actually double the amount shown in the table.

Stride length at Trot = (2 * diagonal length) + (2 * tracking length)

	Stride Length (cm)	Tracking Length (cm)	Diagonal Length (cm)
Collected Trot	250	-7	132
Working Trot	273	4	132.5
Medium Trot	326	27	136
Extended Trot	355	39	138.5

Table 3.1: Stride length, tracking length, and diagonal length for different types of trot. Note that the changes in tracking length and diagonal length occur on the left and right sides of the body, so their effect on stride length is doubled.

Linear Speed and Linear Velocity

Linear speed and linear velocity describe the rate at which a body moves from one location to another. Although the terms are often used interchangeably, they differ in that speed is a scalar quantity, whereas velocity is a vector quantity.

The average speed over a period of time is measured as the distance covered divided by the time taken.

$$\text{Speed} = \frac{\text{Distance}}{\text{Time}}$$

$$\bar{s} = \frac{l}{t}$$

where $\bar{s}$: is the average speed, l is the length of the path (i.e. the distance), and t is the time taken.

The average velocity over a period of time is obtained by dividing the displacement by the time.

$$\text{Velocity} = \frac{\text{Displacement}}{\text{Time}}$$

$$\bar{v} = \frac{d}{t}$$

where $\bar{v}$ is the average velocity, d is the displacement in a given direction, and t is the time taken.

The bars over the *s* and *v* indicates that the values represent averages measured over a period of time.

Speed and velocity are measured using the same units. In the SI system, the units for distance or displacement, which are centimeters (cm), meters (m), and kilometers (km), are divided by the units for time, which are seconds (s), minutes (min), and hours (h). Units of speed and velocity include centimeters per second (cm/s or cms^{-1}), meters/minute (m/min or mmin^{-1}), kilometers/hour (km/h or kmh^{-1}), or some similar combination.

As with linear distances and displacements, linear speed and velocity have equal values only when the motion is in a straight line and in one direction.

Example: For a Quarter Horse racing over a straight track, the average speed is approximately the same as the average velocity. For a 406 m (440 yd) race over a straight course, the displacement is 406 m, but the distance covered is slightly greater, say 415 m. For a race that is completed in 21.7 s, the average velocity and average speed are calculated as follows:

$$\text{Average Velocity} = \frac{\text{Displacement}}{\text{Time}} = \frac{406}{21.7} = 18.71 \, \text{m/s}$$

$$\text{Average Speed} = \frac{\text{Distance}}{\text{Time}} = \frac{415}{21.7} = 19.12 \, \text{m/s}$$

In racing sports, the winner is the horse that completes the course in the shortest time. The relative importance of stride length and stride rate in achieving and maintaining a high speed varies with the distance of the race. Sprinters accelerate quickly, then maintain maximal speed using a high stride rate. Horses that race over middle distances require sufficient stamina to maintain submaximal speed over a longer distance, which is achieved using a longer stride length and slower stride rate than in sprint races. In long-distance races, tactics are important, and the jockey's skill in rating the horse becomes a determinant of success. In this case, the average speed of the entire race is less informative than the average speeds over shorter segments of the race. The split times for each furlong give a clearer picture of how a race was run. Part of the trainer's skill lies in assessing a horse's strengths and weaknesses in terms of speed versus stamina, then using this information to determine the best tactics for that horse over a certain race distance.

In other types of timed sports, the winner is the competitor who fulfills certain technical requirements in the shortest time. In these sports, skills, such as turning or jumping, play a role in determining the outcome.

Example: Barrel racing requires rapid acceleration, combined with an ability to turn sharply in both directions with minimal loss of speed and momentum. It is possible to evaluate an individual horse's performance and determine where improvements could be made by comparing the average speeds of different horses during the same parts of the pattern. To make this type of comparison, the pattern is divided into short segments (e.g., from the start to the first barrel, around the first barrel, between the first and second barrels, etc.), and the time for each segment is determined from video recordings using a stop watch. A shorter time indicates a faster speed. Comparisons between the time profiles for different horses reveal individual strengths and weaknesses and indicate where the race was won and lost. A horse that accelerates more slowly but maintains a faster speed around the barrels may beat a horse that has tremendous acceleration and speed between barrels but loses time by taking wider turns. Furthermore, if an individual horse's performance deteriorates, comparison of videotapes recorded before and after the change in performance may offer clues that are useful for detecting the underlying problem. Video evaluation with details of split times is sometimes offered for a fee at competitions.

Example: In show-jumping, the winner of a jump-off against the clock is the horse that completes the course with the fewest jumping errors in the shortest time, which is indicative of the fastest average speed. A faster time may be achieved by taking a shorter line to reduce the distance covered or by increasing the average speed. Each rider makes a decision regarding the tactics used to achieve a fast time; one rider may choose to reduce the distance by turning more tightly, whereas another rider may gallop faster to keep up the momentum while making wider turns. When a jump off is televised, the commentator often selects one or more places on the course to take a split time and make comparisons between competitors as a means of predicting the final outcome.

Standardization of Linear Variables

Variations in stride length between different horses or within one horse at different speeds or under different conditions make it difficult to compare linear variables. Comparisons are facilitated by standardizing or normalizing the displacements to stride length. This process regards a complete stride as the unit for comparison, and it expresses the linear variables as a percentage of stride length. Standardization to stride length facilitates comparisons between linear variables in strides with different lengths.

Example: In a transition from working trot to medium trot, stride length increases by 53 cm from 273 cm to 326 cm (table 3.1). This is achieved by increasing the tracking length by 23 cm on each side (total 46 cm) and increasing the diagonal length by 3.5 cm on each side (total 7 cm). When the values are standardized to stride length, the overall contribution of diagonal length decreases from 97 percent in working trot to 83 percent in medium trot, while the contribution of tracking length increases from 3 percent to 17 percent.

Instantaneous Speeds and Velocities

The average speed or velocity is measured over a period of time. It is also possible to determine the instantaneous speed or velocity at a specific moment in time rather than the average value over a longer duration.

The instantaneous speed of a body is its average speed measured over such a short distance that the speed does not have time to change.

$$s = \frac{\Delta l}{\Delta t}$$

where s is the instantaneous speed, Δl is the change in distance, and Δt is the change in time.

Δ is the Greek letter delta, which is used to indicate the change in a variable.

The instantaneous velocity of a body is its average velocity measured over such a short displacement that the velocity does not have time to change.

$$v = \frac{\Delta d}{\Delta t}$$

where v is the instantaneous velocity, Δd is the change in displacement, and Δt is the change in time.

Note: In equations, the average and instantaneous speeds and velocities are distinguished by placing a bar above the appropriate letter when the value represents an average value:

s = instantaneous speed, $\bar{s}$ = average speed;

v = instantaneous velocity, $\bar{v}$ = average velocity.

The concept of instantaneous velocity is an important one. In some equestrian activities, instantaneous velocity is a more important determinant of success than the average velocity over a longer period of time or during the entire performance.

Example: When a horse jumps a fence, the velocity at the instant of take-off determines the path of the horse's center of mass during the aerial phase. In other words, the instantaneous velocity at take-off determines the height and width jumped by the horse. (Remember that velocity has magnitude and direction, both of which are important in jumping.) Figure 3.9 compares the take-off velocities and the angles of elevation of a horse jumping a 1.6 m high vertical fence and a 4.5 m wide water jump.

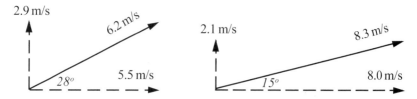

Figure 3.9: Vertical and horizontal components (dashed arrows) of the take-off velocity (solid arrows) for a horse jumping a vertical fence 1.6 m high (left) and a water jump 4.5 m wide (right). Vertical velocity is positive upward, horizontal velocity is positive to the right.

Velocity Vector

Since velocity is a vector, it acts in a certain direction. The vector is often resolved into components acting in directions that are relevant to the understanding of the movement, such as the vertical and horizontal components (figure 3.9). The positive direction is specified for each component, and the velocity in that direction is then described as positive or negative.

Example: If the positive direction of the vertical velocity is specified as being upwards, a jumping horse has positive vertical velocity from take-off to the peak of the flight arc and negative vertical velocity from the peak of the flight arc to landing. If the positive direction of the horizontal velocity corresponds with the direction of movement, its value is positive throughout the jump.

Linear Acceleration

Velocity is rarely constant for long periods of time. When velocity changes, the body undergoes acceleration. Like velocity from which it is derived, acceleration is a vector quantity.

Acceleration is the rate at which velocity changes with respect to time.

$$\text{Acceleration} = \frac{\text{Final Velocity} - \text{Initial Velocity}}{\text{Time}}$$

$$\bar{a} = \frac{v_f - v_i}{t}$$

where $\bar{a}$ is the average acceleration, v_f is the final velocity, v_i is the initial velocity, and t is the time over which acceleration occurs.

The SI units of acceleration are derived from the units of velocity divided by the units of time, as in meters per second per second (m/s^2 or ms^{-2}) or kilometers per hour per hour (km/h^2 or kmh^{-2}).

In everyday parlance, people often talk about acceleration and deceleration as an increase or decrease, respectively, in magnitude of the velocity regardless of direction. While this interpretation may be useful in understanding the movement, it is not appropriate for scientific description. Since acceleration is a vector, the positive direction must be specified, and this determines whether velocity and acceleration are positive or negative, regardless of whether the magnitude of the velocity is increasing or decreasing. Positive acceleration implies an increase in velocity if the body is moving in the positive direction or a decrease in velocity if the body is moving in the negative direction. Negative acceleration implies a decrease in velocity in the positive direction or an increase in velocity in the negative direction. Zero acceleration occurs when velocity is constant.

Example: A Quarter Horse sprints along a straight track with the direction of positive motion being from the starting stalls to the finish line. As the horse comes out of the starting stalls, it accelerates to maximal velocity (positive acceleration), maintains this velocity until it crosses the finish line (zero acceleration), then decelerates (negative acceleration).

Example: A reining horse loping in a straight line in the positive direction performs a sliding stop. Acceleration is negative during the sliding stop. If the horse then does a rollback and lopes in the opposite direction, it undergoes negative acceleration as the magnitude of the loping velocity increases.

Example: A horse moving along the long side of a dressage arena passes the letters H, S, E, V, and K. The following movement is performed:

H to S collected trot

S to V medium trot

V to K collected trot

If the positive direction is designated to be from H to K, the horse accelerates in the transition from collected to medium trot at S, then decelerates in the transition from medium to collected trot at V. During the collected trot and the medium trot, the acceleration is zero.

The horse then changes the rein, returns to K, and performs the movement in the opposite direction:

K to V collected trot

V to S medium trot

S to H collected trot

Because the positive direction has been designated from H to K, the horse decelerates in the transition from collected trot to medium trot and accelerates in the transition from medium to collected trot.

To avoid confusion about positive and negative acceleration, the key is to remember which direction has been designated positive and relate the changes in velocity to this direction.

Relationship between Displacement, Velocity, and Acceleration

Displacement, velocity, and acceleration are closely related. In mathematical terms, velocity is the first derivative of displacement, which means it is calculated from displacement divided by time. Similarly, acceleration is the first derivative of velocity or the second derivative of displacement. Figure 3.10 shows how velocity and acceleration change when displacement takes the form of a simple sine wave. Velocity and acceleration have the same pattern as displacement, but each is offset by one quarter of a cycle. Peaks and troughs in the displacement curve indicate changes in the direction of motion. As the direction of motion changes, it corresponds with zero velocity and a trough or peak in the acceleration. A peak in the displacement curve indicates that velocity is changing from positive to negative, which corresponds with a trough in the acceleration curve. A trough in the displacement curve coincides with the velocity changing from negative to positive, and this corresponds with a peak in the acceleration curve.

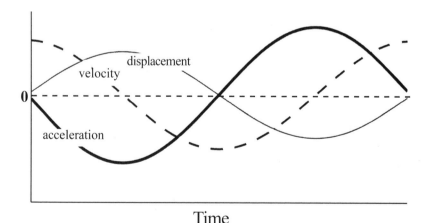

Time

Figure 3.10: Temporal relationship between displacement (light solid line), velocity (dashed line), and acceleration (heavy solid line). The displacement data have been filtered to remove 'noise'.

Noise in Data

The graphs in figure 3.10 are idealized in that the displacement curve is smooth. In real life, displacement data from gait analysis contain 'noise' due to small errors that are introduced during data collection and analysis. Each derivative magnifies the noise, so the velocity and acceleration curves become progressively noisier. Even a small amount of noise in the displacement data, which may not be perceptible to the human eye in the displacement curve, may result in significant amounts of noise in the velocity and acceleration curves (figure 3.11).

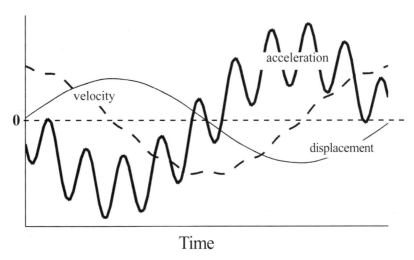

Figure 3.11: Velocity (dashed line) and acceleration (heavy solid line) curves derived from noisy displacement data (light solid line).

Filtering

Filtering is a method of reducing the amount of noise in data. In effect, the noise is 'filtered' out, leaving the real data intact. It is appropriate to filter data before deriving other variables, as in figure 3.10, to avoid magnification of the noise in the derived variables as shown in figure 3.11.

The Effect of Gravity

Gravity is the force exerted by the earth on all other bodies (chapter 7). The force of gravity attracts all bodies toward the center of the earth and maintains the position of bodies on the surface of the earth. For practical purposes, the acceleration due to gravity has a constant value of 9.81 m/s^2, and it is represented by the letter g to differentiate it from other types of acceleration.

During locomotion, the hooves push against the ground to oppose gravity and provide propulsion for locomotion. If the vertical pushing force exceeds the force needed to overcome gravity, the horse is propelled upward into an aerial phase. When the horse loses contact with the ground at the start of an aerial phase, the force of gravity is no longer opposed by the ground reaction force acting through the hooves. Therefore, gravity accelerates the horse's body downward throughout the aerial phase.

Example: Each trot stride has two diagonal stance phases and two aerial phases. During the diagonal stance phases, the hooves push against the ground to generate forces that propel the horse into the aerial phase with a certain vertical velocity. If the upward direction is designated positive, the force of gravity, which is acting downward or in the negative direction, causes the vertical velocity to decrease (deceleration) throughout the aerial phase. This results in a reversal of the upward motion and brings the horse back to earth. The higher the vertical velocity when the horse leaves the ground, the longer it takes for the upward motion to be reversed and the horse to return to the ground.

Although the value of 9.81 m/s^2 is used to represent gravitational acceleration, there are slight variations in its value at different places on the surface of the earth due to the fact that the earth is not perfectly spherical; the diameter is larger at the equator than at the poles. The effect of gravity decreases slightly as the distance from the center of the earth increases, so the gravitational acceleration is lowest in the vicinity of the equator. In human athletics, this has led to speculation regarding the possibility of creating new records for the high jump when track meets are held close to the equator or at high altitude, where gravitational acceleration is slightly lower than at other locations.

One of the characteristics of acceleration due to gravity is that its value is constant (or uniform), which means that an airborne body experiences the same acceleration, in both magnitude and direction, over a period of time. Consequently, the average acceleration is the same as the instantaneous acceleration.

Under conditions of constant acceleration, such as that due to gravity, three important equations of uniformly accelerated motion can be applied. These are based on knowledge of the initial velocity, the magnitude of the acceleration, and either the time elapsed or the displacement. These equations are used to calculate the final velocity of a body after a period of uniform acceleration or the distance traveled during a period of uniform acceleration:

$$v_f = v_i + at$$

$$d = v_i t + \tfrac{1}{2}at^2$$

$$v_f^2 = v_i^2 + 2ad$$

where v_f is the final velocity, v_i is the initial velocity, a (or g) is the acceleration, d is the displacement, and t is the time over which the acceleration occurs.

These three equations apply only under conditions of constant acceleration. In equine locomotion, the effect of gravity is the most frequently encountered condition of constant acceleration. The effects are particularly apparent when the horse is airborne, because, at this time, gravity is the only external force acting on the body.

Example: In years gone by, one of the tourist attractions in Atlantic City was to watch horses, ridden by bathing belles, dive from a platform into a tank of water. From the time the horse and rider lost contact with the platform until they entered the water, they were in free fall being accelerated downward by the force of gravity. For a platform 3 m high and an initial velocity (v_i) of 0 m/s, the horse's final velocity at contact with the water (v_f) is 7.67 m/s. The final velocity is calculated as follows from the equations of constant acceleration:

$$v_f^2 = v_i^2 + 2ad$$
$$v_f = \sqrt{v_i^2 + 2ad} = \sqrt{0 + (2 * 9.81 * 3)} = \sqrt{58.86} = 7.67 \text{ m/s}$$

Example: A jumping horse takes off with an upward velocity. Throughout the aerial phase, the force of gravity accelerates the horse's body toward the ground (positive direction). The upward velocity decreases to zero at the peak of the flight arc (v_f). If the vertical velocity at take-off (v_i) is 3.0 m/s and the positive direction of acceleration is downward, the time taken to reach the peak of the flight arc is calculated from the equations of constant acceleration:

$$v_f = v_i + at$$

$$t = \frac{v_f - v_i}{a} = \frac{0 - (-3)}{9.81} = \frac{3}{9.81} = 0.31 \text{ s}$$

After reaching the peak of the flight arc, the downward velocity increases until the horse lands and the hooves exert a force against the ground to counteract the gravitational force. If the height of the horse's center of mass is the same at take-off and landing, the ascent time equals the descent time. Under these conditions, the total aerial time over the jump is double the ascent time, that is, 0.62 s.

During most jumping efforts, the horse is airborne for less than 1 s. The primary factor affecting aerial time is vertical velocity at take-off (Clayton et al. 1995; Clayton et al. 1996; Colborne et al. 1995). The horizontal velocity at take-off does not affect aerial time, but it does affect the horizontal distance covered during the aerial period. For two horses taking off with the same vertical velocity, the one with the higher horizontal velocity will jump further.

Summation of Linear Scalars and Vectors

Distance and speed are scalar quantities. Summation of scalars is accomplished by simple addition.

Example: A horse trots from point A to point B, a distance of 3 m, then canters from point B to point C, a distance of 4 m. The total distance traveled is calculated as the sum of the two component distances: 3 m + 4 m = 7 m.

Displacement, velocity, and acceleration are vector quantities, which means that they have both magnitude and direction. Summation of vector quantities must take account of the direction in which the vectors act.

The effect of vectors can be depicted by a vector diagram in which each vector is represented by an arrow. The arrow begins at the point of application, its length is scaled to the magnitude, and it points in the direction in which the vector acts. The effect of more than one vector can be determined graphically by "adding" the arrows nose to tail. The summation of the vectors is represented by an arrow that starts at the tail of the first arrow and ends at the head of the final arrow. Vectors can also be added mathematically (Appendix C).

Example: A horse trots from A to B, undergoing a displacement of 3 m, then changes direction by 90° and canters from B to C, undergoing a displacement of 4 m. The total displacement measured as a straight line from A to C, can be determined graphically using arrows scaled in length to the magnitude of the displacement and oriented along the direction of movement (figure 3.12). The arrows are joined end to end, and the magnitude of the displacement is measured with a ruler from the tail of the first arrow (A) to the head of the last arrow (C).

Alternatively, the displacement can be calculated using Pythagoras Theorem:

$$AB^2 + BC^2 = AC^2$$
$$AC = \sqrt{AB^2 + BC^2} = \sqrt{9 + 16} = \sqrt{25} = 5$$

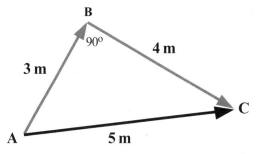

Figure 3.12: The sum of the displacements from A to B and from B to C is the line from A to C. The length can be measured with a ruler or calculated using Pythagoras Theorem.

ANGULAR KINEMATICS

Angular kinematics studies rotational movement. Rotation occurs when a body follows a circular path with all parts of the body traveling through the same angle, in the same direction, in the same time.

Angular kinematics is the study of rotational movement.

The study of angular kinematics is based on the same principles as the study of linear kinematics.

Angular Distance and Angular Displacement

Angular distance and angular displacement describe how far a body rotates over a period of time. Angular distance is a scalar quantity describing the amount of rotation a body undergoes, regardless of the direction of rotation. When a body rotates from one position to another, the angular distance through which it moves is the summation of the rotations between its initial and final positions, measured along the path followed by the body.

Angular distance is a scalar quantity describing the length of the angular path through which a body rotates, regardless of the direction of rotation.

Angular displacement is a vector quantity, which means that it takes account of both the distance and direction of the rotation. The total angular displacement is equal in magnitude to the smaller of the two angles between the body's initial and final positions, with the direction of rotation being specified.

Angular displacement is a vector quantity describing the rotation of a body in terms of the amount of rotation and the direction in which the rotation occurs.

Example: During the swing phase, the front limb is retracted (rotated backward relative to the body) slightly in early swing, protracted (rotated forward) through most of swing, then retracted again in terminal swing. If the angle of the front

51

limb is represented by a line connecting the scapula with the hoof, the angle of the limb during the swing phase can be represented graphically (figure 4.1). When this line is vertical, the angle is zero and the limb is perpendicular to the ground. Negative angles occur when the hoof is behind the scapula; positive angles occur when the hoof is ahead of the scapula. During protraction, the graph slopes upward. As the limb is retracted, the graph slopes downward. In the example in figure 4.1, the minimal and maximal angles are -33° and 20°, respectively, so the range of motion is 53°. The angular displacement, calculated as the difference between the angles at the start (-28°) and end (16°) of the swing phase, is 44°.

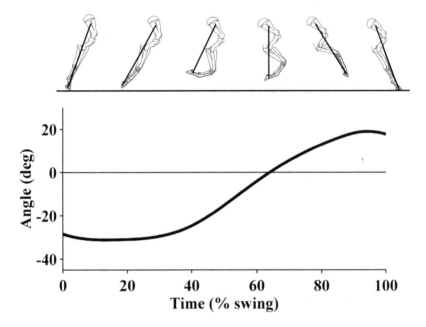

Figure 4.1: Angle-time diagram of front limb rotation during the swing phase, with corresponding diagrams of limb orientation. The angle of the limb is represented by a line from the scapula to the hoof.

The units of measurement of angular distance and angular displacement are revolutions (rev), degrees (deg or °), and radians (rad). One revolution is the angle formed by a complete circle (figure 4.2). If the body rotates through one revolution, it faces in the same direction at the start and end of the turn. There are 360° in a complete revolution. If a body rotates through half a revolution (180°), it ends up facing along the same line but in the opposite direction to its starting position.

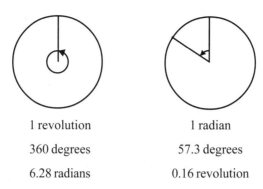

1 revolution	1 radian
360 degrees	57.3 degrees
6.28 radians	0.16 revolution

Figure 4.2: Units of angular distance and angular displacement.

A radian (rad) is defined as the angle formed at the center of a circle by an arc on the circumference that is equal in length to the radius of the circle (figure 4.2). The number of degrees in a radian is calculated from the relationship between the radius and the circumference of a circle:

$$\frac{\text{Circumference}}{\text{Radius}} = \frac{2\pi r}{r} = 2\pi \text{ radians/revolution}$$

The value of π is 3.14 and there are 2π radians in one revolution, so there are 6.28 radians in one revolution. Alternatively, we can say that one radian is 0.16 rev or 57.3°. Biological applications usually use revolutions and degrees, but radians are used extensively in engineering and technical applications.

Conversions:

1 rev = 360 deg = 6.28 rad

1 rad = 57.3 deg = 0.16 rev

In equestrian sports the revolution is the unit of choice for measuring the angular distance of movements that involve rotating around complete circles, such as pirouettes or spins. A full pirouette is one revolution; a triple spin is three revolutions. Angular displacement is always zero for complete revolutions.

When describing movements in which the rotation is less than one revolution, the degree is usually the unit of choice. A dressage horse rotates through 90° in a quarter pirouette and 180° in a half pirouette. A reining horse rotates through 180° in a rollback.

The angular distance through which a body moves and the angular displacement it experiences are equal in magnitude if the rotation occurs through an angle equal to or less than 180° and the rotation occurs in one direction. Otherwise, the angular distance and angular displacement of a rotational motion are different. The total angular distance is the summation of all the rotations.

Example: A horse swings his head and neck to the left through an angle of 60°
and back to the starting position. The angular distance is 120°, the angular
displacement is zero.

Since angular displacement is a vector quantity, the direction of the motion
must be included in its description. The direction of rotation can be described
using the terms clockwise and counterclockwise. In scientific terminology,
rotation is more commonly described as positive and negative; by convention,
the positive direction corresponds with counterclockwise.

Note that in defining angular displacement, the stated direction describes the
direction in which the body would rotate if it followed the shortest path from its
initial position to its final position. It does not necessarily follow the direction
in which the body actually rotated.

Example: A trainer lunges a horse on the left rein (figure 4.3), which is
counterclockwise as seen from above and therefore corresponds to the positive
direction for measurement of angular displacement. After completing the first
quarter circle, the trainer's body has rotated through an angular distance of 90°
and has an angular displacement of +90°. When a half circle has been completed,
the angular distance is 180° and the angular displacement can be described as
+180° or -180°. As the horse continues beyond a half circle and toward a full
circle, the magnitude of the angular distance continues to increase, but the
magnitude of the angular displacement decreases and its value is negative,
because the angle between starting and finishing positions is smaller when
measured in a clockwise direction. After three-quarters of a circle, the angular
distance is 270° and the angular displacement is -90°. When a full revolution
has been completed, the angular distance is 360°, and the angular displacement
is 0°. After two revolutions, the angular distance is 720° and the angular
displacement is 0°.

In studies of equestrian activities, angular distance is usually more useful than
the angular displacement for describing and understanding rotational motion.

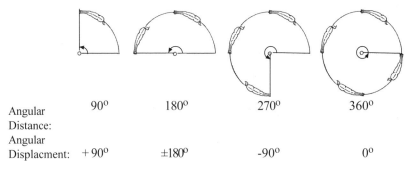

	90°	180°	270°	360°
Angular Distance:	90°	180°	270°	360°
Angular Displacment:	+90°	±180°	-90°	0°

Figure 4.3: Angular distance and displacement of the trainer during longeing.

Angular Speed and Angular Velocity

Angular speed is a scalar quantity derived from the angular distance covered during a period of time.

The average angular speed of a rotating body is obtained by dividing the angular distance through which the body moves by the time taken:

$$\text{Angular Speed} = \frac{\text{Angular Distance}}{\text{Time}}$$

$$\bar{\sigma} = \frac{\phi}{t}$$

where $\bar{\sigma}$ is the average angular speed, ϕ is the angular distance and t is the time.

Angular velocity is a vector quantity derived from the angular displacement occurring over a period of time.

The average angular velocity is obtained by dividing the angular displacement of the body by the time taken:

$$\text{Angular Velocity} = \frac{\text{Angular Displacement}}{\text{Time}}$$

$$\bar{\omega} = \frac{\theta}{t}$$

where $\bar{\omega}$ is the average angular velocity, θ is the angular displacement specifying the direction of rotation, and t is time.

The units of angular speed and angular velocity are those of angular distance or displacement divided by units of time. Examples are revolutions per minute (rev/min), radians per second (rad/s) or degrees per second (deg/s or °/s).

As with angular distances and displacements, the average angular speed and average angular velocity are equal for a body that rotates in one direction through an angle equal to or less than 180°. As the angular distance increases from 180° to 360°, the magnitude of the angular displacement decreases and its sign changes. Average angular velocity is not a very useful measurement in equestrian sports.

Instantaneous values for angular speed and angular velocity are calculated by measuring their values over very short periods of time. The instantaneous values generally yield more valuable information than the average values.

$$\sigma = \frac{\Delta\phi}{\Delta t}$$

where σ is the instantaneous angular speed, $\Delta\phi$ is the change in angular distance and Δt is the change in time.

$$\omega = \frac{\Delta\theta}{\Delta t}$$

where ω is the instantaneous angular velocity, $\Delta\theta$ is the change in angular displacement and Δt is the change in time.

Example: During breakover, the front hoof rotates through $51°$ during a period of 0.08 s. If the rotation is in a counterclockwise direction, the average angular velocity during this period of rotation is:

$$\overline{\omega} = \frac{51}{0.08} = 637.5°/s$$

The instantaneous angular velocity of the hoof during breakover, shown graphically in figure 4.4, is quite different from the average angular velocity.

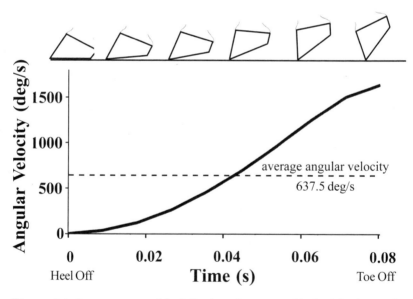

Figure 4.4: Instantaneous (black line) and average (dashed line) angular velocities of front hoof during breakover. The diagrams above show the corresponding hoof orientations.

Angular Acceleration

When the angular velocity changes, the body undergoes angular acceleration. Like angular velocity from which it is derived, angular acceleration is a vector quantity.

Angular acceleration is the rate at which the angular velocity is changing with respect to time.

The average angular acceleration over a period of time is calculated as:

$$\bar{a} = \frac{\omega_f - \omega_i}{t}$$

where $\bar{a}$ is the average angular acceleration, ω_f is the final angular velocity, ω_i is the initial angular velocity, and t is time.

The SI units of angular acceleration are derived from the units of angular velocity divided by the units of time. Examples are revolutions per minute per minute (rev/min^2) and degrees per second per second (deg/s^2, $°/s^2$).

Example: In the example of the hoof rotating during breakover, in a period of 0.8 s it accelerates from an angular velocity of 0°/s to 1,500°/s. The average angular acceleration during this time is:

$$\bar{a} = \frac{\omega_f - \omega_i}{t} = \frac{1500 - 0}{0.8} = 1,875 \ °/s^2$$

Angular Vectors

In linear kinematics, a vector is represented graphically by an arrow scaled in length to the magnitude of the vector and pointing in the direction in which the vector acts. The graphical method of representing vectors associated with angular motion is complicated by the fact that the body is moving along a circular path, so the vectors cannot be adequately represented by a straight arrow. To overcome this difficulty, a convention known as the right-hand thumb rule is used. According to this convention, an angular motion vector is represented by an arrow drawn in the direction indicated by the extended thumb when the curled fingers of the right hand point in the direction of rotation (figure 4.5). The arrow's length is proportional to the vector's magnitude.

This method of representation can be used for any angular motion vector, including angular displacement, velocity, and acceleration. Angular vectors can be added to obtain a resultant, or they can be resolved into components in the same manner as linear vectors (Appendix C).

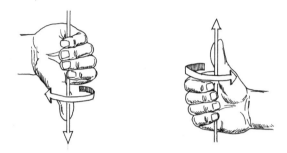

Figure 4.5: Right-hand thumb rule for angular vectors. When the fingers of the right hand are curled in the direction of rotation, the thumb points in the direction of the angular vector.

Example: A bareback rider is thrown from a bucking horse. As he flies through the air, he experiences a combination of twisting and somersaulting motions (figure 4.6). The resultant angular velocity can be determined by summation of the velocity vectors using the right-hand thumb rule.

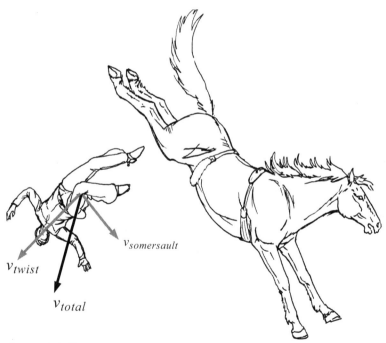

Figure 4.6: Vector summation of twisting (v_{twist}) and somersaulting ($v_{somersault}$) angular velocities is represented by the black arrow (v_{total}). When the right thumb points along the black arrow, the curled fingers of the right hand show the direction of the resultant rotation.

Relationship between Linear and Angular Velocities

Angular velocity may be used to increase the linear velocity of an implement, often with the objective of increasing the effect of an impact. During rotation, all points on a line rotate through the same angle in the same time, but linear velocity varies with the radius of rotation. The farther a point is from the axis of rotation, the greater its linear velocity.

Example: If a polo player swings a mallet through an angle θ, all points on the player's arm and the mallet undergo the same angular displacement and move at the same angular velocity, but different points have different linear velocities (figure 4.7). The linear velocity of the hand is proportional to the length of the player's arm, while the linear velocity of the head of the mallet is proportional to the combined length of the arm and mallet. Linear velocity of the mallet head is faster for a long mallet than a short one. Since momentum is the product of mass and velocity, a longer mallet contacts the ball with more momentum than a short mallet.

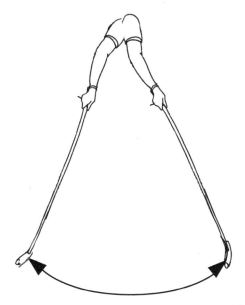

Figure 4.7: The head of the mallet has the same angular velocity as the player's hand but undergoes a greater linear displacement and moves at a faster linear velocity.

CHAPTER 5

AERIAL MOTION

Abbreviation used in this chapter:

CoM: Center of mass

Aerial motion, also known as projectile motion, is a characteristic of many locomotor activities. It affects movements as diverse as the lift in the stride, the trajectory of a horse jumping a fence, and the flight of a polo ball. Knowledge of the principles of aerial motion is important in understanding all these activities.

Example: As a polo ball leaves the head of the mallet, it becomes a projectile. Factors that influence success as a polo player include the ability to hit the ball with appropriate velocity and direction to its aerial motion and to predict the flight path of the ball in preparation for making the next play.

Example: Between take-off and landing, the body of a jumping horse is a living projectile. Success as a jumper is largely dependent on the horse's ability to generate sufficient force during take-off to impart an appropriate upward and forward velocity to the center of mass (CoM) so that all parts of the horse's body clear the fence. The take-off forces act eccentrically (not through the horse's CoM), which causes the body to rotate forward during the aerial phase. This allows the horse to take off from the hind limbs and land on the front limbs.

Factors that Influence Aerial Motion

The path of a projectile is influenced by the initial conditions at the start of the aerial phase and the forces that act on the projectile while it is airborne. The main force acting on a body during the aerial phase is gravity, which cannot be controlled, but an understanding of the effects of gravity enhances the ability to predict what will happen during an aerial phase. This knowledge can be used to develop a better understanding of locomotor performance.

Initial Conditions

The initial conditions of a projectile's flight result from forces applied prior to the start of the aerial phase. These forces determine the direction and velocity of the aerial motion. The direction is measured by the angle of elevation (θ) relative to the horizontal at the instant of release or take-off (figure 5.1). If the take-off velocity (v) and angle of elevation (θ) are known, the vertical (v_{vert}) and horizontal (v_{hz}) components of the take-off velocity can be calculated:

$$v_{vert} = v \sin\theta$$

$$v_{hz} = v \cos\theta$$

The sine (sin) and cosine (cos) of an angle are listed in tables of trigonometric functions, or they can be calculated using the appropriate functions on a hand calculator.

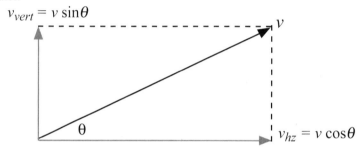

Figure 5.1: Initial conditions of a projectile. The angle of elevation (θ) is measured relative to the horizontal at the instant of release. The velocity (v) is the instantaneous velocity at release. It is resolved into horizontal (v_{hz}) and vertical (v_{vert}) components.

Forces during the Aerial Phase

When a projectile is airborne, its motion is governed by the effect of the gravitational force (g), which produces a constant acceleration of 9.81 m/s^2 in a downward direction. Under the influence of gravity, the vertical component of the velocity of a projectile changes constantly. The effect is to reduce the velocity in an upward direction until, at the peak of the flight arc, the vertical velocity is zero. During the descent, vertical velocity increases continuously in a downward direction until contact with the ground. Horizontal velocity is almost constant throughout the aerial phase. Air resistance may result in a small decrease in horizontal velocity, but for practical purposes, this effect is small enough to be ignored.

Figure 5.2 shows the velocity vector and its vertical and horizontal components at take-off, the peak of the flight arc, and landing. It assumes that horizontal

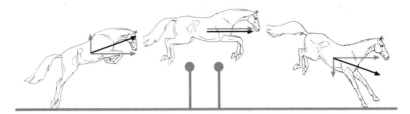

Figure 5.2: Velocity of a jumping horse. The velocity vector (black arrow) and its vertical and horizontal components (gray arrows) are shown at take-off (left), the peak of the flight arc (center), and landing (right).

velocity is constant throughout the aerial phase. Vertical velocity has its highest magnitude in an upward direction at the start of the aerial phase and has its highest magnitude in a downward direction at the end of the aerial phase. It is zero at the peak of the flight arc.

Trajectories

The forces that act during the aerial phase determine the path of a projectile, which is called its trajectory. Regardless of the release velocity and angle of elevation, the trajectory follows the same general form of a smooth curve that is symmetrical on either side of its center. A curve of this type is called a parabola. In the absence of air resistance, which can be regarded as negligible for the purposes of this discussion, a projectile follows a parabolic flight arc.

The height (vertical displacement) and range (horizontal displacement) of a projectile depend on the initial velocity and angle of elevation. Figure 5.3 shows the trajectories of projectiles released at the same angle of elevation but with different release velocities. An increase in release velocity produces increases in both the height and the range.

The effect of varying the angle of elevation, while maintaining a constant take-off velocity, is shown in figure 5.4. The range is maximal when the projection angle is 45°. For angles higher or lower than 45°, the range is reduced. The same range is achieved for angles that differ from 45° by the same amount regardless of whether the angle is larger or smaller. For example, the horizontal range is the same for projection angles of 30° (45° - 15°) or 60° (45° + 15°). However, a projection angle of 60° gives a significant increase in height, and a consequent increase in the aerial time.

If the objective is to cover the maximal horizontal distance during the aerial phase, then the optimal angle of elevation is close to 45°. Other factors may be involved, however, that affect the ideal angle for specific purposes.

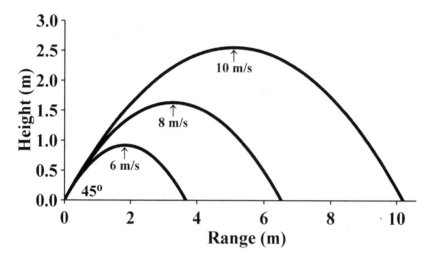

Figure 5.3: Effect of release velocity on the height and range of a projectile released at an angle of elevation of 45°. The magnitudes of the release velocities are 6 m/s, 8 m/s, and 10 m/s.

Example: A polo ball being hit for maximal length must take account not only of the distance covered during the aerial phase, but also the distances covered during the bounce and the roll.

Example: In jumping horses the angle of elevation varies with the type of fence, but it is generally much lower than 45°. A typical take-off angle for a horse jumping a water jump 4.5 m wide is 21°. However, jumping horses are not

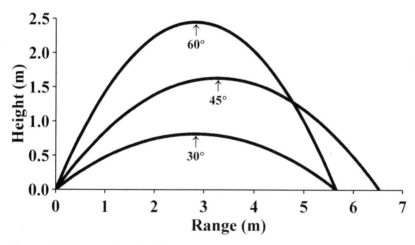

Figure 5.4: Effect of angle of elevation on the height and range of a projectile released with a velocity of 8 m/s. The angles of elevation are 30°, 45°, and 60°.

trying to maximize their range. Even a water jump 4.5 m wide is not substantially longer than a normal gallop stride, which is why horses can clear this width easily with a relatively small angle of elevation (Colborne et al. 1995).

Aerial times and distances are calculated with reference to the position of a projectile's CoM at take-off and at landing. Therefore, the instantaneous position of the CoM must be known to determine how high and how far the body travels during the flight phase. For a spherical body of uniform density, such as a ball, the CoM is at the center of the sphere, equidistant from all points on the surface. In living bodies, the position of the CoM changes slightly as the body parts move relative to each other.

The CoM of the horse-and-rider system is located within the horse's trunk, and its location changes slightly with the positions of the rider's body and the horse's limbs, neck, and head. The fact that the horse's body has a different orientation at take-off compared with landing means that, even when the horse is jumping on level ground, the height of the CoM at landing may be slightly different than at take-off. It should be noted that the CoM is ahead of the hind limbs at take-off and behind the front limbs at landing (figure 5.5), so the total distance from take-off of the hind hooves to landing of the front hooves is about 1.5 m further than the horizontal distance covered by the CoM during the aerial phase (Clayton et al. 1996). The total distance covered from hind hoof take off to front hoof landing is the sum of the take-off distance (horizontal distance from hind limbs to CoM at take-off), the jump distance (horizontal distance covered by the CoM during the aerial phase), and the landing distance (horizontal distance from CoM to trailing front hoof at landing).

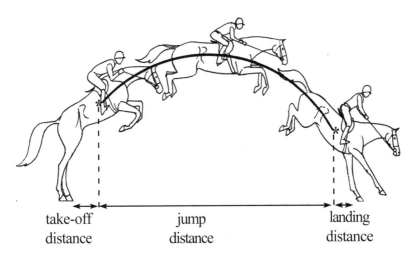

take-off   jump   landing
distance   distance   distance

Figure 5.5: Total distance covered during the jump is the sum of take-off distance, jump distance, and landing distance. Asterisks indicate location of center of mass at take off and landing.

65

Aerial Time

The total aerial time is the sum of the ascent time (t_{up}) and the descent time (t_{down}). The time taken to reach the peak of the flight arc is calculated as:

$$t_{up} = \frac{v_{vert\,i}}{g} = \frac{v\sin\theta}{g}$$

where t_{up} is the time to reach the peak of the flight arc, $v_{vert\,i}$ is the initial vertical velocity, v is the magnitude of the velocity vector at take-off, θ is the angle of elevation, and g is the acceleration due to gravity.

When the horse's CoM has the same height at take-off and landing, the time of the upward flight (t_{up}) is exactly the same time as the time of the downward flight (t_{down}). Under these circumstances the total aerial time (t_{total}) is calculated as follows:

$$t_{total} = t_{up} + t_{down}$$
$$= 2\,\frac{v\sin\theta}{g}$$

This equation shows that if the take-off and landing heights are the same, the only factor that can be manipulated to change the aerial time is the vertical velocity at take-off.

If the take-off and landing heights of the CoM are different, then the descent time is calculated as:

$$t_{down} = \sqrt{\frac{2d_{down}}{g}}$$

where t_{down} is the descent time, d_{down} is the vertical displacement of the CoM during the descent, and g is the acceleration due to gravity.

Vertical Motion

For any angle of elevation, the height (or lift) achieved and the aerial time are entirely dependent on the vertical velocity at take-off. This vertical velocity is imparted to the body prior to the start of the aerial phase, and it changes constantly during the aerial phase under the influence of gravity.

If the magnitude and direction of the take-off velocity are known, the vertical velocity of a projectile is calculated as:

$$v_{vert} = v \sin\theta$$

where v_{vert} is the vertical velocity, v is the magnitude of the velocity vector at take-off, and θ is the angle of elevation.

The vertical elevation of the CoM during the aerial phase is calculated from one of the equations of constant acceleration:

$$v_f^2 = v_i^2 + 2ad$$

$$v_{vert\,f}^2 = v_{vert\,i}^2 + 2gd_{up}$$

$$d_{up} = \frac{v_{vert\,f}^2 - v_{vert\,i}^2}{2g}$$

where $v_{vert\,f}$ is the final vertical velocity, $v_{vert\,i}$ is the initial vertical velocity, d_{up} is the vertical displacement of the CoM during the ascent, and g is the acceleration due to gravity.

Example: A horse takes off to jump a vertical fence with a vertical velocity of 2.5 m/s. The elevation of the CoM *(d_{up})* is:

$$d_{up} = \frac{v_{vert\,f}^2 - v_{vert\,i}^2}{2g} = \frac{(2.5)^2 - (0)^2}{2*9.81} = \frac{6.25}{19.62} = 0.32\,m$$

Horizontal Motion

The horizontal velocity of a projectile is calculated as:

$$v_{hz} = v \cos\theta$$

where v_{hz} is the horizontal velocity, v is the magnitude of the velocity vector at take-off, and θ is the angle of elevation

The only force acting to change the horizontal velocity during the aerial phase is air resistance which, for practical purposes, can be ignored. This means that the same horizontal velocity will be maintained throughout the aerial phase. In other words, the average horizontal velocity during the aerial phase is equal to the initial (instantaneous) horizontal velocity at take-off. The range (horizontal distance) is calculated as the product of the initial horizontal velocity and the aerial time:

$$d_{hz} = v_{hz} * t_{total}$$

where d_{hz} is the horizontal distance covered, v_{hz} is the horizontal velocity at take-off, and t_{total} is the aerial time.

Substituting:

$$d_{hz} = v\cos\theta * t_{total}$$

Example: A horse takes off to jump a water jump with a horizontal velocity of 8.0 m/s and is airborne for 0.4 s. The horizontal distance (d_{hz}) covered by the horse's CoM is:

$$d_{hz} = \bar{v}_{hz} * t_{total} = 8 * 0.4 = 3.2 \text{ m}$$

The magnitude and direction of the take-off velocity and the angle of elevation determine the total distance traveled during the flight phase. The take-off and landing distances (position of hind limbs at take-off and front limbs at landing relative to CoM) have a smaller effect. When the height of the CoM is the same at take-off and landing, the optimal angle of elevation to achieve maximal horizontal range is 45°. Under these conditions, the faster the projection velocity, the further the distance traveled.

CHAPTER 6

KINETICS OVERVIEW

The ancient Greeks believed that a body moved when there was a force acting on it and ceased to move when the force was removed. This theory was rejected by the 16th century Italian scientist Galileo Galilei, the founder of modern concepts of dynamics. His ideas were embraced and developed further by Sir Isaac Newton (1642-1727). Today, our understanding of forces and their effects are encapsulated in Newton's laws of motion, which are the basis of the mechanical laws and formulae that describe motion and the associated forces.

Linear kinetics describes the forces responsible for translational (linear) movements; angular kinetics describes the forces associated with rotations. Kinetics includes the study of external forces acting between the system and an external object and internal forces that act within the system. A complete kinetic analysis considers not only the forces, but also the torques (moments of force), work, power, and mechanical energy.

This chapter introduces kinetic concepts that will be discussed in greater depth in the chapters that follow.

Mass

Mass is a measure of the amount of matter a body contains.

The mass of a body depends on the quantity and type of matter of which the body is composed. A pony has a smaller mass than a draft horse or, to put it another way, a pony is less massive than a draft horse (figure 6.1). Different body tissues vary in density, and this affects their contribution to body mass. For example, muscle is denser than fat, so a certain volume of muscle is heavier than the same volume of fat. Consequently, a muscular horse has more mass than a fat horse of the same size. Mass remains constant regardless of location. A horse that has a mass of 600 kg in New York has the same mass at any other location in the world.

The SI units of measurement of mass include the kilogram (kg) and gram (g).

Figure 6.1: Masses of different breeds and types of equids. Pony – height 1.23 m (12 hands), mass 250 kg (left); Thoroughbred – height 1.64 m (16 hands), mass 500 kg (middle); draft horse – height 1.95 m (19 hands), mass 1000 kg (right).

Mass is a direct measure of the inertia possessed by a body. It is easier for a draft horse to pull a lightly laden cart than a heavily laden one, because the former has a smaller mass and, therefore, less inertia.

Inertia

A body is always reluctant to change its state of movement. This means that a stationary body, usually referred to as a body at rest, tends to remain at rest, whereas a moving body tends to continue moving.

> *Inertia is the resistance of a body to change its state of motion.*

The SI unit of measurement of inertia is the kilogram· meter (kg· m).

Example: A polo ball lies at rest on the field until hit by a mallet. After the ball has been hit and is flying through the air, it tends to maintain its forward velocity until it either returns to the surface of the field under the influence of gravity or strikes an object in its path.

For linear motion, the amount of inertia that a body possesses is directly proportional to its mass. A more massive body has more inertia, which makes it more difficult to change its linear motion. For example, it is easier to pick up a racing saddle than a western saddle, because the racing saddle has a smaller mass and, therefore, less inertia.

When a body is in motion, it is easier to stop or change the motion of a less massive body than a more massive one. For example, it takes less force to stop the smaller, lighter calves used in calf roping than the larger, heavier steers used in team roping.

For angular motion, inertia depends not only on mass, but also on the distribution of that mass relative to the axis of rotation.

Force

The state of a body that is at rest or in motion can be changed by the application of a force. A force describes the pushing or pulling effect of one body on another. As a result of the application of a force, a body that is at rest can be made to move or a body that is in motion can have its speed or direction of motion changed.

A body's state of motion can be changed when another body exerts a force on it.

The SI unit of force is the newton (N), which is defined in terms of the acceleration it produces. A force of 1 N produces an acceleration of 1 m/s² in a body with a mass of 1 kg.

Weight

The weight of a body describes the effect of the earth's gravitational force on that body. Weight is the product of mass and the acceleration due to gravity.

Weight is a measure of the effect of the force of gravity on a body.

$$W = mg$$

where W is the weight, m is the mass, and g is the acceleration due to gravity.

Weight is measured in newtons (N), which is the SI unit of force.

If a horse experiences a force of 6,000 N attracting the body toward the center of the earth, it is said to have a weight of 6,000 N. The mass is calculated as:

$$m = \frac{W}{g} = \frac{6000}{9.81} = 611.6 \, \text{kg}$$

Mass and weight measure different things, though they are closely related and are often confused. For further discussion of this topic, see the section on Newton's laws of motion in chapter 7.

Mass is constant regardless of location. However, the gravitational force varies slightly at different places on the surface of the earth. Since weight is the product of mass and the acceleration due to gravity, there are small changes in weight with geographic location.

LINEAR KINETICS

Abbreviations used in this chapter:

GRF: Ground reaction force

Linear kinetics describes the forces associated with
translational (linear) motion.

Force

Force is a vector, and the direction in which a force acts is important in determining its effect. For example, a compressive (pushing) force acts in the opposite direction to a tensile (pulling) force. Compressive forces and tensile forces of equal magnitude have quite different effects on a body. Like other vectors, forces can be added and subtracted graphically (figure 7.1). For more information on vector addition, see Appendix C.

The application of a force can produce or alter motion if the applied force is of sufficient magnitude to overcome the inertia of the body receiving the force.

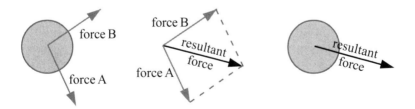

Figure 7.1: Graphical representation of force vectors. Two forces (force A and force B) acting through the center of the body on the left are represented by gray arrows. The force vectors are added by constructing a parallelogram with the forces on adjacent sides (center). The resultant force is the diagonal shown by the black arrow (center and right).

Example: A sulky starts to move when a horse exerts sufficient tension (tensile force) through the traces to overcome its inertia. When this happens, the sulky is no longer at rest, it is in motion. The motion can be speeded up, slowed down, or have its direction changed according to the magnitude and direction of the force exerted on it by the horse.

Sometimes a force is applied that is not large enough to overcome a body's inertia, so the body does not move. However, the force tends to move the body and brings it closer to the point where it would move. If an additional force is also applied, the two forces are additive in their effect.

Example: A small child may not be strong enough to lift a heavy tack trunk, but the force applied by the child tends to move the trunk. If an adult helps the child, the adult does not need to exert as much force as would be required without the child's assistance. Thus, the forces exerted by the child and the adult are additive. These facts are used as a basis for defining force.

> *A force alters or tends to alter a body's state of rest or uniform motion in a straight line.*

Internal and External Forces

The forces acting on a system can be classified as internal or external. Internal forces act within the system, external forces act between the system and another body. Classification of a force as internal or external depends on how the system is defined. If the system is the horse's body, then forces exerted by a rider on the horse or by the horse on a rider are external forces. If the system includes both horse and rider, then forces between horse and rider are regarded as internal forces. In biomechanical research, the system is defined according to the objectives of the study. Sometimes the system is the horse's body or the rider's body, other times the horse and rider are considered as a single system (figure 7.2).

Figure 7.2: Definition of a system. For a horse and rider, the system (shaded area) may be defined as the horse only (left), the rider only (center), or the horse and rider combined (right).

Example: In a study of a horse and rider jumping a fence, the system is defined as the horse's body. Internal forces exerted by the horse's muscles on the bones and joints of the limbs result in external forces being exerted by the hooves against the ground during take-off (figure 7.3). If the rider gets left behind and pulls on the reins, tension in the reins applies an external force to the horse (figure 7.3). If the horse misjudges take-off and hits the jump, the fence exerts an external force against the horse (figure 7.3).

Figure 7.3: External forces (arrows) on a jumping horse: ground reaction force at take off (left), rider pulling on the reins (center), and hitting a fence (right).

Force of Gravity

Forces result from direct contact between bodies, such as the compressive force of a rider sitting on a saddle or the tensile force of a ligament that connects two bones. Forces also exist between bodies that are not in direct contact. These forces cause an attraction between the bodies that tends to make them gravitate (or move) toward each other. Sir Isaac Newton formulated a law of gravitation describing the attraction between bodies.

Law of Gravitation

Two particles of matter attract one another with a force that is directly proportional to the product of their masses and inversely proportional to the square of the distance between them.

Newton's law of gravitation is expressed algebraically as:

$$F \propto \frac{m_1 m_2}{l^2}$$

where F is the force acting on each body, m_1 and m_2 are the masses of the two bodies, and l is the distance between them.

The symbol '$\propto$' means 'is proportional to.'

Since the attractive force decreases in proportion to the square of the distance between the bodies, a small increase in separation results in a relatively large reduction in the attractive force between them.

The masses of the bodies that are studied in biomechanics are not large enough to exert significant attractive forces on each other with one exception: the earth. The earth has a huge mass, and it exerts a gravitational force on all bodies that are either on its surface or in the atmosphere around it. The attractive force of the earth, known simply as gravity (g), imparts an acceleration of 9.81 m/s^2 to a mass of 1 kg.

$$\text{Gravitational Force } (g) = 9.81 \text{ N}$$

The weight of a body is a measure of the effect of gravity on the body's mass.

Example: A draft horse (1,000 kg) has a larger mass than a pony (250 kg) and weighs proportionally more since weight is proportional to mass (figure 7.4).

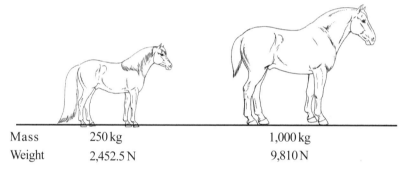

Mass	250 kg	1,000 kg
Weight	2,452.5 N	9,810 N

Figure 7.4: Mass and weight of a pony (left) and draft horse (right).

The effect of the earth's gravitational field on a body varies inversely with its distance from the center of the earth. Since the earth is not exactly spherical, the precise value of the gravitational force differs slightly at different geographic locations. The earth is a little flattened at the north and south poles, with the radius at the poles being about 21 km less than the radius at the equator. Consequently, the gravitational effect is slightly less at the equator than at the poles, and a body weighs less at the equator than elsewhere on the earth's surface. For example, a horse that weighs 6,000 N in Nairobi, Kenya, which is close to the equator, weighs 6,027 N in Helsinki, Finland, which is closer to the North Pole. The value of 9.81 N is generally used to represent the effect of gravity, regardless of geographic location.

The gravitational attraction decreases with height above the earth's surface, though for practical purposes the reduction is too small to be significant. A horse flying in a plane at 3,000 m, experiences almost the same gravitational force as a horse galloping on the beach at sea level. During space travel, however, astronauts are transported hundreds of miles from earth, and at these distances the force of gravity is significantly reduced. The effects on astronauts are well known: weightlessness allows them to float around in the space capsule, but the lack of normal gravitational forces also has important biological effects on the body, such as loss of bone density. This illustrates the importance of the earth's gravitational effect in maintaining a body's normal structure and function. Forces between the limbs and the ground during locomotion stimulate adaptations of the horse's musculoskeletal tissues. In performance horses, conditioning exercises make use of this effect to strengthen the locomotor system in a manner appropriate for the sport (Clayton 1991a).

Laws of Motion

The laws of motion describe the relationships between forces and the effects of forces on linear motion.

First Law of Motion

Every body continues in a state of rest or motion in a straight line unless it is acted upon by an external force.

This law summarizes some of the concepts that were introduced in the descriptions of mass, force, inertia, and momentum (chapter 6). It predicts the effect of forces generated by contact between two bodies.

Example: A show jumper hits a rail with a front hoof. The hoof exerts a force on the rail and, if the magnitude of the force is large enough to overcome the inertia of the rail, then the rail is dislodged. A lighter (less massive) rail has less inertia and is easier to dislodge than a heavier (more massive) one.

Example: A horse bucks with sufficient force to eject the rider from the saddle. Under the influence of gravity, the falling rider accelerates toward the ground. Upon hitting the ground, the rider's motion ceases abruptly due to the force exerted by the earth's surface.

Second Law of Motion

The acceleration of a body is proportional to the force causing it, and the change takes place in the direction in which the force acts.

The second law of motion is expressed by the familiar formula:

$$F = ma$$

where F is the force acting on the body, m is the mass of the body, and a is the acceleration imparted to it.

To be maximally effective in causing motion in a specific direction, the force should be aligned, as closely as possible, with the direction of intended motion.

Example: When a polo ball is struck by a mallet, the magnitude and direction of the force applied by the mallet determine the velocity and direction of the ball. Since the mass of the ball is constant, its acceleration is directly proportional to the force applied to it ($F = ma$; $a = F/m$). In other words, the harder the ball is hit (greater force), the larger its acceleration.

Forces that act in directions other than the intended direction of motion either retard motion or waste energy.

Example: Poorly coordinated muscular contractions producing forces that are not optimally directed are characteristic of unskilled performers, human or equine, who are learning a new technique. With practice, muscular coordination improves, the forces are applied more effectively, and efficiency increases.

When a force is applied to a body that is already moving, the change in velocity is related to the magnitude and direction of the force in relation to the direction of movement.

Example: A polo ball that is hit with a certain force will acquire a higher velocity if it is already rolling in the direction in which the force acts.

An alternative way of stating the second law of motion is as follows:

> *The rate of change of momentum of a body is proportional to the force causing it and takes place in the direction in which the force acts.*

Relationship between Mass and Weight

In an earlier section, it was shown that mass and weight measure different things. The mass of a body measures the amount of matter it contains, and it is constant regardless of location. The weight of a body is a force representing the effect of gravity, which is accelerating the body toward the center of the earth (figure 7.4). The relationship between weight, mass, and gravitational acceleration is derived from the second law of motion:

$$F = ma$$

If the force F is the weight of the horse (W) and the acceleration a is due to gravity (g), then by substitution:

$$W = mg$$

This formula can be used to calculate a horse's weight from its mass. For a horse with a mass of 500 kg:

$$W = 500 * 9.81 = 4,905 \text{ N}$$

Third Law of Motion

The interaction between two bodies that exert forces on each other is expressed in the third law of motion:

For every force that is exerted by one body on another body, there is an equal and opposite force exerted by the second body on the first.

This law is often expressed more succinctly, but perhaps less obviously, in the form:

For every action there is an equal and opposite reaction.

Action and reaction refer to the forces acting in opposite directions. We usually designate the action to be the force exerted *by* the horse, rider, or implement of interest, and the reaction to be the opposing force exerted *on* the horse, rider, or implement. This law indicates that the opposing forces are equal in magnitude, though the effect of the force is usually much more apparent on one body than on the other as a result of a discrepancy in their masses.

Example: After a calf has been roped, it continues to run unimpeded until reaching the end of the rope, which is dallied to the horn on the front of the saddle. When the calf reaches the end of the rope, it exerts a force against the saddle, which is securely attached to the horse. The horse and saddle can be considered as a single system, which exerts a reaction force through the rope on the calf (figure 7.5). The calf has a relatively small mass (around 130 kg) compared with the horse (~ 500 kg). From our knowledge of the second law of motion it is obvious that the force will have more effect on the calf than the horse. A heavier (more massive) rope horse will be less disturbed than a lighter (less massive) horse.

Example: A surcingle is used by vaulters to assist in mounting and performing gymnastic maneuvers on a horse that is cantering slowly on a lunge line. The surcingle must be adjusted tightly so that it doesn't slip and, under these conditions, the horse and surcingle can be regarded as one body. Forces are applied by the vaulter (mass ~ 50 kg) to the surcingle-horse system (mass ~ 700 kg), which exerts an equal and opposite reaction force on the vaulter (figure 7.6). Since the horse is so much more massive than the vaulter, it is relatively undisturbed by the forces applied by the vaulter.

Figure 7.5: Action and reaction between calf and rope horse. The roped calf exerts a force on the horse (gray arrow), which is resisted by the reaction force exerted by the horse on the calf (black arrow). The action and reaction forces are transmitted through the rope.

Figure 7.6: Action and reaction forces between vaulter and vaulting horse. The vaulter exerts a downward force (gray arrow) against the horse acting through the surcingle and the horse exerts an equal and opposite force (black arrow) against the vaulter.

Example: When a rider mounts a horse from the ground, the left foot is placed in the stirrup, and the right foot pushes against the ground (action). The ground pushes back against the right foot with an equal force acting in the opposite direction (reaction), which elevates the body. The stirrup then accepts the force of the left foot pushing against it (action), and pushes back with an equal and opposite force (reaction), which allows the body to continue its upward motion (figure 7.7). Of course, the saddle must be securely anchored by a tight cinch or girth if the stirrup is to offer an effective reaction force.

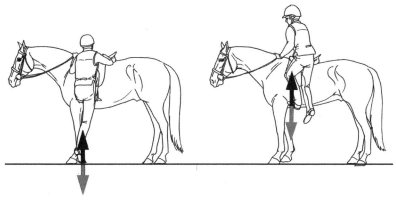

Figure 7.7: Action (gray arrows) and reaction (black arrows) forces during mounting.

Locomotion is produced as a result of external forces exerted by the hoof against the ground during the stance phase. The ground pushes back against the hoof with an equal force acting in the opposite direction, which is called the ground reaction force or GRF (figure 7.8). The magnitude and direction of the GRF determine the speed and direction of locomotion.

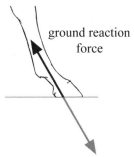

ground reaction force

Figure 7.8: Ground reaction force. The hoof exerts a force against the ground (gray arrow) and the ground exerts a reaction force against the hoof (black arrow) that is equal in magnitude and acts in the opposite direction.

A force vector, such as the GRF, can be resolved into components, which makes it easier to understand the effect of the force. See Appendix C for details on how to resolve a vector into components. The GRF is typically resolved into components acting in the vertical, longitudinal, and transverse directions. The vertical GRF is always directed upward. Its functions are to overcome the downward acceleration due to gravity and to project the horse's body upward into the aerial phase. The longitudinal GRF, which is directed from back to front (tail to nose) along the horse's body, acts to accelerate and decelerate forward motion. The transverse GRF acts from side-to-side across the horse's body.

83

When the horse moves in a straight line, the transverse force is small, but its magnitude increases when the horse turns or performs lateral movements. GRFs are described in detail in chapter 15.

Example: In gaits that have an aerial phase, such as the trot, the GRF propels the horse's body into the air. In order to prolong the aerial phase, the horse increases the vertical component of the force exerted by the hooves against the ground. An increase in vertical GRF creates more lift (greater upward propulsion) in the stride (figure 7.9).

Figure 7.9: Effect of vertical ground reaction force on the aerial phase at the trot. The western pleasure horse (left) has a low vertical ground reaction force and, consequently, the jog trot has no aerial phase. The dressage horse (right) generates a large vertical ground reaction force that propels it into a lofty aerial phase.

Example: A barrel racer makes a left turn around a barrel by leaning to the left and pushing against the ground with the front limbs at an angle. When viewed from the front (figure 7.10), the force exerted by the front hooves acts in a direction pointing downward and to the horse's right. The GRF, which is equal in magnitude and acts in the opposite direction, pushes the horse's body upward and to the left around the barrel.

The forces between the hoof and the ground have very different effects on the horse and the earth. The explanation is found in the second law of motion, which indicates that the acceleration a body experiences is proportional to its mass:

$$F = ma$$
$$a = \frac{F}{m}$$

Figure 7.10: Action and reaction forces during turning. To initiate a turn to the left, the barrel racer leans to the left and pushes against the ground with a force acting downward and to the horse's right (gray arrows). The ground reaction force (black arrows) pushes the horse's body to the left in a small circle around the barrel.

The effect of a force depends on the mass and, consequently, the inertia of the body on which the force acts. If forces of equal magnitude are exerted on the horse and on the earth, it is to be expected that the effect on the small mass of the horse will be considerably more obvious than the effect on the enormous mass of the earth. Consequently, the earth does not move measurably in response to the force exerted by the horses' limbs, whereas the horse may show considerable movement.

Example: In the example of the barrel racer (figure 7.10), the force of the hooves against the ground does not cause a perceptible movement of the earth, whereas the GRF causes the horse to turn rapidly around the barrel.

Impulse

Force is expressed as an instantaneous value, though usually a force acts over a period of time and its value may change during that time. Impulse is the sum of the forces acting over a period of time.

The magnitude of the vertical component of the GRF changes throughout the stance phase. It has a certain magnitude for a very short period of time, then a slightly different magnitude for the next short period of time, and so on. A graph showing the vertical GRF plotted against time is called a force-time

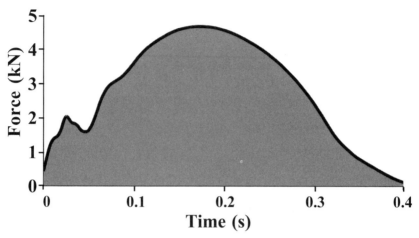

Figure 7.11: Force-time graph showing the vertical component of the front limb ground reaction force during the stance phase of the trot. The vertical impulse is represented by the shaded area.

graph, and it is usually shown for a complete stance phase (figure 7.11). The vertical impulse is the area under the force-time curve, which is the summation of the vertical forces exerted during the entire stance phase.

> *Impulse is the sum of the forces acting over a period of time. It is calculated by integration of the force-time curve.*

The mathematical term for measuring the area under a curve is integration; the impulse is calculated by integration of the force-time curve during a specific period of time.

The SI units of impulse are those obtained by multiplying the units of force by the units of time, which are newtons·seconds (N·s).

The same impulse can be achieved by applying a large force for a short time or maintaining a smaller force over a longer time. If the objective is to generate maximal propulsion, both the magnitude of the GRF and the duration of the stance phase should be increased.

Example: When a draft horse pulls a heavy load, high GRFs are developed and the hooves retain ground contact for as long as possible during each stride to maximize the time over which they are applying a propulsive force.

Example: During jumping, the hind limbs have long stance durations at take-off to allow the generation of large propulsive impulses (Clayton and Barlow 1991).

At high velocities, stance duration decreases, and the magnitude of the ground reaction force must increase to maintain the necessary impulse. Consequently, peak GRF is higher at faster velocities. The muscles in the hind limbs that generate propulsive forces become stronger with training, which facilitates the generation of larger forces during a shorter stance phase. In racehorses, the ability to generate large GRFs limits maximal stride rate, which is the ultimate determinant of speed. In dressage horses, higher GRFs allow the necessary propulsion to be generated during a shorter stance phase (Back et al. 1995b), and the resulting prolongation of the swing phase makes the strides appear less earthbound.

Momentum

Every moving body has momentum, which measures the amount of motion the body possesses. It is calculated as the product of mass and velocity.

Momentum is the quantity of motion a body possesses.

$$\text{Momentum} = mv$$

where m is the mass of the body and v is its velocity.

The SI units of momentum are those of mass and velocity. For example, if momentum is calculated by multiplying mass in kilograms by velocity in meters/second, the units of momentum are kilograms·meters/second (kg·m/s).

The effects of momentum are particularly relevant in determining the outcome of a collision between two bodies. A collision occurs every time a hoof contacts the ground, and collisions are a feature of equestrian sports that involve hitting a ball (polo, polocrosse), contact between horses (polo), or contact between horses and other objects (jumping).

The outcome of a collision depends on the momentum of each body at the instant of impact. The greater the momentum of a body, the more effect it has on other bodies in its path. Since momentum is the product of mass and velocity, a body can have a large momentum by virtue of having a large mass and/or by moving with a high velocity.

Example: A draft horse with a mass of 1,000 kg walking at 2 m/s has considerably more momentum (2,000 kg·m/s) than a pony with a mass of 250 kg trotting at the same speed (500 kg·m/s). In a collision with a post and rail fence, the draft horse would be much more likely to break the rails than the pony. However, if the pony increases its velocity to 8 m/s, it has the same momentum (2,000 kg·m/s) as the draft horse and is equally likely to break through the fence.

To summarize the effects of mass and velocity on momentum:

· for bodies moving at equal velocities, the more massive body has more momentum

· for bodies with equal masses, the body with the higher velocity has more momentum

· a small body can increase its momentum by traveling faster

Example: When one polo pony bumps another, the outcome depends on the masses and velocities of the two ponies (and the angle between them, which will not be considered here). A small pony needs a faster velocity to bump a more massive one off the line. The rules of the game take this into account by regulating the relative speeds (and angles) of bumping to avoid accidents due to large discrepancies in momentum between two ponies.

Free Body Diagrams

When several forces act on a body, their effect can be determined by drawing a free body diagram, in which the body of interest is depicted completely free of its environment, and all the forces acting on it are represented as vectors. The external forces are resolved into their components, and the components acting in a particular direction are added or subtracted, to determine the overall effect of the forces in that direction.

Example: The forces acting on a standing horse are the body weight and the GRFs on the four hooves. In a free body diagram showing a two-dimensional lateral view of the horse (figure 7.12), the following forces are present:

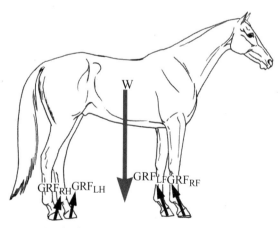

Figure 7.12: Free body diagram of the forces (arrows) acting on a standing horse in the lateral view. The forces are the horse's weight (W) and the ground reaction forces on the left hind limb (GRF$_{LH}$), the right hind limb (GRF$_{RH}$), the left front limb (GRF$_{LF}$), and the right front limb (GRF$_{RF}$).

· the body weight *W* acting vertically downward through the center of mass

· the GRFs of the four limbs, which can be resolved into a vertical component acting upward and a smaller longitudinal component that acts forward in the hind limbs and backward in the front limbs.

The downward force of the body weight is exactly equal to the sum of the upward vertical components of the GRFs on the four limbs, so the net vertical force is zero. The longitudinal GRF components, comprising the forward forces on the hind limbs and the backward forces on the front limbs, also sum to zero.

Example: The forces acting on a draft horse trying to pull a heavy load (figure 7.13) are:

· the body weight of the horse *W* acting vertically downward

· the GRFs of the limbs that are in the stance phase, in this case the right hind (GRF_{RH}), the left hind (GRF_{LH}), and left front (GRF_{LF})

· the resistance force (*R*) acting through the collar

The effect of air resistance is small enough to be ignored.

If the horse exerts a large enough longitudinal force to overcome the resistance, the load will be moved, but if the resultant force is insufficient, the horse will struggle unsuccessfully. To determine whether the horse will be successful in moving the load forward, the forces are resolved into vertical and longitudinal components. The longitudinal components are summed, and if the resultant longitudinal force acts in a forward direction, the horse will overcome the resistance of the load. In other words, the sum of the longitudinal forces exerted by the limbs must exceed the longitudinal force acting through the collar.

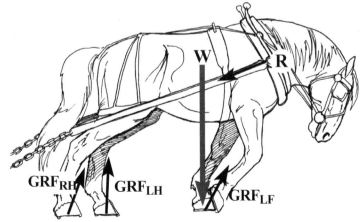

Figure 7.13: Free body diagram of the forces on a draft horse attempting to pull a load. The forces are the horse's weight (W), the ground reaction forces on the right hind limb (GRF_{RH}), left hind limb (GRF_{LH}), and left front limb (GRF_{LF}), and the resistance acting through the collar (R).

If one of the forces is unknown, the free body diagram can be used to predict the marginal value of that force. For example, if the GRFs are known, the maximal load the horse is capable of pulling under those conditions can be calculated.

Pressure

Pressure is the force per unit area.

$$\text{Pressure} = \frac{\text{Force}}{\text{Area}}$$

When a force is distributed over a small area, pressure is high. If the same force is applied over a larger area, the pressure is reduced.

Hoof Pressure

A standing horse has only a small area of support between the four hooves and the ground. When the horse lies down, it has a larger area of contact between its body and the ground. Pressure relates the force, in this case the horse's body weight, with the area over which that force is distributed: when the force (body weight) is distributed over the small area of the hooves, pressure is higher than when it is distributed over the larger area provided by the side of the horse's body.

During locomotion, the GRFs are transmitted through the small contact areas between the hoof and the ground. The practice of allowing the frog and sole to participate in weight-bearing reduces pressure on the wall.

Landing from a Height

In human sports that involve landing from a height, such as high jumping and pole vaulting, athletes reduce pressure on the contact area by landing on their backs on a soft pad. A falling rider should follow the same principles, spreading the impact force over a large, well-padded area of the body. Jumping horses do not have this option; they must land on their front hooves on a surface that offers sufficient resistance to generate the ground reaction forces needed to continue cantering forward to the next fence. Landing on a very soft, deformable surface would be like landing on pillows, and is incompatible with the need to resume a normal stride as quickly as possible. Horses jumping large fences experience higher impact forces than during normal locomotion. These forces are imposed over a small area on the hoof and are transmitted across small contact areas at the joint surfaces as they are transmitted up the front limbs. Since pressure on the hoof and the joints is high, it is not surprising that jumpers are prone to wear and tear injuries of their limbs.

90

Saddle Pressure

The rider's weight is transmitted through the saddle to the horse's back. Saddles that have small panels are associated with higher pressure than saddles with larger panels. Western saddles with their large weight-bearing area, have lower pressure than close-contact saddles that have a very small weight-bearing area. The practice of making English saddles with a wedged panel that extends behind the cantle increases the weight-bearing area, thus reducing the pressure over the contact surface.

The size of the area of contact is not the only consideration in saddle fitting. It is also important that the pressure be spread as evenly as possible throughout the weight-bearing area, which happens only when the shape of the panels matches the shape of the horse's back. Since the development of the horse's back muscles changes with training and general condition of the horse, saddle fit must be reevaluated periodically.

Saddle pads deform under pressure to distribute the forces more evenly over the area of contact. The material used should deform when pressure is applied and return to its original shape after the pressure is removed. Some materials fulfill this function better than others. Materials that do not rebound to their original shape become permanently compressed over time and lose their cushioning properties.

Stress and Strain

Stress describes the amount of force applied per unit of area. Strain is the resulting deformation expressed in terms of the original measurements, so its units are dimensionless. For most materials, there is a linear relationship between stress and strain within a certain range.

Limb loading during locomotion stresses the musculoskeletal tissues. When tensile stress is applied to a tendon, it responds by stretching. The amount of tension relative to the cross-sectional area of the tendon is the stress. A tendon with a large cross-sectional area, such as the deep digital flexor tendon, experiences less stress for the same amount of loading than a tendon with a smaller cross-sectional area, such as the superficial digital flexor tendon. The amount of elongation of the tendon expressed relative to its original length is the strain.

Example: When a limb is loaded during the stance phase, extension of the fetlock is controlled by the flexor tendons and suspensory ligament. The amount of loading (stress) increases with speed, leading to more elongation (greater strain) of the flexor tendons and suspensory ligament, which allows more extension of the fetlock at faster speeds.

Stiffness and Compliance

Stiffness is the amount of force needed to deform a body by one percent of its length. Compliance, which is defined as the amount of elongation per unit of force, is the inverse of stiffness. A stiffer (less compliant) body requires a larger force to produce a certain amount of deformation. Stiffness is often described in terms of Young's modulus, which is the stress required to elongate the body to double its original length. Since most materials break before their length can be doubled, Young's modulus is an abstract quantity.

Example: The outer surface of the hoof is covered with a keratinized protein (horn) that protects the sensitive internal structures. The moisture content of hoof horn varies, and this affects its stiffness. The horn of the wall has a lower moisture content that makes it stiffer than the horn of the frog. The hoof wall is drier and harder in horses that live in a desert than in horses that inhabit marshy areas. Differences in hardness affect the amount and type of wear experienced by the hoof wall, and the ease with which a farrier can trim the foot.

ANGULAR KINETICS

Abbreviations used in this chapter:

CoM: Center of mass

GRF: Ground reaction force

Angular kinetics is the study of the forces associated with angular motion. The concepts of angular kinetics are closely related to those of linear kinetics.

Angular kinetics is the study of forces that cause rotation.

Forces that Cause Rotation

When the line of action of a force passes through the center of mass (CoM) of the body on which it acts, it causes translational motion of the entire body. If the line of action of a force does not pass through the center of a body, it tends to cause the body to rotate around its CoM as it moves. A force that does not act through the CoM is called an off-center or eccentric force. Angular motion results from the application of an eccentric force.

An eccentric force is one that does not pass through the center of mass of the body on which it acts. An eccentric force causes both translation and rotation.

Example: A rubber mat is lying on the floor in the center of a stall. If someone pushes with his or her foot against the middle of the left side of the mat, the force vector acts through the CoM of the mat (figure 8.1). If the force is large enough, the whole mat is moved to the right; there is translation but no rotation. If the same force is applied eccentrically to the upper left side of the mat (figure 8.2), the mat is translated to the right and, at the same time, it is rotated in a clockwise direction.

This example illustrates how the same force produces different effects when applied to the same object in different locations. When the line of action of a force passes through the CoM of an object, it causes translation in the direction

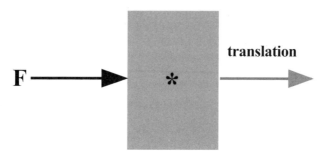

Figure 8.1: Force causing translation. A force (black arrow F) acting through the center (*) of the mat causes translation without rotation in the direction shown by the gray arrow.

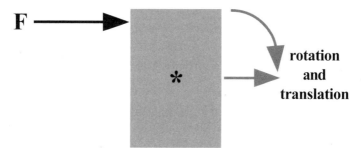

Figure 8.2: Force causing translation and rotation. An eccentric force (black arrow F), which does not act through the center (*) of the mat, causes a combination of translation and clockwise rotation as shown by the gray arrows.

in which the force acts. If the force does not pass through the CoM, it causes simultaneous translation and rotation, with the direction of rotation being determined by the line of action relative to the center.

A special situation exists when a body is constrained to rotate around one point, for example a gate that rotates around hinges or a bucket that swings around its handle. In this case, a force applied at any point tends to cause rotation and is regarded as an eccentric force.

To continue the example of moving a mat across the floor, imagine that the mat in a wash rack has been displaced, and it is lying at an angle to the walls. It needs to be turned so that the long edges of the mat lie parallel to the walls (figure 8.3). This mat is too heavy to be moved by one person, so two people position themselves at opposite corners, where they exert equal and opposite parallel forces (F_1 and F_2) against the mat. F_1 tends to rotate the mat clockwise and to translate it to the right. F_2 tends to rotate the mat clockwise and to translate it to the left. The force components that tend to translate the mat are equal in magnitude but act in opposite directions, so they cancel each other

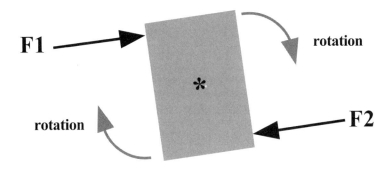

F1

rotation

rotation

F2

Figure 8.3: Force couple causing rotation. Two parallel forces (black arrows F1 and F2), that are equal in magnitude, opposite in direction, and act at equal distances from the center of mass (*), cause rotation without translation (gray arrows).

out. The remaining tendency of both forces is to rotate the mat clockwise so their turning effects are additive. The net result is that the mat is simply rotated clockwise around its center. This arrangement of forces is called a couple.

> *A couple is a force combination that tends to cause rotation without translation.*

In chapter 1, three types of motion were described: translation, rotation, and simultaneous translation and rotation (general motion). The forces responsible for each type of motion are as follows:

· translation results from a force directed through the CoM of the body

· rotation results from a force couple

· simultaneous translation and rotation result from the application of an eccentric force.

Torque

The effect of a force couple is to produce rotation. Two factors determine the rotary effect of a couple: the magnitude of the forces and the distance between their lines of action (figure 8.4). In the example of the rubber mat in the wash rack, the harder the two people push (higher forces), the more the mat will be turned. The turning effect can also be increased by applying the forces further apart, that is, closer to the corners of the mat rather than close to its center.

The product of these two factors, the magnitude of the forces and the distance between their lines of action, is a measure of the turning effect of the couple, which is called the moment of the couple or the torque (figure 8.4). The distance between the lines of action of the forces is called the moment arm.

95

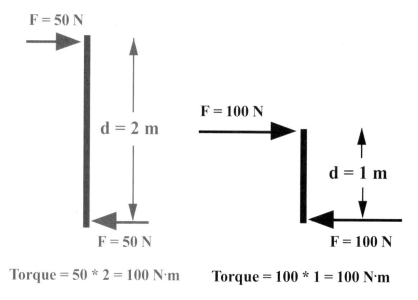

F = 50 N

d = 2 m

F = 50 N

F = 100 N

d = 1 m

F = 100 N

Torque = 50 * 2 = 100 N·m   Torque = 100 * 1 = 100 N·m

Figure 8.4: Turning effect (torque or moment) of a couple on a vertical bar. The torque, which is the product of the force (F) and the moment arm (distance d) between the lines of action of the forces, is the same for the two examples.

The torque (moment) of a couple measures the turning effect.

$$T = Fd$$

where T is the torque of the couple, F is the magnitude of one of the forces, and d is the shortest (perpendicular) distance between the lines of action of the two forces (moment arm).

The SI units of torque are obtained by multiplying the units of force by the units of distance as in newton·meters (N·m).

The word torque is also used to describe the turning effect produced when a force is exerted on a body that pivots around a fixed point, such as a gate that opens on hinges or a limb segment that rotates around a joint. When a gate is pulled outwards, it swings around its hinges regardless of the magnitude of the force or its point of application. Since the gate simply rotates around an axis, the hinges must exert a force that is equal in magnitude, opposite in direction, and parallel to the force used to open the gate. This opposing force at the hinges cancels the tendency to translate and results in a couple that rotates the gate. When rotation occurs around a fixed point, it is customary to ignore the force exerted at the pivot (hinge) and to describe the magnitude and direction of the turning effect in terms of the torque of the applied force. In this case, torque is calculated from the force multiplied by its distance from the fixed point of rotation, with the distance between the force and the point of rotation being measured perpendicular to the force direction.

Example: When a force F of 100 N is applied perpendicular to a gate at a distance d of 1.2 m from the hinges (figure 8.5), the torque is calculated as:

$$T = Fd = 100 * 1.2 = 120 \text{ N·m}$$

If the force of 100 N is applied to the gate at an angle of 65° (figure 8.5), the resulting torque is calculated by resolving the force into two components, a tangential force (F_T) acting perpendicular (tangential) to the gate and a radial force (F_R) acting along its length (radially).

The force component F_R acting along the gate is:

$$F_R = 100 * \cos65 = 100 * 0.42 = 42 \text{ N}$$

The tangential force F_T acting perpendicular to the gate is:

$$F_T = 100 * \sin65 = 100 * 0.91 = 91 \text{ N}$$

Because the radial component of the force passes through the axis at the hinges, it has no tendency to cause the gate to swing. The rotational effects are entirely due to the tangential component acting perpendicular to the gate. In this case the torque is:

$$T = Fd = 91 * 1.2 = 109.2 \text{ N·m}$$

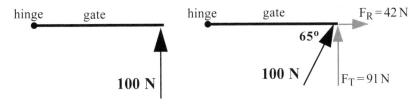

Figure 8.5: A gate rotating around a hinge as viewed from above. On the left, a force is applied perpendicular to the gate. On the right, a force applied at an angle of 65° is resolved into a radial component (F_R) acting along the gate and a tangential component (F_T) acting perpendicular to it.

The above examples show that the most effective way to produce rotation about a fixed point is to direct the force perpendicular (tangential) to the object and to apply that force as far as possible from the axis of rotation. Practical experience supports this; the force required to open a gate is smallest when the force is applied perpendicular to the end of the gate.

There are numerous equestrian examples in which rotation occurs around a fixed point. In most of these examples, it is possible to adjust the rotation by altering the force or by changing the length of the moment arm.

Example: The stirrup pivots around its suspension point on the stirrup leather, and the entire stirrup leather pivots around its suspension point on the bar (figure 8.6). When a rider exerts an eccentric force acting downward through the heel, the stirrup rotates so that the heel is lowered relative to the toe without changing the position of the upper part of the leg. Riders who adopt a chair seat push their whole leg forward causing the entire stirrup leather to rotate forward around the bar.

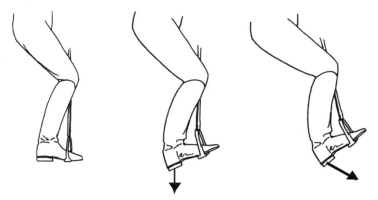

Figure 8.6: The stirrup is horizontal when the foot rests lightly (left). An eccentric force acting downwards through the rider's heel causes the stirrup to pivot around the leather (center). When the leg is pushed forward in a chair seat, the entire stirrup leather rotates around the bar (right).

Example: The cheeks (shanks) of a curb bit rotate around the mouthpiece. The length of the lower cheek determines the moment arm of a force applied through the reins (figure 8.7). The longer the lower cheek, the greater the torque and the larger the angle through which the cheek rotates for a certain rein tension. The length of the upper cheek determines the amount of pressure applied to the poll and to the chin groove. The longer the upper cheek, the further forward the cheek piece moves and the more pressure is applied to the poll and chin groove for the same amount of rein tension.

Muscles as Torque Generators

Muscles exert forces on bones that are constrained to rotate around the joints. In other words, muscles act as torque generators. The amount of torque generated depends on the force applied, the angle at which the muscle attaches to the bone, and the distance from the muscular attachment to the joint. Slight differences in the attachment point can produce significant differences in the muscular torque.

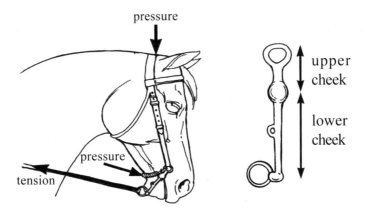

Figure 8.7: Action of the curb bit. The length of the lower cheek determines the torque resulting from rein tension. The length of the upper cheek determines the amount of forward displacement of the cheek piece and the resulting pressure on the poll and chin groove.

One of the characteristics of the muscular system is the seemingly large amount of redundancy. Most joints have more than one muscle capable of performing the same, or at least similar, functions. These muscles work in harmony to stabilize and move the joints, and coordination between the various muscles produces smooth movements. When different muscles have the same effect at a joint, they are called *agonists* and their actions are said to be *agonistic*. For example, the superficial digital flexor and the deep digital flexor muscles are both flexors of the fetlock, so they are agonists. Muscles that have opposite actions at a joint are called *antagonists*, and their actions are *antagonistic*. For example, the common digital extensor is an extensor of the fetlock and is thus antagonistic to the digital flexors.

Contraction of the superficial or deep digital flexor muscle creates a torque on the flexor side of the fetlock. Contraction of the common digital extensor muscle creates a torque on the extensor side of the fetlock. These muscles may act individually or together. The magnitude of the torque produced by each muscle is calculated by multiplying the component of the force that acts perpendicular to the bone by its moment arm, which is the distance from the line of action of the muscle to the center of rotation of the joint.

The net or resultant torque across a joint is the summation of the flexor and extensor torques, which can also be expressed as the difference between the total flexor torque and the total extensor torque.

Angular Momentum

During linear motion, momentum is the product of mass and velocity. For rotational motion, angular momentum is the product of moment of inertia and angular velocity.

$$H = I\omega$$

where H is the angular momentum, I is the moment of inertia, and ω is the angular velocity.

Moment of Inertia

For linear motion, a body's mass is a measure of its inertia. For rotational motion, resistance to changes in angular momentum are due to angular inertia or moment of inertia. A body's moment of inertia is determined not only by its mass, but also by how the mass is distributed relative to the axis of rotation.

The moment of inertia is the resistance of a body to change its state of angular motion.

The smaller the moment of inertia, the easier it is to change the angular momentum and rate of rotation. Moment of inertia is decreased by shortening the total length to bring all parts of the body closer to the axis of rotation or by moving more of the mass or the heavier components closer to the axis of rotation (figure 8.8). Conversely, the moment of inertia is increased by lengthening the entire body or by moving more of the mass or the denser components away from the axis of rotation (figure 8.8). A larger moment of inertia requires more force to change the rate of rotation.

Figure 8.8: Effect of mass distribution relative to the axis of rotation (*) on moment of inertia. For an object of uniform density, moment of inertia is higher for the shape on the left than for the shape in the center. If density is proportional to depth of shading, moment of inertia is higher for the object on the right than the one in the center.

Moment of Inertia of the Equine Limbs

Horses have evolved as cursorial (running) animals. Long limbs are advantageous for speed, because the body mass is vaulted further forward over the supporting limb strut during the stance phase. During the swing phase, however, long limbs are a disadvantage due to their greater moment of inertia. By flexing the joints, the entire limb can be compressed and brought closer to the axis of rotation during swing. The moment of inertia of the equine limbs is further reduced by confining the large heavy muscles to the proximal part of the limb, and minimizing the weight of the distal limb by having a single digit comprised of relatively lightweight tissues.

Angular Velocity

Angular velocity describes the rate of rotation. When a body is airborne, the total angular momentum is constant, and angular velocity varies with the moment of inertia. For a body with articulated segments, moment of inertia can be adjusted by changing the orientation of the segments.

Example: In a vaulter performing a somersault during a dismount, moment of inertia is large when the limb joints are extended, which moves the segments away from the CoM, and smaller when the joints are flexed bringing the limb segments closer to the CoM. Consequently, moment of inertia decreases and angular velocity increases progressively from the layout position (back straight and limb joints extended), to the piked position (folded at the waist), to the tucked position (back and limb joints flexed).

Laws of Angular Motion

The applications of the laws of motion to linear motion and linear kinetics were described in chapter 7. Analogous laws can be applied to angular motion.

First Law of Angular Motion

A rotating body will continue to turn about its axis of rotation with constant angular momentum, unless an external couple or eccentric force is exerted upon it.

This law is also known as the principle of conservation of angular momentum. It indicates that a spinning body will continue spinning indefinitely, with the same angular momentum, unless acted upon by a couple or an eccentric force that modifies its angular momentum.

Example: Jumping horses rotate around their CoM during the aerial phase. At take-off the GRF imparts a certain amount of linear and angular momentum. The linear momentum projects the horse upward and forward to clear the height and width of the fence. The angular momentum rotates the horse's body so that, after pushing off with the hind limbs, the entire trunk rotates forward around the CoM throughout the aerial phase to enable the horse to land on its front limbs (figure 8.9). The angular momentum can be altered only by an external couple or an eccentric force (principle of conservation of angular momentum). Therefore, angular momentum is constant from the time the horse leaves the ground until it contacts an external object. Usually this external object is the ground on the landing side, though sometimes the horse's rotation is changed by hitting the fence, especially a solid cross country obstacle.

Since angular momentum cannot be changed during the aerial phase, it is important for a jumping horse to exert appropriate eccentric forces during take-off. A horse that takes off without enough angular momentum fails to rotate sufficiently during the aerial phase and lands with a very flat angle to the ground. This occurs most often in hurdlers racing at high speeds over small fences. Occasionally, there is so little angular momentum that the hind limbs land before the front limbs. Conversely, a horse may misjudge a fence and take-off with too much angular momentum. In this case, the horse may over-rotate during the aerial phase or be unable to control the high angular velocity at landing, causing it to fall and somersault forward over the front limbs.

Angular momentum is constant during an aerial phase, but angular velocity (speed of rotation) can be adjusted by changing the moment of inertia. When a horse tucks the limbs more tightly, the moment of inertia around the CoM decreases and angular velocity increases. Conversely, the horse's angular velocity can be reduced by extending the limbs to increase the moment of inertia. Jumpers sometimes extend their hind limbs between the rails of an oxer to reduce the angular velocity and prevent over-rotation.

Figure 8.9: Rotation during the aerial phase of jumping. The horse's body rotates forward around its center of mass (*) with constant angular momentum from take off to landing.

Second Law of Angular Motion

The rate of change of angular momentum of a body is proportional to the torque causing it, and the change takes place in the direction in which the torque acts.

$$T = I\alpha$$

where T is the applied torque (moment of force), I is the moment of inertia, and α is the angular acceleration.

Example: In order to swing a gate around its hinges, a force is applied that causes a torque (figure 8.5). Since the moment of inertia of the gate does not change, an increase in force (torque) is associated with an increase in angular acceleration.

Third Law of Angular Motion

For every torque that is exerted by one body on another, there is an equal and opposite torque exerted by the second body on the first.

When a torque causes part of a body to rotate in one direction, there is an equal and opposite reaction torque causing some other part of the body to rotate, or tend to rotate, in the opposite direction.

Example: When a roper's arm rotates above his head in one direction, the trunk tends to rotate in the opposite direction. However, since the trunk has a much larger moment of inertia than the arm, the effects of the equal torques appear to be quite different. While the arm swings in large circles, the remainder of the body exhibits only a slight tendency to rotate in the opposite direction. Furthermore, because the roper is sitting firmly in the saddle, the tendency to rotate is transmitted to the horse, which has a considerably larger mass and greater inertia.

Example: When a polo player makes a swing, the trunk tends to rotate in the opposite direction to the swing of the arm and mallet (figure 8.10). For a fore shot, rotation of the arm and mallet (counterclockwise in figure 8.10) tends to cause the player's body to rotate forward (clockwise). For a back shot, the upper body tends to rotate backward. As with the roper, the effect on the player's body is relatively small, because the body has more inertia than the arm and mallet and, when the player is securely anchored in the saddle, the effect on the horse and player is imperceptible.

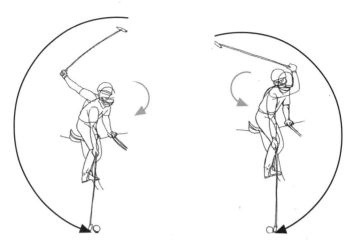

Figure 8.10: Torque causing rotation of a polo player's arm (black arrow) is opposed by a reation torque that tends to rotate the trunk in the opposite direction (gray arrow). The body tends to rotate forward during a fore shot (left) and backward during a back shot (right).

Transfer of Momentum

Total angular momentum is constant when a body is airborne. However, it is possible for the angular momentum of different parts of the body to change, while maintaining the overall angular momentum of the entire body. When the angular momentum of one part of the body decreases, some part (or all) of the rest of the body must experience a compensatory increase in angular momentum to conserve the total angular momentum.

Example: A jumping horse rotates forward with constant angular momentum throughout the aerial phase. As the horse prepares for landing, the head and neck are elevated relative to the trunk. This backward rotation of the neck is compensated by a small increase in forward angular velocity of the trunk.

Motion through a Turn

When a body moves on a curved path, it tends to accelerate out of the circle unless a centripetal (center-seeking) force is applied to maintain its circular motion. The tendency to fly off at a tangent is often referred to as the centrifugal force. The tendency to leave the curved path increases with an increase in mass or velocity, or a decrease in radius of rotation.

Example: When a racehorse negotiates a turn at racing speed, the tendency to drift to the outside of the track is overcome by a centripetal force provided by the hooves, which exert a large transverse force acting toward the outside of the turn. The opposing GRF is directed toward the inside of the turn. It acts eccentrically around the horse's CoM and tends to rotate the body outward. The horse combats the tendency to rotate outward by leaning into the turn, so the vertical component of the GRF acts eccentrically on the CoM in the opposite direction, and tends to rotate the body inward.

The safe speed for a turn is the maximal speed at which a horse can negotiate it safely. If this safe speed is exceeded, the ground is no longer able to provide sufficient centripetal force. Unless speed is reduced, the horse will drift outward during the turn or risk falling. If all other factors are the same, the safe speed gets slower as the radius of curvature of the turn decreases (tighter turn). One way to increase the safe speed is to increase the radius of the turns, but this may not be an option when a racetrack has to fit into a small space and provide good visibility of the backstretch from the stands. An alternative method of increasing the safe speed is to bank (elevate) the turns. The effect of the banked slope is that a component of the horse's weight acts down the slope, thus contributing to the centripetal force. Depending on the amount of banking, the need for a transverse GRF directed to the inside of the turn may be reduced or eliminated.

There has been considerable research on the effect of the radius of curvature and the amount of banking in human sports, such as cycling and sprinting. In equine sports this information was applied in Standardbred racing (Fredricson et al. 1975a). Traditionally, Standardbred racetracks had two straights joined by semicircular turns with a relatively small radius of curvature. In order to negotiate these turns, the horses had to lean inwards. When the hooves were placed flat on the track with the limbs angled toward the center of the turns, large mediolateral strains were created in the joints of the distal limbs. Thermographic evaluations of Standardbreds after they worked on a track with under-banked turns revealed heat in the fetlock joints (Fredricson et al. 1975b). With adequately banked turns, the hooves and limbs are aligned perpendicular to the track, thus avoiding the damaging effects of leaning into the turns.

Even when the turns are adequately banked, however, a sudden change from a straight track to a fully-banked, semicircular turn is a difficult adjustment for a horse to make at racing speed, so it is preferable to include a transition curve between the straight and the turn. The transition curve incorporates a gradual decrease in radius of curvature, together with a gradual increase in the amount of banking. When Standardbreds race on tracks that are constructed in this manner, their gait is more regular and they are likely to stay sounder (Dalin et al. 1973). However, correctly banked tracks are more difficult to maintain, because the surface material tends to roll toward the inside rail in the banked areas.

105

A centripetal force acts on a rotating body but is provided by another body. In a racehorse moving through a turn, the other body is the surface of the track. A swinging polo mallet maintains its curved path due to a centripetal force exerted by the player's hand. If the grip on the mallet is released part way through the swing, the centripetal force exerted by the hand on the mallet ceases to exist. Consequently, the mallet tends to continue traveling in the direction in which it was moving at the moment of release. That is, it leaves the player's hand at a tangent to the arc of rotation (figure 8.11), not radially outward away from the axis of rotation. The mallet has a loop that fits around the player's hand to prevent this from happening if the grip on the handle is loosened.

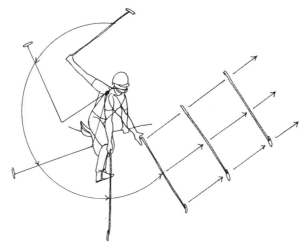

Figure 8.11: Tangential path of an object when centripetal force ceases. If the player's grip on the mallet is lost, it flies off at a tangent to the arc of rotation.

A lever is a device used to facilitate moving an object by creating a torque. Levers are present throughout the musculoskeletal system, and the principles of leverage are applied in the design of implements used to facilitate the performance of many chores around the barn.

A lever consists of a rigid bar revolving around a fixed axis known as the fulcrum. A force is applied at some point on the bar to overcome a resistance that is also acting at some point on the bar (figure 9.1). The relative positions of the force, the fulcrum, and the resistance determine whether the lever acts to increase the effect of the force or to increase the speed or distance through which the resistance is moved.

A lever is a rigid structure, hinged at one point, and to which a force and a resistance are applied at two other points.

How Leverage Works

In chapter 8, it was shown that torque is the product of a force and its moment arm. The effectiveness of a force applied to move a resistance depends on the relative torques created by the force and the resistance. These torques are calculated as the product of the force or resistance and its moment arm, measured as the perpendicular distance from the force or resistance vector to the fulcrum.

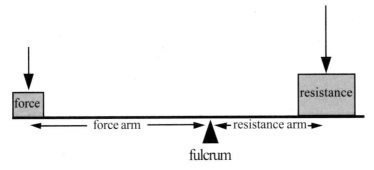

Figure 9.1: Parts of a lever.

When the torques generated by the force and resistance are equal, the lever is in balance. If the torque generated by the force exceeds that of the resistance, it overcomes the resistance and movement occurs. If the torque generated by the force is smaller than that of the resistance, movement does not occur or it occurs in the direction of resistance.

The relative lengths of the force arm and the resistance arm determine whether a lever acts to increase the effect of the force or to increase the distance or speed of its action. In general, a long force arm increases the effect of a force and allows a large resistance to be overcome, whereas a long resistance arm allows a small resistance to be moved rapidly or through a large distance.

Using Leverage to Increase the Effect of a Force

When lifting an object without the aid of a lever, a force must be exerted that is at least as large as the weight of the object. With the aid of a lever, however, it is possible to lift or hold a weight using a much smaller force if the force arm is longer than the resistance arm (figure 9.2).

Example: A person with a mass of 60 kg can move a rock, mass 80 kg, using a long board as a lever and a small rock as a fulcrum. The key to success is to make the force arm longer than the resistance arm.

Figure 9.2: Effect of relative lengths of the force arm and resistance arm. When the force arm is short and the resistance arm is long, a small force (F) is unable to move a large resistance (R) (left). When the force arm is long and the resistance arm is short, a small force overcomes a large resistance causing movement in the direction shown by the arrow (right).

Using Leverage to Increase the Speed or Distance of Movement

When a lever rotates around its fulcrum, all points on the force arm and lever arm rotate through the same angle but the amount of linear motion increases with the distance from the fulcrum (chapter 4). Therefore, the relative lengths of the force arm and resistance arm determine the distance through which the force and resistance move and their relative speeds of movement. Leverage can be used to increase the speed or distance through which a small resistance is moved by making the resistance arm longer than the force arm (figure 9.3).

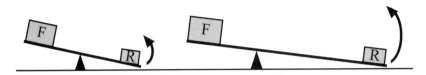

Figure 9.3: Effect of relative lengths of force arm and resistance arm on the distance through which the resistance moves. A short resistance arm moves the resistance through a small arc (arrow on left). A longer resistance arm moves the resistance through a wider arc (arrow on right).

Types of Levers

Levers are classified as first, second, or third-class according to the relative placements of the force, resistance, and fulcrum (figure 9.4).

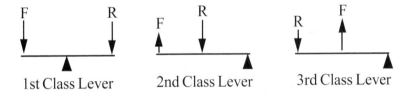

1st Class Lever   2nd Class Lever   3rd Class Lever

Figure 9.4: Positions of force (F), resistance (R) and fulcrum (arrow) in different types of levers.

First-Class Levers

In a first-class lever, the fulcrum lies between the force and the resistance. The relative lengths of the force arm and resistance arm determine the mechanical effect of a first-class lever. When the force arm is shorter than the resistance arm, speed of movement is increased. If the force arm is longer than the resistance arm, the effect of the force is increased.

Seesaw

A seesaw is a classical example of a first-class lever. The seesaw is balanced when the torques are approximately the same on both sides of the fulcrum. This is achieved by adjusting the seating positions so the heavier person sits closer to the fulcrum to shorten the moment arm.

Pitchfork

A pitchfork is used as a first-class lever in which the relative lengths of the force arm and resistance arm can be adjusted by the user. The hand placed part way down the shaft acts as the fulcrum about which the two ends rotate. The other hand applies a force at the end of the shaft to lift something that acts as the resistance, such as a pile of manure. If the pile of manure is small and is to be lifted through a wide arc, the fulcrum hand should be placed close to the lifting hand, which gives a short force arm and a long resistance arm (figure 9.5). The lever effect then acts to increase the distance or speed of movement. On the other hand, if the objective is to lift a heavy pile of soiled bedding, it is better to move the fulcrum hand further down the shaft toward the tines of the pitchfork (figure 9.5). This lengthens the force arm and shortens the resistance arm, which has the effect of increasing the effect of the force. In practice, a pitchfork is not used purely as a lever. The leverage it provides is used to overcome inertia and establish momentum of the material being lifted, after which it acts as an extension of the arms to throw the material into a wheelbarrow or other container.

Figure 9.5: Pitchfork as a lever. When the fulcrum hand is placed close to the handle, it increases the speed of lifting (left). When the fulcrum hand is placed close to the tines it increases the effect of the lifting force (right).

Second-Class Levers

A second-class lever is one in which the force and resistance are located on the same side of the fulcrum, with the resistance applied closer to the fulcrum than the force. Since the force arm is longer than the resistance arm, a second-class lever increases the effect of the force, not the speed of movement.

Wheelbarrow

A wheelbarrow is a second-class lever (figure 9.6). The wheel is the fulcrum, the force is applied to the handles, and the bucket supports the resistance. The force arm is relatively long, providing a mechanical advantage that allows a heavy resistance to be lifted by a smaller force. It is easier to lift the wheelbarrow if the load in the bucket is placed closer to the wheel (shorter resistance arm), than if it is placed closer to the handles (longer resistance arm).

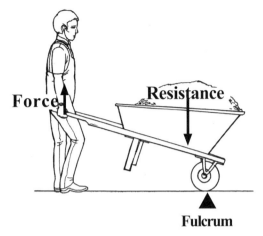

Figure 9.6: Wheelbarrow as a lever.

Girth Tightener

A girth tightener acts as a second-class lever by applying more tension to the girth tabs than the fingers alone (figure 9.7). The fulcrum at the end of the tightener is placed against the panel of the saddle. The girth tab is grasped by the jaws of the tightener fairly close to its fulcrum, and a force is applied at the end of the handle, giving it a long force arm. An upward force on the handle rotates the tightener around its fulcrum and pulls the girth tab through the buckle. The leverage provided by the relatively long force arm increases the effect of the force and tightens the girth. The girth tightener is a useful device for people who are unable to grasp the girth strap between their fingers or whose strength is compromised. For those with normal strength, however, the leverage creates a danger of over-tightening the girth.

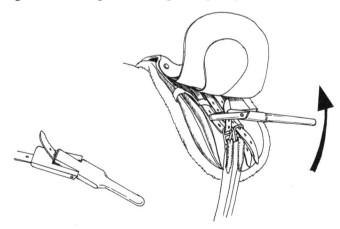

Figure 9.7: Girth tightener (left) is used as a lever to tighten the girth by applying a force to the handle in the direction shown by the arrow (right).

111

Third-Class Levers

In a third-class lever the force and resistance act on the same side of the fulcrum, with the force being applied closer to the fulcrum than the resistance. Since the resistance arm is longer than the force arm, this type of lever always acts to increase the distance or speed of movement.

Locomotor Muscles

The musculoskeletal system has numerous examples of muscles that act as third-class levers. These muscles usually attach close to a joint, so the force arm is short. Muscles that are active during the swing phase overcome the small inertial resistance of the more distal segments and swing the limb rapidly through a wide range of motion. During stance, however, the ground reaction force provides a large resistance to limb movement, so muscles that act as third-class levers are less effective in providing propulsion during stance.

The *tibialis cranialis* muscle runs from the tibia, across the front of the hock joint, to the hind cannon bone (figure 9.8). Its action is to flex the hock joint during the swing phase of the stride, when resistance to flexion is due to inertia of the limb segments below the hock joint. The force arm, which is the distance from the fulcrum at the hock to the line of action of the muscle, is much shorter than the resistance arm, measured from the hock to the center of mass of the distal limb. Thus the *tibialis cranialis* acts as a third-class lever.

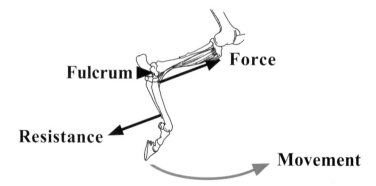

Figure 9.8: Tibialis cranialis *muscle exerts a force that overcomes the inertial resistance of the distal limb, causing the cannon bone to rotate around its fulcrum at the hock joint. The muscle acts as a third-class lever to rotate the hoof through a wide arc during the swing phase.*

FRICTION 10

Friction is a force that occurs when one body moves or tends to move across the surface of another. The frictional force opposes the motion or impending motion.

Friction is the force that opposes motion or impending motion when one body moves or tends to move across the surface of another.

Friction has both beneficial and detrimental effects. For example, a driving horse needs sufficient friction between its hooves and the ground to generate a tractive force, but the vehicle's wheels or runners should have low friction to reduce the tractive force needed to pull the vehicle.

Energy lost due to friction is dissipated as heat (thermal energy).

Example: The belt of an equine high speed treadmill is made of non-slip material. When a horse exercises on a treadmill, considerable heat is generated as a result of friction between the hooves and the treadmill belt. If the moving belt is photographed with a thermographic (heat detecting) camera, the hoof prints are clearly visible as hot spots.

Friction is classified according to the type of motion that is occurring. This chapter will consider two types of friction: sliding friction occurs when one body slides over the surface of another, and rolling friction occurs when one body rolls over the surface of another. In both cases, limiting friction must be overcome to initiate motion, then sliding or rolling friction must be overcome to maintain motion.

Example: A sled is parked on a level floor. The weight of the sled acts downward through the runners and is supported by an upward force exerted by the ground. There is no tendency to slide over the ground, and there is no friction. If a horse is hitched to the sled and pulls on the shafts, the sled tends to start sliding forward, and friction then acts to oppose the tendency to slide (figure 10.1).

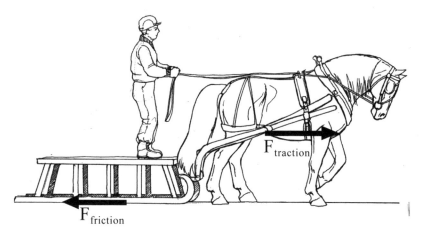

Figure 10.1: The force of friction ($F_{friction}$) opposes movement when the horse applies a tractive force to the shafts. $F_{traction}$ represents the horizontal component of the force applied to the shafts.

How Sliding Starts

Limiting friction controls the initiation of sliding. Until movement actually commences, the magnitude of the frictional force is exactly equal to the magnitude of the force tending to move the body. In other words, up to the point at which movement occurs, friction cancels the force that tends to cause movement. When friction reaches its upper limit, movement is about to begin.

In the example of the sled, the frictional force increases at the same rate as the force exerted by the horse until the limiting frictional force is reached. At this point the sled is about to slide forward.

Suppose the magnitude of the limiting friction between the sled and the ground is 2,000 N. If the horse exerts a tractive force of 1,200 N, this is matched by a frictional force of 1,200 N and no sliding occurs. If the horse increases the tractive force to 2,000 N, the limit of the frictional opposition has been reached. The sled still does not slide, but it is on the verge of doing so. When the tractive force reaches 2,001 N, it overcomes the limiting frictional force of 2,000 N and the sled begins to slide forward.

Factors that influence limiting friction are the nature of the surfaces and the forces that hold the surfaces together. These effects are expressed in the law of friction.

Law of Friction

Friction between two surfaces depends on the properties of the surfaces and the force that holds them in contact with each other.

For two dry surfaces, the limiting friction is equal to the normal reaction force multiplied by a constant, the value of which depends only on the nature of the surfaces.

This is expressed by the formula:

$$F = \mu R$$

where F is the limiting friction, R is the normal reaction force, and μ is a constant known as the *coefficient of friction*.

The normal reaction force is the component of the force between the two surfaces that acts perpendicular to the surface over which sliding occurs. On a level surface, the normal reaction force is equal to the weight of the sliding object. On a slope, the normal force is calculated from the weight of the sliding object and the angle of elevation *(θ)* of the surface over which it is tending to slide (chapter 15).

Normal Force = Weight * $\cos\theta$

Example: A horse is pulling a sled over level ground. The weight of the sled (which is equal to the normal reaction in this example) is 1,500 N, and it requires a longitudinal tractive force of 600 N to overcome the limiting friction. The coefficient of limiting friction is calculated as:

$$\mu = \frac{F}{R} = \frac{600}{1,500} = 0.4$$

The coefficient of limiting friction between the material comprising the runners of the sled and the ground surface is 0.4. The value is constant for the two materials regardless of the magnitude of the normal force or the limiting friction.

The force between two bodies affects the friction between them. Therefore, if weight is placed on a sled, a larger tractive force is required to overcome the limiting friction and start forward motion than if the sled were empty.

Example: If two people weighing 600 N and 900 N ride on the sled, the normal reaction force increases by 1,500 N to a total of 3,000 N. The coefficient of limiting friction is still 0.4. In this case, the tractive force needed to overcome the limiting friction is:

$$F = \mu R = 0.4 * 3,000 = 1,200 \text{ N}$$

This example illustrates how an increase in the normal forces, which is due to the additional weight on the sled, results in a proportional increase in the limiting friction, with the magnitude of this increase being determined by the value of the coefficient of friction. When μ is small, an increase in the normal force is associated with a smaller increase in the limiting friction force than when μ is high. The value of μ depends on the materials comprising the two surfaces that are sliding over each other. If one or both of the materials change, the coefficient of friction also changes.

Example: The coefficient of limiting friction is higher between asphalt and hoof horn than between asphalt and steel. Therefore, a barefoot horse is less likely to slip on an asphalt surface than a shod horse. The coefficient of friction between steel and hard soil is higher than that between steel and asphalt, so a shod horse is less likely to slip on hard soil than on asphalt.

Control of Sliding

Sliding friction controls slipping of one surface over another surface. Until sliding commences, the magnitude of the friction force is exactly equal to the force tending to cause the body to slide. As soon as the limiting friction is overcome, however, it requires less force to maintain the sliding than to initiate it. This is because the coefficient of sliding friction is always smaller than the coefficient of limiting friction.

$$F_S = \mu_S R$$

where F_S is the sliding friction force, R is the normal reaction force, and μ_S is a constant known as the coefficient of sliding friction.

The coefficient of sliding friction is generally in the range 0.1 to 1.0.

Example: A pair of draft horses pulling a heavy load lunge forward to initiate movement, but once the load begins to move, a steady pull is adequate to keep the load moving against the opposing force due to sliding friction.

Both limiting friction and sliding friction depend on the coefficient of friction between the two surfaces and the normal force holding the surfaces together. A heavier horse is less likely to slip than a lighter horse because it has a larger normal force. The same horse is less likely to slip on a rubber mat than on a smooth cement floor due to the higher coefficient of friction between hoof horn and rubber than between hoof horn and cement.

Experience indicates that a sled slides much more easily over snow or ice than over asphalt. However, the mechanics of gliding over snow and ice involve considerations other than simple sliding friction, that are beyond the scope of this discussion.

116

When the hoof makes contact with a soft surface, it penetrates the surface as it decelerates. On a hard surface, the hoof is unable to penetrate and may slide across the surface if there is insufficient friction to overcome the longitudinal force of the hoof (figure 10.2). For a horse traveling over slippery ground (low coefficient of friction), the horse is most likely to lose control of hoof movement and slide uncontrollably at the start of the stance phase, when the longitudinal component of the ground reaction force is high.

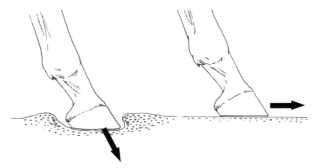

Figure 10.2: Hoof motion during the impact phase. On a soft surface (left), the hoof is gradually brought to rest as it penetrates forward and downward into the surface. On a hard surface (right), downward motion of the hoof ceases abruptly, but the hoof may slide forward if the surface offers insufficient frictional resistance to oppose the longitudinal force and decelerate the forward motion.

In the later part of stance, the hoof exerts a propulsive force to drive the horse forward. An ideal surface allows some penetration of the toe, but offers sufficient resistance for the hoof to push off against the surface and generate propulsion. On a hard surface, the toe is unable to penetrate the surface, and, if the coefficient of friction is low, the hoof may slide out behind the horse (figure 10.3).

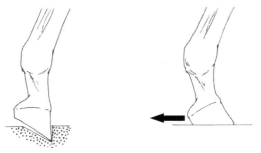

Figure 10.3: Hoof motion during push off. On a soft surface (left), the toe penetrates the ground, which stabilizes the hoof during push off. On a hard surface (right), the propulsive longitudinal force may cause the hoof to slide backward (black arrow) if the surface offers insufficient frictional resistance.

Studs or calks are sometimes used to reduce the risk of slipping by converting the longitudinal force into a torque around the calk, which acts as a fulcrum (figure 10.4).

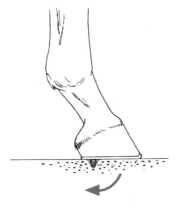

Figure 10.4: Effect of studs or calks. During impact, the calk penetrates the surface and acts as a fulcrum about which the hoof tends to rotate (gray arrow).

Rolling Motion

Rolling friction is a consideration when one surface rolls over another, which causes both surfaces to be deformed slightly. Although the deformations may not be large enough to be visible, they are sufficient to create some opposition to the rolling motion.

$$F_R = \mu_R R$$

where F_R is the rolling friction force, R is the normal reaction force, and μ_R is a constant known as the coefficient of rolling friction.

The coefficient of rolling friction is generally of the order of 0.001 to 0.01, which is much smaller than the coefficient of sliding friction. Consequently, the force opposing rolling motion is considerably less than the force opposing sliding over the same surface. This is why it is easier to roll a wheel across a surface than to slide it across the same surface.

Example: It is much easier for a driving horse to pull a vehicle over an asphalt surface when the wheels are rolling than when the wheels are locked. If the brakes are applied hard enough to lock the wheels, it becomes much more difficult for the horse to maintain forward motion because the coefficient of sliding friction is so much higher than the coefficient of rolling friction.

Sometimes a driver makes use of the effect of friction by applying the brakes on a vehicle to slow the forward motion of an over-enthusiastic horse or team.

Rolling friction is a factor in equestrian sports that involve a ball or wheels. The main factors that affect rolling friction are the nature of the surfaces, the normal reaction force, and the diameter of the ball or wheel. Because these factors can influence performance, the rules of a sport usually dictate the size and type of ball or wheel to be used.

Example: The ease with which a polo ball rolls over a field depends on the length of the grass, the way the grass is lying (called the grain), whether the grass is wet or dry, and the softness of the underlying soil. When long grass covers a soft surface, the ball doesn't roll easily, and the playing field is described as 'slow.' A hard, smooth surface with short turf provides a much faster playing field.

Example: For the driving enthusiast, the firmness of the ground and the type of wheels on the vehicle (wood, metal, solid, pneumatic) have a large influence on how easily the wheels roll over the ground and this, in turn, influences the energy expended by the horse to pull the vehicle over a distance. A loose deep surface that allows the wheels to sink into it is much more tiring for a driving horse than a uniformly firm surface.

Grip and Slip in Equestrian Sports

There are many situations in equestrian sports in which riders or drivers try to increase the limiting friction or grip between two surfaces to prevent sliding. This can be accomplished by changing the nature of the contact surfaces or by interposing a substance that binds the two surfaces together.

Example: To prevent the reins slipping through the rider's fingers, the reins may be held more tightly between the thumb and first finger (increased normal force). Additionally, the rider may use reins and gloves made of materials that have a high coefficient of friction, such as rubberized gloves with leather reins.

Example: Losing the stirrups is a problem that may be related to friction (or lack of it). The boot is less likely to slide out of the stirrup if the rider pushes down firmly against the stirrup (increased normal force) or uses stirrup treads and/or special soles on the riding boots to increase the coefficient of friction and so reduce slipping of the boot sole across the stirrup. It is also beneficial to clean the soles of the boots before mounting since the presence of sand grains allows the boot sole to roll across the stirrup tread.

IMPACT 11

Collisions

When two bodies collide, they are in contact for a short period of time during which each body exerts a force on the other. An impact is a collision characterized by the transient nature of the interaction and the large magnitude of the contact force. Impacts are an integral part of locomotion and of many equestrian activities, for example, a hoof contacting the ground, a polo mallet striking a ball, or a jumper hitting a fence.

Hoof Contact with the Ground

Every time the hoof contacts the ground it constitutes an impact, and the effect of these repetitive impacts has implications for the horse's soundness and longevity as an athlete. The hoof is moving forward and downward at the instant of ground contact and its velocity is reduced to zero soon after impact. The forces associated with hoof deceleration during impact cause energy to enter the limb in the form of a shock wave that has potentially damaging effects on the bones and joints as it travels up the limb.

If the surface is composed of a deformable material, the hoof is decelerated more gradually and impact occurs over a longer time, which decreases the magnitude of the force between the hoof and the ground. Consequently, a horse moving on a compliant surface, such as wood fiber or rubber, experiences lower impact forces and accelerations than when moving over a harder surface, such as cement, asphalt, or packed clay. The use of shoes or hoof pads made of a resilient material may also help to reduce impact forces.

Driving a Farrier's Nail

The ease with which a farrier pounds a nail into a horse's hoof depends on the mass of the hammer head and its velocity at impact with the nail. The dynamic nature of the hammer's impact makes it easy to drive the nail. It would be much more difficult to push a nail into the hoof wall by static loading, since this would require thousands of newtons of force on the nail head.

121

Impact in Sports

Several sports involve impacts; some are deliberate, others are accidental or incidental. In polo, impacts occur when a mallet hits a ball or when one pony bumps another. In jumping competitions, impact between a horse and a fence may cause a rail to be dislodged or it may result in a fall of horse and/or rider.

Example: A polo ball lying at rest on a field has mass but no velocity, so its momentum is zero. When a mallet strikes the ball, it imparts momentum to it. The momentum gained by the ball is equal to that lost by the mallet. If the objective is to maximize the velocity of the ball, this can be achieved by increasing the momentum (mass or velocity) of the mallet head at the instant of contact. The total momentum after impact (momentum of mallet plus momentum of ball) is equal to the momentum before impact (momentum of mallet).

Example: When a jumping horse dislodges a rail with its front limbs (figure 11.1), the momentum gained by the rail is equal to the momentum lost by the horse. Because the mass of the rail is small relative to the mass of the horse, the velocity of the rail changes much more than the velocity of the horse. A horse with a mass of 500 kg and a horizontal velocity of 7 m/s contacts a rail with a mass of 5 kg and knocks it forward with a velocity of 2 m/s. The initial momentum of the horse before the impact is:

$$\text{Horse Mom}_{initial} = \text{Mass} * \text{Velocity} = 500 * 7 = 3{,}500 \text{ kg·m/s}$$

The momentum acquired by the rail after the impact is:

$$\text{Rail Mom}_{final} = \text{Mass} * \text{Velocity} = 5 * 2 = 10 \text{ kg·m/s}$$

From the principle of conservation of momentum, the total momentum after impact is equal to the total momentum before impact:

$$\text{Horse Mom}_{initial} + \text{Rail Mom}_{initial} = \text{Horse Mom}_{final} + \text{Rail Mom}_{final}$$

$$\text{Horse Mom}_{final} = \text{Horse Mom}_{initial} + \text{Rail Mom}_{initial} - \text{Rail Mom}_{final}$$

$$\text{Horse Mom}_{final} = 3{,}500 + 0 - 10 = 3{,}490 \text{ kg·m/s}$$

The horse's velocity after dislodging the rail is:

$$\text{Momentum} = \text{Mass} * \text{Velocity}$$

$$\text{Velocity} = \frac{\text{Momentum}}{\text{Mass}} = \frac{3{,}490}{500} = 6.98 \text{ m/s}$$

Therefore, in imparting a velocity of 2 m/s to the rail, the horse's velocity is reduced by only 0.02 m/s, which reflects the difference in mass between the horse and the rail.

Figure 11.1: A 500 kg jumping horse makes impact with a fence dislodging a 5 kg rail. In imparting a horizontal velocity of 2 m/s to the rail, the horse's horizontal velocity is reduced from 7 m/s to 6.98 m/s.

Falls

Injuries during falls are usually a consequence of a collision with the ground or another object. The amount of force on the body during impact depends on the body's momentum, which is the product of its mass and velocity.

Example: A small child sliding off a stationery pony has little momentum (small mass, small velocity). On the other hand, a large adult who is thrown from a tall, galloping horse has a larger mass and hits the ground with higher horizontal and vertical velocities giving a much higher momentum.

The damaging effects of a fall are reduced if the momentum is decreased gradually. This can be achieved by absorbing the force of impact over a longer time by landing on a well-padded area of the body or wearing protective clothing to prolong the duration of the impact and absorb some of the force.

Conservation of Momentum

The third law of motion indicates that the forces on two impacting bodies are equal in magnitude and act in opposite directions. Since impulse is the product of force and time, the impulse one body receives is exactly equal in magnitude and opposite in direction to the impulse received by the other body. Impact also changes the momentum (mass * velocity) of each body, with the changes in momentum of the two bodies being equal in magnitude and opposite in direction. These ideas are summarized in the principle of conservation of momentum, which is an extension of the first law of motion.

In any system of bodies that exert forces on each other, the total momentum of the system remains constant unless some external force acts on the system.

Elasticity and Plasticity

When one body collides with another, both bodies are slightly compressed. Most bodies tend to return to their original shape when the compressive force is removed. The property that allows a body to regain its original shape after it has been deformed is called elasticity. Some bodies do not return to their original shape after being deformed, instead they retain the new shape. This property is called plasticity. Plasticine is an example of a plastic material; when it is molded into a new shape, it retains that shape without any tendency to return to its original shape.

The properties of the material determine whether it behaves in an elastic or a plastic manner. An elastic material has a memory for its original shape, whereas a plastic material does not. Most of the bodies involved in impacts during locomotion show elastic behavior, though elasticity differs from one body to the next. Some bodies return to their original shape almost immediately, others take much longer.

Example: A rubber ball is a good example of an elastic body. When it impacts the ground, one side of the ball is flattened, but as it rebounds into the air the spherical shape is restored (figure 11.2)

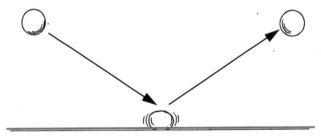

Figure 11.2: Response of an elastic body to deformation. A rubber ball flattens when it contacts the ground, then regains its spherical shape as it rebounds.

Example: The digital cushion, which lies within the palmar part of the hoof, contains much elastic tissue. During stance, the digital cushion is compressed between the phalangeal bones above and the frog and sole of the hoof below. During the swing phase, the digital cushion rebounds to its original shape.

Example: A saddle pad may be used to distribute the weight of the saddle and rider more evenly on the horse's back. If the shape of the saddle does not conform to the shape of the horse's back, the pad is compressed under areas of higher pressure. Saddle pads are made of a variety of materials. The elastic properties of the pad determine whether it returns to its original shape or retains the new shape after repeated loading.

Law of Impact

The law of impact describes the changes in velocity that occur during an elastic impact.

> *If two bodies move toward each other along the same straight line, the difference between their velocities immediately after impact bears a constant relationship to the difference between their velocities at the moment of impact.*

The way two bodies move after impact depends on how they were moving before impact and on a constant known as the coefficient of restitution *(e)*. The value of this coefficient is always less than one, so the sum of the rebound velocities is always less than the sum of the impact velocities.

Even if the two bodies are not traveling along the same straight line before impact, they still obey the law of impact. In this case, their rebound velocities along a line perpendicular to the surface of contact depend on the components of their original velocities in that direction.

The value of the coefficient of restitution depends largely on the nature of the two impacting bodies. In the simple example of a ball bouncing off different surfaces, the value of *e* would be very different for asphalt and sand. Furthermore, two balls of different materials would have different values for *e* on the same surface. Therefore, the coefficient of restitution depends on the nature of both of the impacting bodies. It is also influenced by the temperature of the bodies and the velocity at which they collide.

Angle of Impact

Impact between two bodies may be direct or oblique. In a direct impact, the two bodies are moving along the same straight line immediately prior to impact or one of them is at rest and other is moving along a line perpendicular to the surface where contact occurs. Examples of this type of impact include a jumping horse hitting a fence or a mallet hitting a stationary polo ball.

On other occasions two bodies collide at an angle, which is called an oblique impact. Oblique impacts occur when one polo pony bumps another or when a polo ball strikes the wall of an arena at an angle. The outcome of an oblique impact depends on both the principle of conservation of momentum and the coefficient of restitution. The angle between the velocity vector and a line perpendicular to the contact surface before impact is called the angle of incidence (figure 11.3). Its value is always smaller than the corresponding angle after impact, which is called the angle of reflection (assuming the effect of friction is negligible). Since the value of the coefficient of restitution is always less than one, the velocity after impact is less than the velocity before impact.

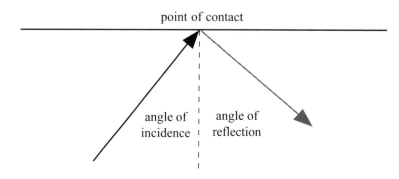

Figure 11.3: Angle of incidence is smaller than the angle of reflection and the velocity before impact (black arrow) is larger than the velocity after impact (gray arrow) for a ball bouncing off a rigid surface.

Shock Absorption

The forces generated during impact may have deleterious effects on body tissues. Shock absorptive materials provide protection from impact forces by absorbing some of the impact energy, or prolonging the duration of the impact.

Protective Clothing

Many injuries are the result of a direct impact that occurs either during a fall or as a result of being kicked. Protective clothing is worn to reduce the risk of injury during a fall. Padded clothing, such as a body protector vest, dissipates some of the energy associated with impact by deformation and by spreading the effects of the forces over larger areas of the body. Protective headgear reduces the risk of brain injuries by absorbing energy and by distributing the load through the thickness of the helmet structure and its component materials.

Hoof Pads

Hoof pads are sometimes inserted between the hoof wall and the shoe. When the hoof strikes the ground, it is rapidly decelerated and energy enters the horse's limb. Compression of the pad dissipates some of the impact energy. For pads to perform effectively, they must return (rebound) to their original shape before the next impact. Not many materials are able to do this. Instead, after a number of loading cycles, the pads become permanently flattened with loss of their energy absorbing abilities. Loose nails and risen clenches are signs that this has happened.

CHAPTER 12

BALANCE AND EQUILIBRIUM

Abbreviations used in this chapter:

CoM: Center of mass

GRF: Ground reaction force

GRF_{long}: Ground reaction force, longitudinal component

GRF_{vert}: Ground reaction force, vertical component

GRF_{LH}: Ground reaction force of left hind limb

GRF_{RH}: Ground reaction force of right hind limb

GRF_{LF}: Ground reaction force of left front limb

GRF_{RF}: Ground reaction force of right front limb

A body is in a state of equilibrium when all parts of the body are at rest or are moving with the same constant velocity.

A body can be in equilibrium when it is stationary (static equilibrium) or when it is moving (dynamic equilibrium). Being in a state of equilibrium implies that the forces acting on the body are evenly distributed. Application of an external force disturbs the state of equilibrium. If the body tends to return to its original balanced position when the force is removed, it is in stable equilibrium. If the body tends to fall away from its balanced position when the force is removed, it is in unstable equilibrium.

Static Equilibrium

Static equilibrium refers to a state of equilibrium in which the body is at rest.

Static equilibrium is demonstrated by a horse and rider that are motionless in the halt, a horse performing a perfectly balanced levade, or a saddle supported on a saddle rack. In each of these examples, the body (horse, rider, saddle) is not moving in any direction; in other words, it is at rest.

The Standing Horse

A horse standing motionless illustrates the characteristics of a body in static equilibrium: The horse is balanced, it is bearing weight on its four limbs, and all parts of the body are perfectly still. A free-body diagram shows that the horse's body is acted on by five external forces: W, the horse's weight, and the ground reaction forces on the four limbs $(GRF_{RH}, GRF_{LH}, GRF_{RF},$ and $GRF_{LF})$. The vertical components of the GRFs on the four limbs exactly balance the horse's weight (W) and the sum of the longitudinal components is zero (figure 12.1).

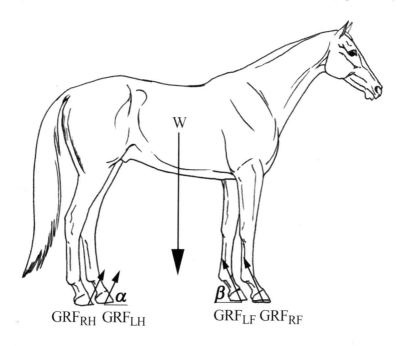

Resultant Vertical Force

$$GRF_{RH}\sin\alpha + GRF_{LH}\sin\alpha + GRF_{RF}\sin\beta + GRF_{LF}\sin\beta - W$$

Resultant Longitudinal Force

$$(GRF_{RH}\cos\alpha + GRF_{LH}\cos\alpha) - (GRF_{RF}\cos\beta + GRF_{LF}\cos\beta)$$

where GRF_{RH}, GRF_{LH}, GRF_{RF}, and GRF_{LF} are the resultant forces between each hoof and the ground, W is the horse's weight, α is the angle between hind limb GRFs and the ground, and β is the angle between the front limb GRFs and the ground.

Figure 12.1: Standing horse in static equilibrium. The equations show summation of vertical and longitudinal forces. Vertical force is positive upward, longitudinal force is positive toward the horse's head.

For equilibrium to exist, the sum of the moments around any point in a plane must be zero. In the standing horse, we can consider the resultant moments around the right hind limb, the right front limb, and the horse's center of mass (CoM) in the sagittal plane shown in figure 12.2. For each of the forces acting on the horse, the moment is calculated as the magnitude of the force multiplied by its perpendicular distance from the point around which the moments are being calculated.

If the resultant moment around any of these points has either a positive or a negative value, the horse will rotate about an axis through that point. Since we know that the horse is not rotating, the resultant moments must all equal zero.

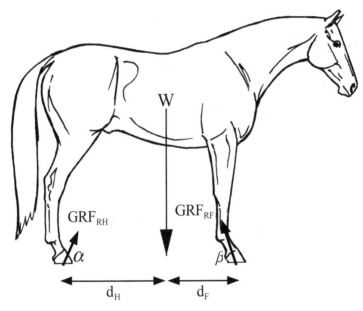

Resultant Moment around RH $= [GRF_{RF} \sin\beta * (d_F + d_H)] - [W * d_H]$

Resultant Moment around RF $= [W * d_F] - [GRF_{RH} \sin\alpha * (d_F + d_H)]$

Resultant Moment around CoM $= [GRF_{RF} \sin\beta * d_F] - [GRF_{RH} \sin\alpha * d_H]$

where d_F is the horizontal distance from front limb to line of gravity, d_H is the horizontal distance from hind limb to line of gravity, $d_F + d_H$ is the distance between front and hind limbs, W is the weight of the horse, $GRF_{RF} \sin\beta$ is the component of the right front GRF acting perpendicular to the ground, and $GRF_{RH} \sin\alpha$ is the component of the right hind GRF acting perpendicular to the ground.

Figure 12.2: Summation of moments in standing horse. Counterclockwise is positive.

129

Dynamic Equilibrium

*Dynamic equilibrium refers to a state of equilibrium in which
all parts of the body move with the same constant velocity.*

Dynamic equilibrium exists when the body undergoes translational motion. If all or part of the body is rotating, then different parts of the body have different angular momenta, and the conditions of dynamic equilibrium are not fulfilled.

Example: When a polo ball flies without any spin, all parts of the ball move in the same direction at the same velocity. The ball is in dynamic equilibrium. However, if the ball spins as it travels through the air, different parts of the ball move at different velocities; a point on the surface of the ball moves faster as it spins than a point in the center of the ball. Therefore, a spinning ball is not in dynamic equilibrium.

Example: A vaulter maintaining a stationary position on a cantering horse is in dynamic equilibrium. During the dismount, the vaulter's body rotates into an appropriate landing position, so dynamic equilibrium no longer exists.

Center of Mass

When gravity acts on a body, every particle within the body is attracted toward the earth (chapter 7). The resultant of all these attractive forces is the weight of the body. Its line of action passes through the center of mass (CoM).

*The center of mass is a point at which the mass of a body is
considered to be concentrated and around which the weight is
equal on all opposite sides.*

One method of finding the location of the CoM is to balance the body on a sharp edge. When the body is balanced, the CoM lies directly above the fulcrum. Alternatively, when a body is suspended it comes to rest with its CoM vertically below the point of suspension.

Example: A whip feels balanced in the rider's hand when it is grasped around its CoM. The location of the CoM can be found by balancing the whip on the edge of a finger, which acts as a fulcrum. If the finger is placed beneath the middle of the whip, the handle rotates downwards, because the mass is concentrated at that end. If the fulcrum (finger) is moved gradually toward the handle it reaches a point at which the whip balances and this indicates the location of the CoM. The purpose of weighting the handle of a long whip is to move the CoM close to the end of the whip, so that it feels balanced when held by the handle.

Example: When a riding helmet hangs on a hook it swings back and forth until it comes to rest with its CoM vertically below the point of suspension (figure 12.3). If it is then suspended from a different part of the helmet, it again comes to rest with its CoM vertically below the point of suspension. Vertical lines drawn through the two points of suspension intersect at the CoM. In the case of the riding helmet, the lines intersect within the cavity of the helmet. In other words, the CoM lies outside the material of the helmet, but within the space surrounded by it. Other examples of objects that have their CoM outside of their substance are a horse shoe and a riding boot.

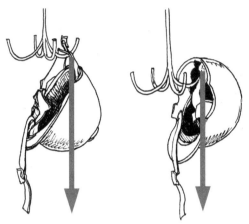

Figure 12.3: Locating the center of mass of a riding helmet by the suspension method. When the helmet hangs from a hook, it comes to rest with its center of mass vertically below the point of suspension, along the lines indicated by the gray arrows.

Rider Center of Mass

In a standing person the CoM is located on the midline of the body at about 55 percent of the person's height, which is between the hips. The exact location varies from one individual to another depending on body proportions. It is usually lower in women than in men and lower in adults than in children. Within an individual, the location of the CoM is not stationary, however. Movements of the body parts relative to each other are associated with slight changes in CoM location (figure 12.4). If the arms are raised the CoM moves upwards. If one arm is extended to the side the CoM moves toward that side. Bending forward in a piked position moves the CoM outside of the body into the angle between the torso and the thighs.

131

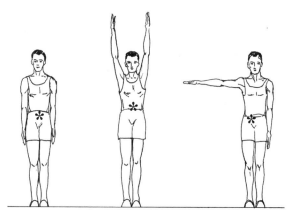

Figure 12.4: Location of the center of mass (*) of a person standing with the arms in three positions.

Different equestrian sports are associated with different styles of riding. The positions of the body segments and the joint angles of the dressage rider are very different from those of a jockey (figure 12.5). However, both riders maintain a secure and balanced position, with the CoM positioned over the base of support. For the dressage rider, most of the weight is supported by the seat, assisted by the thighs and stirrups. Most of the jockey's weight is supported by the stirrups, assisted by the thighs and sometimes the hands and reins forming a bridge across the neck.

Figure 12.5: Body segment orientation and location of the rider's center of mass (*) in a dressage rider (left) and a jockey (right).

Horse Center of Mass

For a standing horse the CoM is located just below a line connecting the point of the shoulder (greater tubercle of the humerus) with the point of the buttock (tuber ischium), and at the approximate level of the 13th rib (figure 12.6).

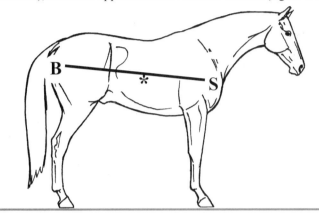

Figure 12.6: Position of the center of mass in a standing horse. The center of mass (*) lies at approximately the level of the thirteenth rib, just below a line from the point of the shoulder (S) to the point of the buttock (B).

The precise location of the horse's CoM changes slightly according to the orientation of the various segments of the body. The head and neck have a relatively large effect due to their large mass. The head accounts for about 4 percent of body mass, and the neck accounts for about 6 percent of body mass. The length of the neck gives the head a long lever arm, which increases the influence of head movements on the location of the total body CoM.

When a horse stands with its head and neck in a neutral position, about 58 percent of the horse's weight is carried by the front limbs and about 42 percent by the hind limbs. Therefore, the CoM is located closer to the front limbs than the hind limbs. When the head and neck are stretched forward, the CoM moves forward so that about 60 percent of the horse's weight is carried on the front limbs (figure 12.7). Conversely, when the neck is retracted, the CoM moves backward so the front limbs carry only about 56 percent of the body weight. If the head and neck are raised without moving their CoM forward or backward, the horse's CoM is raised but the weight distribution on the front and hind limbs does not change.

During locomotion, the position of the head and neck segments has only a small effect on CoM location. Dynamic movements of the neck, however, cause a larger shift in weight distribution between the front and hind limbs by creating a torque around the trunk at the base of the neck (Vorstenbosch et al. 1997). In a lame horse, for example, the rhythmical raising and lowering of the head and neck changes the weight distribution between front and hind limbs.

133

Figure 12.7: Effect of head and neck position on the location of the horse's center of mass shown by the gray circle for the neutral position. Stretching the head and neck forward moves the center of mass forward (black asterisk on left). Retraction and elevation of the head and neck moves the center of mass backward and upward (black asterisk on right).

Calculation of Center of Mass Location

In biomechanical studies, there are many situations when it would be useful to know the location of the horse's CoM, but it is not practical to measure this by balancing or suspending the entire horse. Instead, we calculate the location of the horse's CoM from the locations of the body segment CoMs combined with knowledge of segmental parameters that have been derived from analyses of horse cadavers. The cadavers were cut into segments that represent the main parts of the body: head, neck, trunk, shoulder, arm, forearm, thigh, gaskin, cannon, pastern, and hoof. Each segment was weighed and its mass expressed as a percentage of the total body mass of the horse. The CoM of each segment was determined using precision methods based on balance or suspension of the segment. The segmental CoM can then be located relative to bony landmarks that are easily identified in the live horse during gait analysis (Sprigings and Leach 1986; Buchner et al. 1997). The overall location of the horse's CoM is calculated by summation of the individual segmental CoMs.

Example: The CoM of the cannon segment lies exactly half way along a line connecting the intercarpal joint with the fetlock joint (figure 12.8).

During gait analysis, markers are attached to the horse's skin overlying bony landmarks that are used to calculate the position of the CoM for each of the body segments. Typical marker locations for two-dimensional analysis are shown in figure 12.9. Videos are recorded and analyzed. During the analysis, the markers are digitized to determine the location and orientation of each segment and the precise location of the segmental CoM is calculated. From a knowledge of the segment masses and CoM locations for all the body segments (head, neck, trunk, limb segments) on both sides of the body, the position of the overall CoM for the entire body is calculated.

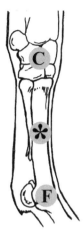

Figure 12.8: Location of the center of mass of the cannon segment. The center of mass (*) lies 50 per cent of the distance along a line from the intercarpal joint (C) to the fetlock joint (F).

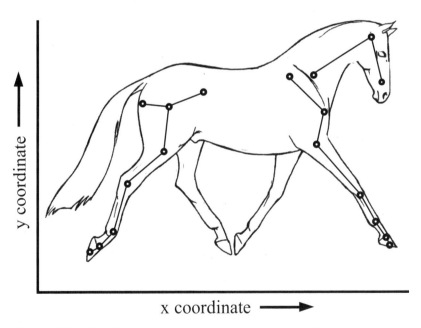

Figure 12.9: Two-dimensional, sagittal plane analysis. Markers, shown as circles, are attached to the skin over bony landmarks. The markers are digitized and their coordinates in the horizontal (x) and vertical (y) directions are used to define the body segment orientations and to calculate the position of the center of mass of each segment, from which the total body center of mass is determined.

135

What Makes the Horse Stable

A body that is in equilibrium is balanced. If a large enough force is applied, the body will be displaced from its equilibrium position. Stability describes balance in terms of a body's tendency to return to its original position after being displaced. If a body returns to its original balanced position when the destabilizing force is removed, it is in stable equilibrium. If it continues to move away from the original balanced position when the force is removed, it is in unstable equilibrium.

Stable Equilibrium

> *A body that is in stable equilibrium tends to return to its equilibrium position after being displaced.*

When an object hangs freely from a suspension point, it always settles with its CoM vertically below the point of suspension. This is an example of stable equilibrium.

Example: A bridle hanging on a hook suspended from the ceiling is free to move in any direction. If someone brushes against the bridle and displaces it to one side, it swings back and forth a few times, then returns to its original position of balance. Since the hook and bridle tend to return to the original position of balance, they are in stable equilibrium.

When a body is supported from below, its tendency to return toward or move further away from its equilibrium position after being displaced depends on the location of the CoM relative to the base of support. The larger the base of support and the more centrally the line of gravity is located within that base of support, the more stable the equilibrium. This is because the body can be displaced further before the line of gravity falls outside the base of support.

Unstable Equilibrium

> *A body that is in unstable equilibrium tends to move away from its equilibrium position after being displaced.*

When a body has a small base of support, the line of gravity is easily displaced outside the base of support, causing the body to become unbalanced and move further away from its original position.

Example: A vaulter standing on a horse's back is in equilibrium under the action of two forces: the body weight and the reaction forces through the feet, which provide a narrow base of support (figure 12.10). The body can be

136

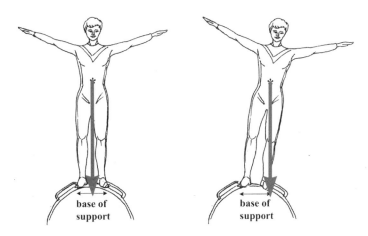

Figure 12.10: A vaulter is in unstable equilibrium (left). A small displacement of the vaulter's body to the side moves the line of gravity (gray arrow) outside the base of support (right), which tends to cause the vaulter to rotate further away from the original balanced position.

displaced only a small distance to one side before the line of gravity falls outside the base of support, and the vaulter becomes unbalanced. When this happens, the body tends to rotate farther away from the original balanced position, causing the vaulter to fall to the side. This tendency to move farther away from the equilibrium position after the body has been displaced is characteristic of unstable equilibrium.

Neutral Equilibrium

> *A body in neutral equilibrium has no tendency to return to its original position or to move further away from it after being displaced.*

Bodies that maintain the line of gravity within the base of support when changing position are in neutral equilibrium. A spherical object on a horizontal surface falls into this category.

Example: A polo ball lying on a field is in a state of equilibrium. In response to being tapped by a mallet it rolls forward to a new location and stops. It has no tendency to either return to its original position or to move still further away from it. No matter what position the ball is in on a level surface, its weight and the reaction forces are exactly equal and opposite.

137

Stability versus Maneuverability

Stability is achieved at the expense of maneuverability. Activities that require good balance need stability, whereas maneuverability is important in activities that depend on the ability to accelerate, decelerate, or turn rapidly.

Stability is important in sports like vaulting and roping. A vaulting horse should be sufficiently stable that its balance is not unduly affected by the activities of the vaulters. A rope horse should not be pulled off balance by the jerk of a calf meeting the end of the rope. On the other hand, maneuverability is important in sports like cutting and reining, in which the horse needs to accelerate and turn rapidly in either direction.

Maneuverability is enhanced by reducing the distance the CoM must move to clear the base of support. To accelerate quickly in a given direction the CoM should be moved as close as possible to the edge of the base of support in the desired direction of movement. If the direction of movement is not known in advance, a compromise position is adopted that allows rapid movement in either direction, as in a cutting horse.

Factors that affect the stability of balance are:

· location of the line of gravity relative to the periphery of the base of support

· size of the base of support

· weight of the body

· height of the CoM relative to the base of support

Location of the Line of Gravity

The line of gravity is drawn vertically from the CoM to the ground. A body that is in equilibrium is stable when the line of gravity contacts the ground within the base of support. The more centrally the CoM is located within the base of support, the greater the stability. Moving the line of gravity closer to the perimeter increases maneuverability. If the line of gravity falls outside the base of support, the body is no longer in stable equilibrium.

If the direction of an intended movement is known in advance, the motion is facilitated by shifting the CoM toward the periphery of the base of support in the intended direction of movement before the movement commences.

Example: When a racehorse prepares to accelerate out of the starting stalls, it leans forward or retracts the front limbs so the line of gravity lies close to the front edge of the base of support. When the gate opens the state of equilibrium is easily disrupted to initiate forward motion with a minimum of effort.

If the horse anticipates the action of a force that will disrupt its balance, the disruptive effect can be countered by leaning into the force or shifting the line of gravity away from the direction in which the body will tend to be displaced. As a result, the CoM must be moved further before it reaches the periphery of the base of support and balance is lost.

Example: A polo pony that anticipates a bump by leaning toward its opponent is less likely to be unbalanced by the force applied during the bump.

Size of the Base of Support

The horse's base of support is defined by the hoof contacts with the ground. The greater the area circumscribed by the base of support, the more stable the balance. The horse's base of support is longer from back to front, than from side to side. The easiest way for a standing horse to increase its stability is to increase the width of the base of support by spreading the limbs wider apart. For example, when a horse has difficulty staying balanced during a trailer ride, it adopts a wide-based stance to broaden the base of support. Horses suffering from neurological diseases that interfere with balance stand with their limbs abducted and hooves displaced laterally. Horses that have difficulty balancing during locomotion may move with a wide-based locomotor pattern, for example, when learning to walk on a treadmill. By contrast, maneuverability is increased by having a small base of support, which makes it easier to displace the CoM outside the area of support.

Weight of the Body

Stability is affected by weight and by the mass distribution within the body. For a body in stable equilibrium, when a force is applied that tends to displace the body, the opposing torque is the product of the body weight multiplied by the distance from the CoM to the fulcrum about which the body tends to rotate. Thus, stability is improved by increasing the weight of the body or by distributing the mass in such a way that it increases the distance between the CoM and the fulcrum around which it is being turned.

It is advantageous to select a more massive horse with a broad base of support for sports that rely on stability (e.g., roping) and a less massive horse with a relatively narrow base of support for sports that emphasize maneuverability (e.g., cutting).

Height of the Center of Mass

For two horses with equal mass, the same base of support, and the same location of the line of gravity relative to the base of support, the one with the higher CoM is less stable. This is because it requires a smaller angular

139

displacement to move the line of gravity outside the base of support when the CoM is higher.

The CoM can be lowered by crouching down. The horse that stands with a wide base of support during a trailer ride or moves with its hooves further apart on the treadmill is better balanced not only by virtue of having a wider base of support, but also as a consequence of having a slightly lower CoM. The presence of a rider raises the CoM of the horse-rider system compared with the horse alone, which slightly decreases the stability but increases maneuverability.

Conformational Considerations

Overall, stability is enhanced by having a large mass located close to the ground and centrally placed within a large base of support. Maneuverability is increased by having a small mass located close to the periphery of a narrow base of support. In the animal kingdom, there are examples of animals that show morphological features consistent with increasing the stability of the body, such as a rhinoceros, and animals that show features consistent with increasing maneuverability, such as a gazelle. The horse world has examples of similar adaptations. A draft horse with its large mass, short legs, and a wide base of support in relation to its height is designed for stability at the expense of maneuverability. By comparison a Thoroughbred is lighter in weight, taller in relation to its mass, and has a relatively narrow base of support. These design features enhance maneuverability. Even within breeds, different body types are favored for different uses. In the Quarter Horse breed, the stock horse is broader and heavier making it more stable than a cutting or reining horse, which requires more maneuverability.

Example: The farrier's stand has design features consistent with the need for stability. The stand is heavy (large mass), the mass is concentrated in the base (low CoM), and the line of gravity contacts the ground centrally within the large round base of support. The hoof support is centered above the base, and the horse must exert a large horizontal force to create sufficient torque to displace the top of the stand. The stand is in stable equilibrium, so when the force is removed, it returns to its original position. It can be displaced quite far in any direction before the line of gravity contacts the ground outside the base of support and it falls over (figure 12.11).

Balance

The word balance is used in equestrian terminology to indicate that a horse performs movements and exercises easily and without any apparent difficulty in maintaining its equilibrium. In mechanical terms, a horse is able to maintain static balance when its line of gravity contacts the ground within its base of support. During locomotion, the area of support is usually much smaller than

base of support

Figure 12.11: The farrier's stand has the hoof support located centrally above a large, round, heavy base.

during standing because there are fewer limbs in contact with the ground, and there are many stages of the stride when the line of gravity does not lie within the base of support. In spite of having its line of gravity outside the base of support, the horse does not fall because it is carried forward by momentum. The mechanics of static balance and balance during locomotion will be considered separately.

Balance in the Standing Horse

The line of gravity projects vertically downwards from the CoM. If the horse is to stay balanced in a stationary position, the line of gravity must meet the ground within the area circumscribed by the ground contact points that support the body. For a standing horse, the ground contact points are the hooves.

When the horse is standing squarely on four limbs, the CoM is fairly centrally located within the base of support but is a little closer to the front limbs than the hind limbs (figure 12.12). If one of the horse's hooves is picked up, the base of support becomes triangular. In order for the horse to remain balanced, the CoM must lie within the new base of support. Figure 12.12 shows that when a hind limb is raised, the CoM is still within the support triangle but lies closer to the periphery than when the horse stands on all four limbs. Consequently, the equilibrium is less stable. When a front limb is lifted, the line of gravity falls so close to the edge of the base of support that the CoM must be shifted sideways or backward to keep it safely within the base of support and maintain the horse's balance (figure 12.12). The horse achieves this by leaning away from the front limb that will be lifted. This need to shift the CoM when raising a front limb explains why it is easier for a horse to pick up a hind limb than a front limb.

Certain balance skills, such as the levade and pessade, require the horse to maintain static balance in a position that has a very small base of support. In

141

 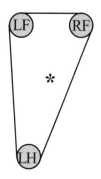 

Figure 12.12: Location of the horse's center of mass (*) relative to the perimeter of the base of support. The horse standing squarely on four limbs has an approximately rectangular base of support (left), which becomes triangular when a hind limb (center) or a front limb (right) is picked up. LF: left front limb; RF: right front limb; LH: left hind limb; RH right hind limb.

both of these movements the horse balances on the two hind limbs, and the base of support comprises a line joining the hind hooves (figure 12.13). The levade is performed with a smaller angle of elevation and lower CoM than the pessade, and this gives it more stability, which allows the horse to be displaced sideways through a larger angle before becoming unstable.

To execute balance skills effectively, the horse must develop adequate strength to support the body in the required position, together with the ability to shift the body weight quickly into the correct position at the right time. If the CoM moves outside the base of support, a quick adjustment must be made to regain balance. This can be achieved by moving or enlarging the base of support or repositioning a body part to return the CoM to its position over the base of support. Recovery of balance may not be possible if the CoM has been allowed to move too far outside the base of support or if too much falling speed has developed.

Example: In the levade, balance is maintained by muscular activity that overcomes the tendency of the forehand to fall forward and descend to the ground. The muscles of the hind limbs create a propulsive (positive) GRF, and the resulting torque around the CoM tends to rotate the forehand in an upward direction. If the body falls too far forward, the forehand descends, ending the levade.

Balance during Locomotion

Balance is different during locomotion than during standing because the base of support is constantly moving and changing shape. Locomotion results from loss of balance followed by hoof placement to establish a new base of support

142

base of support

Figure 12.13: The levade has a small base of support. Stability is increased by lowering the center of mass.

and regain balance. The CoM moves forward continuously as it passes over each new base of support. Locomotor progression is the result of three forces:

- muscular forces that produce the GRF to move the horse's body

- gravity, which pulls the body downward when it is off balance

- momentum, which tends to keep the body moving in the same direction at constant speed

Example: The support sequence at the gallop alternates between unipedal and bipedal support phases, with the base of support comprising a single hoof or a line joining two hooves. The body keeps moving under the influence of momentum and the GRFs provided by the supporting limbs. As the CoM descends under the influence of gravity, its downward motion is arrested, and it is elevated by the next limb to contact the ground; the limbs catch the body before it falls too far and raise it again. The faster the speed of progression, the less the horse relies on balance and the more it relies on momentum.

Many locomotor activities depend on deliberate loss of balance to make use of the effect of gravity, pulling the body downward, combined with the action of the limbs in catching the body before it falls too far. Recovery movements must be quick and precise to establish the new base of support before the body gains too much downward velocity, which would result in loss of control. Locomotor stability is enhanced by lowering the CoM, enlarging the base of support, and using short, choppy steps to re-establish the base of support more often.

Rider Balance

Horses are accustomed to balancing themselves during some athletic leaping and turning maneuvers. The presence of a rider, however, complicates the issue because the horse now has to deal with an added mass that does not always move predictably.

Not surprisingly, early studies of jumping horses showed that it was easier for a horse to jump carrying a sandbag than with a rider of equal weight. More recent studies have confirmed that horses are able to compensate for an inanimate mass of 90 kg without changing limb kinematics at walk, trot, or canter, and a competent rider has an equivalent effect to a sandbag of equal mass (Sloet et al. 1995).

When the rider's CoM is positioned vertically above the horse's CoM, the horse does not have to adjust its locomotor pattern to compensate for the effect on balance, though the magnitude of the GRFs must be increased to accommodate the increase in mass of the horse-rider system. A good rider is able to accommodate to moving at different speeds and in different directions by keeping his or her CoM vertically above that of the horse.

Example: Barrel horses lean into the turn when circling a barrel, which places the horse's CoM to the inside. The rider should sit vertically to avoid displacing the overall horse-rider CoM even further to the inside.

Example: During the approach to a fence, a jumping rider's CoM is directly above that of the horse. As the horse takes off, the rider folds forward at the hips to avoid being left behind as the horse pushes off. In order for the rider's CoM to stay centered over that of the horse, the rider's hips need to slide back as the trunk folds forward, making it easy for the horse to maintain balance. This is in contrast to the disturbing effect of the rider who flings his or her body forward during take-off.

Example: When riding up and down hills the horse's trunk is not perpendicular to the ground. Since the line of gravity is always vertical, it contacts the ground closer to the hind limbs on an uphill grade and closer to the front limbs on a downhill grade. To stay aligned with the horse's line of gravity, the rider leans forward when going uphill and backward when going downhill. On a steep incline, the rider may need to stand in the stirrups to get far enough forward. When going downhill, the rider can achieve alignment either by leaning backward or, on a gradual decline, by rounding the back.

During locomotion at high speed, momentum is the primary method of maintaining balance; the hooves have short stance durations and the base of support is re-established frequently. Highly collected gaits and movements, such as piaffe or pirouettes, have little momentum, so the ground contact times of the hooves (stance durations) are increased to compensate for the lack of momentum.

144

ENERGETICS

Abbreviations used in this chapter:

CoM: Center of mass

GRF: Ground reaction force

KE: Kinetic energy

PE: Potential energy

Biomechanics measures performance in terms of movements and forces. The movements are produced and controlled by muscular contractions, which result from the conversion of chemical energy into mechanical energy. Chemical energy is consumed in the diet, primarily in the form of carbohydrates and fats. It is converted into mechanical energy by the coordinated activities of the cardiovascular, respiratory, and muscular systems, which are studied by the discipline of exercise physiology. Gait energetics links biomechanics with muscle physiology. For example, kinematic and ground reaction force (GRF) data can be combined to calculate the amount of work performed and the net mechanical energy generated or absorbed by the muscles across a joint. This chapter will describe the variables measured in a study of gait energetics and will explore their importance in understanding equine biomechanics.

Role of the Muscles

The only tissue in the body that converts chemical energy into mechanical energy is muscle. Muscles use mechanical energy to generate tension. Muscular actions are classified as concentric, isometric, or eccentric according to the change in muscle length as tension is developed. A concentric muscular action is one in which a muscle shortens as it generates tension. During a concentric muscular action, a flexor muscle flexes a joint or an extensor muscle extends a joint. An eccentric muscular action is one in which a muscle acts in opposition to another (larger) force, so the muscle lengthens as it generates tension. For example, an extensor muscle acts eccentrically to control the rate at which a joint flexes under the influence of gravity. An isometric muscular action is one in which muscle length does not change as tension is developed.

Work

In everyday language, we regard work as any process that involves physical or mental effort. In biomechanics, however, the term work has a precise, and much more limited, definition.

> *Work is done when a force acts on a body and causes it to move. Time must elapse and movement must occur for work to be done.*

The work done by a force is equal to the product of its magnitude and the distance moved by the body in the direction of the force, while the force is being applied to it.

$$W = Fd$$

where W is the work done by the force, F is the magnitude of the force, and d is the distance moved in the direction of the force.

The SI unit of work is the joule (J). One joule is the work done by a force of 1 newton over a distance of 1 meter.

The definition of work indicates that movement must occur for work to be done. If a draft horse strains to pull a heavy load without actually moving it, no work is done regardless of the amount of effort expended in the attempt.

Work is described as positive or negative according to the direction in which the movement occurs. When the movement occurs in the same direction as the force acts, positive work is done. This occurs during a concentric muscular action. When the movement occurs in the opposite direction to the action of the force, negative work is done and the muscle acts eccentrically. Negative work is often done against the effect of gravity or some other external force.

Example: When a rider mounts a horse, positive work is done by the rider's muscles as they extend the joints of the left leg to raise the body against the effect of gravity. When dismounting with a stirrup, the same muscles in the rider's leg do negative work in controlling the rate of descent.

Example: When lifting a saddle from a saddle rack onto a horse's back, a force is applied to raise the saddle against the effects of gravity (figure 13.1). An upward force is used to raise the saddle, so the saddle moves in the same direction as the force acts. Positive work is done to raise the saddle. When the saddle is removed from the horse and returned to the saddle rack, a force must

146

Figure 13.1: Work done in lifting a saddle. Positive work is done in lifting the saddle from the saddle rack onto the horse's back. Negative work is done in lowering the saddle from the horse's back onto the saddle rack.

be applied to control the downward movement of the saddle under the influence of gravity. In this case, an upward force controls the downward movement of the saddle. Negative work is done to lower the saddle.

Example: A saddle with a mass of 10 kg (weight = 10 kg * 9.81 = 98.1 N) is lifted from a saddle rack that is 1.0 m high onto a 1.62 m horse. It is raised a distance of 0.62 m. The work done (W) is calculated as:

$$W = Fd = 98.1 * 0.62 = 60.82 \text{ J}$$

The work done in lowering the same saddle from the horse onto the saddle rack is –60.82 J.

Internal and External Work

In chapter 7, forces were described as external (forces acting between the system and the external environment) and internal (forces acting within the system). External forces perform external work. Internal forces perform internal work.

> *External work is work done by the body on the external environment. The body's energy level changes when external work is done.*

> *Internal work is work done within the body. When internal work is done, body energy is conserved.*

External work is done by a draft horse pulling a load or by a riding horse carrying a rider. In both cases, the horse's body energy decreases as a result of performing external work. Internal work is done across the joints of the limbs during locomotion but, in this case, total body energy does not change.

Power

Time must elapse for work to be done, but the amount of work done is independent of the length of time taken. The same amount of work can be accomplished by applying a small force for a long time or by applying a larger force for a shorter time. Power measures the rate of working by relating the amount of work done to the length of time taken. It is calculated from the work done divided by the time taken to perform it.

Power is the rate at which work is performed.

$$P = \frac{W}{t}$$

where *P* is the power developed, *W* is the work done, and *t* is the time taken to do the work.

The SI unit of power is the watt (W). One watt is the power developed when 1 joule of work is done over a time of 1 second. Before the SI system was adopted, power was measured in units of horsepower (HP). The term horsepower was coined by James Watt, who later gave his name to the SI unit of measurement of power. One horsepower was originally defined as 33,000 foot-pounds of work per minute, and is equivalent to 746 W.

Example: When putting tack on a horse, one person may lift the saddle slowly from the saddle rack onto the horse over a period of 3 s, while another person my take only 2 s. Both people do 60.82 J work in lifting a 10 kg saddle a distance of 0.62 m, but they produce different amounts of power. The power produced by the person raising the saddle in 2 s is:

$$P = \left[\frac{W}{t}\right] = \left[\frac{60.82}{2}\right] = 30.41 \text{ W}$$

For the person who takes 3 s to raise the saddle, the power produced is:

$$P = \left[\frac{W}{t}\right] = \left[\frac{60.82}{3}\right] = 20.27 \text{ W}$$

Example: In a pulling contest, a team of draft horses pulls a heavy load over a distance of 8.1 m (27.5 ft). For a load of 1,800 kg (weight 17,658 N), the amount of work done (143,030 J) is independent of the time taken to perform it. One team may take 6 seconds, a second team may take 7 seconds, and a third team may take 8 seconds. Table 13.1 shows the power developed by the three teams.

Work (J)	Time (s)	Power (W)	Power (HP)
143,030	6	23.838	31.9
143,030	7	20,433	27.4
143,030	8	17,879	24.0

Table 13.1: Power developed during a draft horse pull.

Energy

Energy exists in many forms including electrical, chemical, mechanical, thermal, acoustic, and nuclear. In biomechanics, the most important type of energy is mechanical energy, though chemical (or metabolic), thermal (or heat), and acoustic (or sound) energy also play a role in locomotion and athletic performance.

Principle of Conservation of Energy

The principle of conservation of energy tells us that the total amount of energy is maintained at a constant level through exchanges between the different forms of energy.

Energy can neither be created nor destroyed.

No athlete, equine or human, can use more energy than the body contains in one form or another. However, exchanges between different forms of energy are constantly occurring. Within the horse's body, mechanical energy is derived from the chemical energy consumed in the diet. Muscles are the only tissues in the body that are capable of converting chemical energy into mechanical energy.

The horse ingests chemical energy, usually in the form of carbohydrates and fats. The energy content of the diet is measured by its caloric content, with fats having a higher caloric density than carbohydrates. The foodstuffs are digested and the products of digestion, in the form of sugars and fatty acids, are absorbed into the bloodstream and transported to the muscles where they are converted to mechanical energy. Sugars and fatty acids that are not needed immediately for mechanical energy generation are stored in the body tissues from which they can be retrieved when needed.

The conversion from chemical energy to mechanical energy proceeds via aerobic and anaerobic metabolic pathways. These are inefficient processes with only about 20 percent of the chemical energy from the food substrates appearing as mechanical energy; the remainder is converted to thermal energy (heat), which is a waste product of the process. During prolonged exercise it is important for the horse to dissipate the heat that accumulates as a by-product of mechanical energy production in the muscles, otherwise hyperthermia develops, necessitating a reduction in exercise intensity. For more information on energy metabolism during exercise the reader should consult an exercise physiology text (Clayton 1991a; Hodgson and Rose 1994; Nankervis and Marlin, 2002).

In this chapter, the focus is on mechanical energy. However, exchanges between mechanical energy and other forms of energy should not be neglected when considering the horse's overall athletic performance.

Mechanical Energy

A body possesses mechanical energy as a result of its motion (kinetic energy), position (gravitational potential energy), and state of deformation (elastic potential energy). The amount of mechanical energy is expressed in terms of the capacity to do work, which is not too different from the use of the word *energy* in everyday language. An individual with a great deal of energy can perform a large amount of work.

Mechanical energy is the capacity to do work.

Since energy measures the capacity for doing work, the SI units of measurement are the same as the units of work, such as joules (J).

Kinetic Energy

A body possesses kinetic energy by virtue of its linear and angular motion.

Kinetic energy (KE) is calculated separately for translational (linear) motion and rotational (angular) motion.

150

Translational Kinetic Energy

Translational KE is due to linear motion. The amount of translational KE depends on a body's mass and velocity.

$$KE_{trans} = {}^1/_2 mv^2$$

where KE_{trans} is the translational KE, m is the mass and v is the translational (linear) velocity.

At a given velocity, a body with a larger mass has more KE. Velocity has a greater effect than mass on KE, since the term for velocity is squared in the calculation of KE. If two horses have equal masses, a small difference in velocity results in a relatively large difference in KE. Figure 13.2 shows the linear relationship between mass and KE, and the curved relationship between velocity and KE. An increase in velocity causes a relatively large increase in KE compared with an increase in mass.

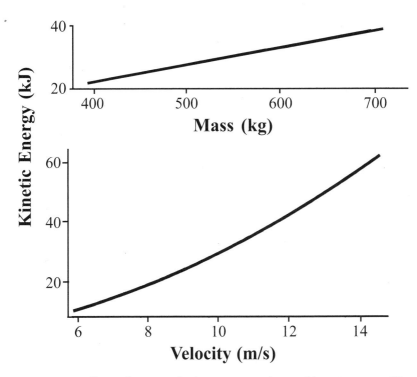

Figure 13.2: Effects of mass and velocity on translational kinetic energy. The graphs show the effect of a change in mass at constant velocity (above) and the effect of changes in velocity when mass stays the same (below). The same scale is used for kinetic energy on the two graphs.

Rotational Kinetic Energy

Rotational KE is due to angular motion. The amount of rotational KE depends on a body's moment of inertia and angular velocity.

$$KE_{rot} = {}^1\!/_2 I \omega^2$$

where KE_{rot} is the rotational KE, I is the mass moment of inertia, and ω is the angular velocity.

Similar to translational KE, a change in angular velocity has more effect on rotational KE than a comparable increase in mass of the horse.

Example: A reining horse (mass 450 kg) performing a spin has more rotational KE than a warmblood (mass 600 kg) performing a canter pirouette, because the greater angular velocity of the spin, which is squared in the calculation of KE, more than compensates for the smaller size of the reining horse.

Potential Energy

Potential energy (PE) is energy that is stored in the system in latent form as a result of the position (gravitational PE) or state of deformation (elastic PE or strain energy).

Gravitational Potential Energy

Gravitational PE is due to a body's location in a gravitational field. The amount of gravitational PE depends on the body's mass and its elevation relative to the surface of the earth.

A body possesses potential energy by virtue of being raised to a certain height in opposition to the force of gravity.

$$PE = mgh$$

where *PE* is the gravitational potential energy, *m* is the mass, *g* is the gravitational acceleration, and *h* is the height.

Since the gravitational acceleration is constant, PE varies directly with the mass of the horse and its elevation. A larger horse has more gravitational PE than a smaller horse at the same elevation. A horse jumping a fence has more gravitational PE at the apex of the flight arc than at take-off or landing due to the elevation of its center of mass (CoM) during the aerial phase (figure 13.3).

Example: A horse with a body mass of 500 kg jumps a fence. The height of the CoM at lift-off is 1.5 m and at the peak of the flight arc is 2.0 m, an increase of 0.5 m. The increase in gravitational PE is calculated as:

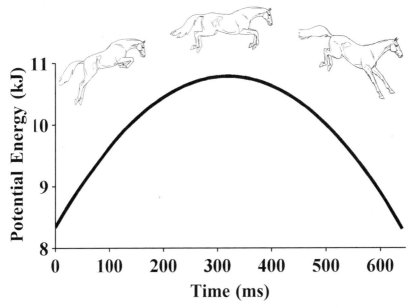

Figure 13.3: Change in potential energy during jumping due to elevation of the horse's center of mass. Time is measured from take off to landing.

$$PE = mgh = 500 * 9.81 * 0.5 = 2,452.5 \text{ J} \ (2.45 \text{ kJ})$$

When a jumping horse is airborne and gravity is the only external force acting on the body, the total mechanical energy is constant, though exchanges occur between the different forms of mechanical energy. During the ascent, PE increases with the horse's height above the ground. At the same time, translational KE decreases as a result of the reduction in vertical velocity under the influence of gravity. The increase in PE is equal to the decrease in KE. During the descent, the reverse process occurs: PE decreases as the horse descends and, at the same time, translational KE increases as vertical velocity increases. This exchange between different types of mechanical energy illustrates the principle of conservation of energy.

Elastic Potential Energy or Strain Energy

Elastic PE or strain energy is due to deformation. A body may change shape (deform) as a result of the application of a force. Most bodies tend to rebound elastically to their original shape after being deformed. During the process of deformation, an elastic body stores strain energy, which is released in the process of rebounding to the original shape.

A body possesses strain energy by virtue of its tendency to return to its original shape after being deformed.

153

Example: During the stance phase of the stride, the lengths of the suspensory ligament and flexor tendons change with the angle of the fetlock joint (figure 13.4). As the fetlock extends in early stance, the suspensory ligament and flexor tendons are stretched, storing elastic energy in their elastic fibers. Negative work, shown by the light shading in figure 13.4, is done in storing energy. Later in the stance phase, the fetlock flexes and the stored elastic energy is released as the suspensory ligament and flexor tendons recoil. Positive work, shown by the darkly shaded area in figure 13.4, is done as energy is released.

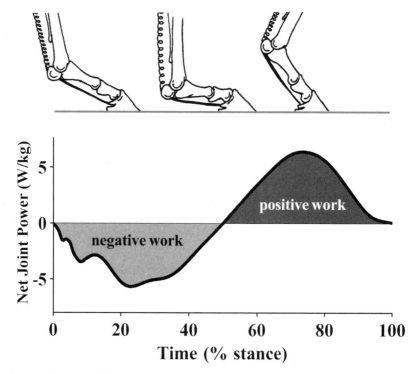

Figure 13.4: Work done across the fetlock joint during the stance phase. In early stance, negative work is done (light shading) as the fetlock extends and elastic energy is stored in the suspensory ligament and flexor tendons, which are represented as a spring in the diagram. In late stance, positive work is done (dark shading) as the fetlock flexes and the elastic tissues recoil.

Storage of elastic energy during limb loading and release of the stored energy during unloading is widely used in the equine limbs as a means of increasing the efficiency of locomotion.

Energy Generation and Absorption

The work done by a body may be positive or negative. Similarly, energy expenditure may be positive or negative. When positive work is done during a concentric muscular action, power is positive and energy is generated. When negative work is done during an eccentric muscular action, power is negative and energy is absorbed. Work and energy are related: the energy level of a body is the sum of the work done on it or, to put it another way, the energy level indicates how much work the body contains. When a muscle acts concentrically (shortening), it performs positive work and the mechanical energy of the system increases. Conversely, when a muscle acts eccentrically (lengthening), it performs negative work, and the mechanical energy of the system decreases. It should be noted that both concentric (adding mechanical energy) and eccentric (removing mechanical energy) muscular actions require the use of chemical energy within the muscle.

Example: During the swing phase of the stride, the entire front limb is raised and protracted, which swings the distal limb forward around its rotation point in the upper limb. In preparation for ground contact, the rate of protraction is slowed and eventually the direction of limb rotation is reversed, so the distal limb is retracted relative to the body in terminal swing. The purpose of the swing phase retraction is to reduce the velocity of the hoof relative to the ground at the moment of contact. The elbow is the key joint in protracting and retracting the front limb during swing. The *biceps* tendon recoils and the *brachiocephalicus* and *brachialis* muscles work concentrically in early swing to flex the elbow and protract the limb. Thus, energy is generated on the flexor aspect of the elbow in early swing. The extensor muscles of the elbow, primarily the *triceps brachii*, reverse the direction of limb motion in the later part of swing. Initially, as the *triceps* starts to generate tension, the elbow joint continues to flex; at this stage, the *triceps* acts eccentrically to slow the rate of flexion, and mechanical energy is absorbed. Then, after the limb changes its direction of movement and the elbow joint starts to extend, the *triceps* acts concentrically and mechanical energy is generated.

Energy Exchanges

Although the total amount of energy is maintained (principle of conservation of energy), energy exchanges occur within and between bodies and between different types of energy. During locomotion, the body loses mechanical energy when external work is done. These energy losses are replaced through the conversion in the muscles of chemical energy from the diet into mechanical energy.

Example: When a course builder constructs a fence, the rails are lifted manually onto cups supported by standards. As the rails are raised, they gain PE. If a jumping horse hits a rail and dislodges it from the cups (figure 13.5), the horse loses KE during the collision, which slightly reduces the horse's velocity. KE lost by the horse is converted into KE in the rail and acoustic energy, which is heard as the sound of the impact. The rail is displaced forward losing the support of the cup, which allows it to accelerate toward the ground under the influence of gravity. As it falls, the rail loses gravitational PE as it descends, and gains KE as its velocity increases. When the rail hits the ground, its KE is converted to acoustic energy, which is the sound of the rail hitting the ground, and strain energy, which causes deformation of the rail and the ground; the rail bends and bounces, while the ground may be slightly indented.

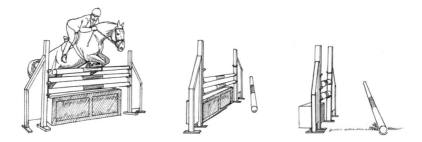

Figure 13.5: Energy exchanges when a jumper dislodges a rail. During impact, kinetic energy is lost by the horse and gained by the rail (left). The falling rail loses gravitational potential energy and gains kinetic energy as it descends under the influence of gravity (center). On hitting the ground, the rail loses kinetic energy, which is converted into acoustic (sound) energy and strain energy (deformation of rail and ground) (right).

Kinetic Analysis of Equine Locomotion

Gait analysis involves a combination of measurements and calculations. Kinematic variables and GRFs are measured directly using motion analysis systems and force plates, respectively. Other forces are measured directly using transducers attached to bones, ligaments, and tendons. The laws of dynamics can be used to estimate the forces responsible for an observed motion (inverse dynamics) or to predict the motion that will occur from knowledge of the forces (forward dynamics).

Inverse Dynamics

In an inverse dynamics analysis, the locomotor system is considered to consist of a series of rigid rods with adjacent segments articulated (linked) at frictionless hinge joints (figure 13.6).

Studies have been performed in which equine cadavers were dissected into segments and the physical properties of each segment were measured to determine the mass, location of the CoM, and the inertial properties (mass moment of inertia, radius of gyration). Inverse dynamics analysis uses these inertial properties to estimate the segmental values of living horses. Of course, there are inaccuracies in the technique: the segments are not completely rigid, the joints do not behave as perfect hinges, and the horses being studied do not have identical conformation and inertial properties to those used to determine the segmental properties. Even so, the calculations yield useful and interesting information regarding the functions of the limbs.

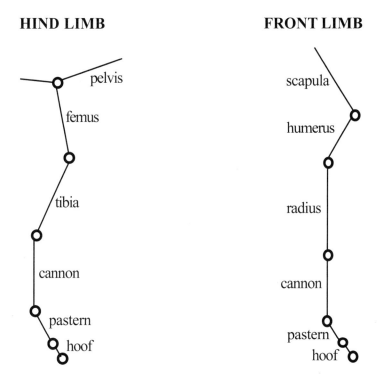

Figure 13.6: Linked segment models of the horse's hind limb (left) and front limb (right). Each segment is represented as a rigid rod. Adjacent segments articulate at frictionless hinge joints represented by circles. Note that in these models, the long pastern bone and short pastern bone are represented as a single pastern segment.

Inverse dynamics calculates the torques acting at the joints and indicates which muscle groups are generating and absorbing energy across the joints. This information can be applied, for example, to assess whether a joint is generating energy to provide propulsion or absorbing energy to damp concussion.

Identical kinematic profiles can be produced by different patterns of muscle activity. Inverse dynamic analysis indicates the net effect of the muscles acting across each joint and detects changes in internal limb kinetics that are not apparent from measurements of limb kinematics and GRFs alone.

Mechanical power measures the mechanical work done across a joint; it is calculated by multiplying net joint torque by the angular velocity of the joint:

$$\text{Power (W)} = \text{Torque (N} \cdot \text{m)} * \text{Joint Angular Velocity (rad/s)}$$

If net joint torque acts in the same direction as the joint angular velocity, power is positive, and the muscles perform positive (concentric) work (figure 13.7). If net joint torque acts in the opposite direction to the joint angular velocity, power is negative, energy is absorbed, and the muscles perform negative (eccentric) work (figure 13.7). Energy absorption occurs when the muscles act to restrain the rate of joint motion against gravity or some other external force.

The net work performed over a period of time by the muscles crossing a specific joint is calculated by mathematical integration of the power curve with time. There may be periods of positive work and negative work at the same joint.

Forward Dynamics

In a forward dynamic analysis, the muscle forces are known, and they are used to calculate the resulting movements by solving the differential equations of motion. This method was used by van den Bogert (1989) to develop a computer simulation of locomotion in the horse.

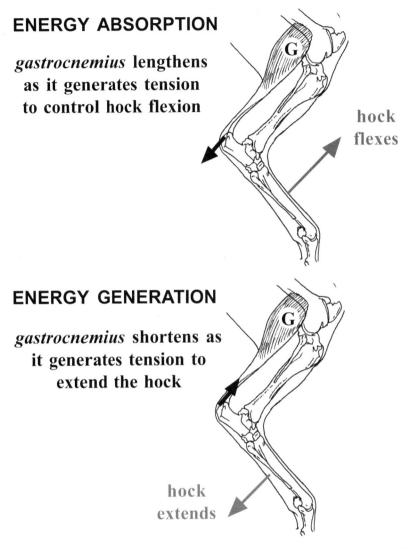

ENERGY ABSORPTION

gastrocnemius lengthens
as it generates tension
to control hock flexion

hock
flexes

ENERGY GENERATION

gastrocnemius shortens as
it generates tension to
extend the hock

hock
extends

Figure 13.7: Energy absorption and generation. The gastrocnemius *muscle (G) attaches to the point of the hock, where it generates an extensor torque across the hock joint. Movements of the point of the hock (black arrows) and the corresponding movements of the cannon segment (gray arrows) are shown for hock flexion (above) and hock extension (below). If the* gastrocnemius *generates an extensor torque as the hock flexes, energy is absorbed and negative work is done. If the* gastrocnemius *generates an extensor torque as the hock extends, energy is generated and positive work is done.*

PART 3

LOCOMOTION

THE ACT OF MOVING FROM PLACE TO PLACE

Abbreviations used in this chapter:

F: Front limb

H: Hind limb

L: Left

R: Right

Ld: Leading

Tr: Trailing

A gait is defined as a characteristic limb coordination pattern recognized by the sequence and timing of the limb movements. Each animal species has a repertoire of gaits, and horses are particularly versatile in the number and variety of gaits they perform naturally. Training may enhance the manner in which the natural gaits are performed or it may be used to teach horses to perform gaits that are not part of their natural repertoire.

Gaits are classified as symmetrical or asymmetrical according to the symmetry of movement between the left and right sides of the body. The natural symmetry of the gait must be taken into account when evaluating asymmetries associated with lameness. Gaits are also classified according to the presence or absence of aerial phases; stepping gaits have no aerial phases, leaping gaits have one or more aerial phases in each stride.

Gait Symmetry

Gait symmetry is defined by the rhythm of the right and left footfalls.

Symmetrical Gaits

A symmetrical gait is one in which the left and right footfalls have a regular rhythm.

163

In a symmetrical gait, the footfalls of the front limbs and the hind limbs are evenly spaced in time. In other words, the left front step duration is equal to the right front step duration, and the left hind step duration is equal to the right hind step duration.

The footfall timing of the left (L) and right (R) front and hind limbs in a symmetrical gait has equal time intervals between successive footfalls:

$$L — R — L — R — L — R — L — R$$

Horses perform a number of symmetrical gaits, including the walk, running walk, rack, paso largo, paso corto, classic fino, paso llano, sobreandando, marcha picada, marcha batida, fox trot, tölt, pace, stepping pace, trot, passage, piaffe and rein back.

The symmetrical gaits are distinguished from each other by the coordination between the hind limbs and the front limbs, the speed of progression, the relative durations of stance and swing phases, and the presence/absence of aerial phases. Gait diagrams for three common symmetrical gaits — the walk, trot, and pace — are compared in figure 14.1. Although the left and right footfalls are evenly spaced in time in the three gaits, coordination between hind and front limbs is quite different.

Asymmetrical Gaits

An asymmetrical gait is one in which the footfalls of the front limbs and/or the hind limbs are not evenly spaced in time. Instead, the rhythm of the footfalls alternates between a long and a short interval and, consequently, the footfalls occur as couplets.

> *An asymmetrical gait is one in which the footfalls of the front limb pair and/or the hind limb pair occur as couplets.*

The first (1) beat of the couplet is the footfall of the trailing (Tr) limb, the second (2) beat of the couplet is the footfall of the leading (Ld) limb, and the rhythm of the couplets is such that there is a shorter interval from trailing to leading limb than from leading to trailing limb. This naming convention sometimes causes confusion when people assume that the first beat should be the leading limb. However, the naming actually describes the visual appearance, in which the leading limb is the one that appears to reach further forward.

The footfall timing of the trailing (Tr) and leading (Ld) pairs of limbs in an asymmetrical gait is as follows:

$$1 — 2 —— 1 — 2 —— 1 — 2 —— 1 — 2$$

$$Tr — Ld —— Tr — Ld —— Tr — Ld —— Tr — Ld$$

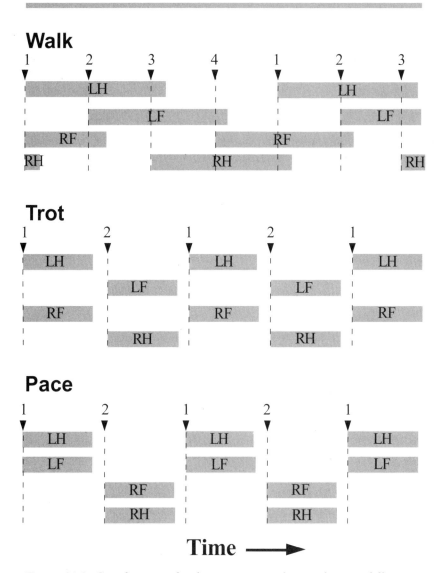

Figure 14.1: Gait diagrams for three symmetrical gaits showing differences in coordination between hind and front limbs for the walk (above), trot (middle), and pace (below). Shaded bars represent the stance phases of the limbs, open areas between bars represent swing phases. The numbered arrows and vertical dashed lines indicate the timing of the footfalls. LH: left hind limb; RH: right hind limb; LF: left front limb; RF: right front limb.

In horses, the common asymmetrical gaits are the lope, canter, and gallop. In all of these gaits, the footfalls of both the front limbs and hind limbs occur as couplets (figure 14.2). Typically, horses use a transverse limb placement sequence in the asymmetrical gaits, in which the leading limbs are on the same

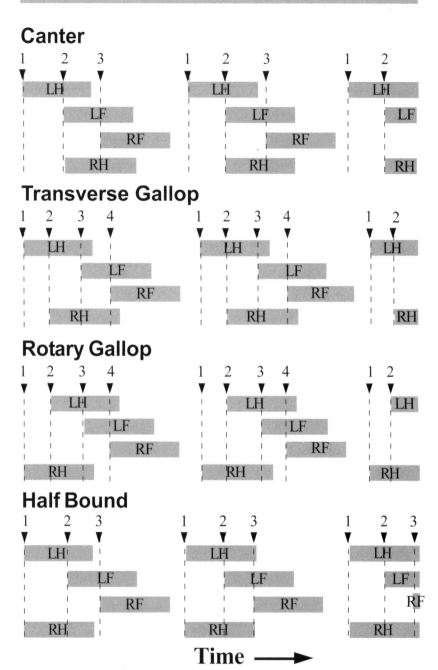

Figure 14.2: Gait diagrams showing coordination patterns for asymmetrical gaits on the right lead. Shaded bars represent stance phases, open areas between bars represent swing phases, and numbered arrows show footfall timing. LH: left hind limb; RH: right hind limb; LF: left front limb; RF: right front limb.

side of the body for the hind and front limb pairs. The name *transverse* indicates that the limb placement sequence transverses or crosses the body axis, so the footfalls alternate between left and right. Occasionally horses canter or gallop using a rotary sequence, in which the footfalls follow a circular pattern, with the leading limbs on opposite sides for the hind and front limbs. This is also described as being *disunited* or *on a crossed lead*. The overall lead for the gait is named according to the leading front limb.

Another asymmetrical gait sometimes performed by horses is the half bound in which the two hind limbs move synchronously while the front footfalls occur as a couplet (figure 14.2). The half bound is often seen in race horses as they leave the starting stalls; the front limbs adopt a lead within the first few strides, while the two hind limbs move together for several strides before settling into the same lead as the front limbs.

Other animal species perform asymmetrical gaits that are not used by horses. In the bound, the hind limbs move synchronously and the front limbs also move synchronously, but the front limbs are out of phase with the hind limbs. In the pronk or stott, all four limbs contact the ground together in a leaping gait in which a quadripedal support phase alternates with an aerial phase.

Aerial Phases

The distinction between a stepping or walking gait and a leaping or running gait is based on the overlaps between the stance phases of the limbs, which determine whether the stride has an aerial phase or phases.

A stepping gait always has at least one limb in contact with the ground. There is no aerial phase during the stride.

A leaping gait has one or more aerial phases during each stride when none of the limbs is in contact with the ground.

The presence or absence of an aerial phase has several functional implications. In stepping gaits, the horse's weight is transferred smoothly from limb to limb, and the body moves along a relatively flat trajectory. In leaping gaits, the horse is projected into the air with more vertical motion of the body than the stepping gaits. The presence of an aerial phase affects the magnitude of the forces on the limbs. Compared with stepping gaits, leaping gaits have higher vertical ground reaction forces to propel the horse's body into the air and larger impact spikes when the limbs contact the ground at the end of the aerial phase.

The *easy gaits* are stepping gaits in which the movements of the horse's trunk are so smooth and easy to sit that the rider has the feeling of gliding over the ground without uncomfortable bouncing. This is in contrast to leaping gaits, in which vertical motion of the horse's body requires the rider to use abdominal, trunk, leg, and shoulder muscles to follow the horse's motion.

Limb Coordination Patterns

One of the characteristic features of a gait is the way in which the movements of the four limbs are coordinated. Limb movements are controlled by specialized neural circuits located in the spinal cord called central pattern generators, that regulate the rhythm and frequency of limb movements. The hind limbs and the front limbs are controlled by separate spinal centers, and these are coordinated by long neurons that connect them.

The central pattern generators establish the stepping frequency (tempo), and they determine whether footfalls of the front limbs and the hind limbs occur symmetrically or as couplets. The connecting neurons control the phase relationship between the hind and front limbs. Coordination between the central pattern generators for the hind and front limbs is particularly interesting in relation to the easy gaits, all of which are four-beat gaits with a lateral sequence of limb placements. Differences in the frequency of the footfalls and the coordination between hind and front limb movements gives rise to a range of rhythms and tempos. Transitions from one easy gait to another often occur almost seamlessly, in contrast to the more abrupt transitions between other types of gaits.

When the time interval between footfalls in a four-beat, lateral sequence gait is exactly one quarter of the stride duration, the gait is described as regular or square. If the time between footfalls of the hind and front limbs on the same side is less than one quarter of the stride duration, the lateral footfalls occur as couplets giving a lateral or pacing rhythm. If the time between the hind and front footfalls is longer than one quarter of the stride duration, then the footfalls of the front limb and the diagonal hind limb occur as couplets, which is called a diagonal rhythm. Gait diagrams of a symmetrical, four-beat, lateral sequence gait performed with a regular rhythm, lateral couplets, and diagonal couplets are illustrated in figure 14.3.

The rhythm of the left and right footfalls defines gait symmetry, while the coordination of the hind and front footfalls affects the regularity of the gait.

Temporal Characteristics of Symmetrical Gaits

An interesting graphical method of representing the temporal characteristics of symmetrical gaits involves plotting lateral advanced placement on the vertical axis against hind stance duration on the horizontal axis (Hildebrand 1965). Both measurements are expressed as a percentage of stride duration. Figure 14.4 shows this method of classification applied to the symmetrical gaits of horses.

Lateral advanced placement represents the coordination between hind and front limbs. For the two-beat gaits, lateral dissociation is close to 0 percent for

168

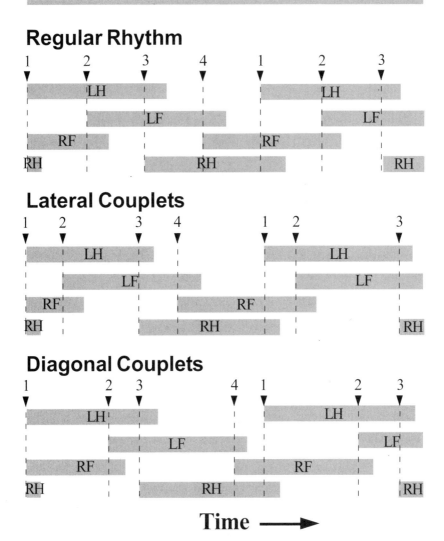

Figure 14.3: Gait diagrams for symmetrical, four-beat, lateral sequence gaits performed with a regular rhythm (above), lateral couplets (middle), and diagonal couplets (below). Shaded bars represent the stance phases of the limbs and open areas between bars represent swing phases. The numbered arrows and vertical dashed lines show the timing of the footfalls. LH: left hind limb; RH: right hind limb; LF: left front limb; RF: right front limb. Note that contacts of the LH and RH occur at the same time in all three diagrams.

the pace and 50 percent for the trot. For the pace, values below and above 0 percent indicate negative and positive lateral dissociation, respectively. For the trot, values below and above 50 percent indicate negative and positive diagonal dissociation, respectively. For the four-beat gaits, lateral advanced

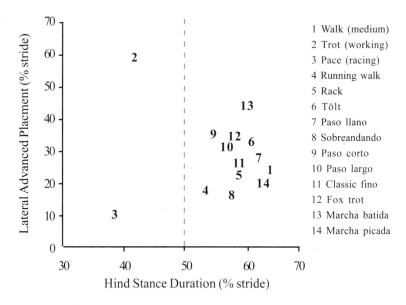

Figure 14.4: Graphical representation of the temporal characteristics of symmetrical gaits of horses.

placement is 25 percent in a square gait, less than 25 percent in gaits with lateral couplets, and greater than 25 percent in gaits with diagonal couplets.

Hind stance duration is an indicator of whether the gait is leaping or stepping. Hind stance duration greater than 50 percent of the stride indicates a stepping gait, because each hind limb is on the ground for more than half of the stride. If hind stance percentage is less than 50 percent, it may be a leaping gait, but the hind-front limb coordination and front limb stance percentage must also be taken into consideration before determining whether an aerial phase is present.

Horses perform a large number of gaits, that will be described in the following sections. Some of these gaits are present naturally, others are developed or enhanced by training. There are differences between breeds, and even within breeds, in the gaits performed naturally. In addition to being classified as symmetrical or asymmetrical and as stepping or leaping, gaits are described in terms of the number of footfalls (beats) per stride, sequence and rhythm of the footfalls, and limb-support sequences (chapter 2). The rhythm of the stride is characterized by the time between footfalls of the hind and front limbs on the same side (lateral step), the time between footfalls of the front and diagonal hind limbs (diagonal step), the time between footfalls of the two front limbs (front step), and the time between footfalls of the two hind limbs (hind step). For the sake of consistency, the stride will be considered to start at the instant of ground contact of the left hind limb (LH), which is an arbitrary choice and does not imply that the LH has any special functional significance; it is merely a convenient and repeatable point in the stride pattern. It does not indicate that the horse initiates the stride with the LH, nor that the hind limbs are in any way more important than the front limbs.

The Gaits

This section describes temporal and linear characteristics of a variety of equine gaits that have been studied and reported in the scientific literature.

Walk

The walk is a symmetrical, four-beat, stepping gait with a lateral footfall sequence. The footfall sequence, beginning with the left hind limb is:

LH : LF : RH : RF : LH : LF : RH : RF : LH : LF : RH : RF etc.

Ideally, the four footfalls of the walk are equally spaced in time, so the lateral step duration is equal to the diagonal step duration. This type of rhythm is described as regular or square. Many horses, however, walk with an irregular rhythm (Clayton 1995). The irregularity most often involves lateral couplets, in which the front limb is placed relatively early in the stride, so the lateral step has a shorter duration than the diagonal step. Other horses walk with diagonal couplets, in which front limb placement is delayed so the lateral step has a longer duration than the diagonal step. In both cases, it is the relationship between the footfalls of the hind and front limbs that is changed, not the relationship between the left and right limbs, which remains symmetrical (figure 14.3).

The walk is a stepping gait and does not have an aerial phase. In a medium walk there are eight distinct support phases during each stride, which alternate between periods of support by three limbs (tripedal support) and two limbs (bipedal support) (figure 14.5).

LIMB-SUPPORT SEQUENCE MEDIUM WALK

TEMPO: 55 strides/min

3 : 2 : 3 : 2 : 3 : 2 : 3 : 2

RH-RF-LH : RF-LH : RF-LH-LF : LH-LF : LH-LF-RH : LF-RH : LF-RH-RF : RH-RF

Bipedal support always consists of one front limb and one hind limb, and alternates between diagonal and lateral limb pairs. Tripedal supports alternate between two hind/one front and one hind/two front limbs (figure 14.5).

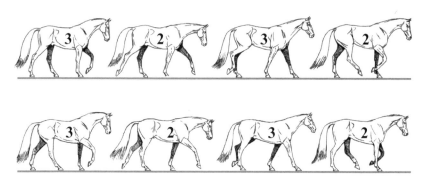

Figure 14.5: Support phases during the walk stride alternate between tripedal (3) and bipedal (2) support.

As walking speed increases, the periods of tripedal support decrease and the periods of bipedal support increase. This is due to shortening of the stance durations of individual limbs leading to reductions in duration of overlaps between limbs. At faster speeds, the horse becomes more reliant on forward momentum and is able to remain balanced with fewer supporting limbs (chapter 12). Conversely, at a slow or collected walk, tripedal support time increases, and the fact that there are more limbs on the ground facilitates balance.

Four types of walk are performed in dressage competitions: collected, medium, extended, and free. (There is no working walk.) The free walk, in which the horse is allowed freedom to stretch the neck, is only performed in lower levels of competition. Speed of the medium and extended walks is significantly faster than that of the collected walk (table 14.1) as a result of a longer stride length and a slightly quicker stride rate. The difference in speed, stride length, and stride rate between medium and extended walks is relatively small.

In gaits that have no aerial phase, such as the walk, lengthening of the stride involves moving the horse's body further forward over the grounded hoof during the stance phase. Stride length in the walk can be measured as the sum of the lateral length (distance between the hind hoof print and the lateral front hoof print) plus the tracking length (distance between the front hoof print and the next lateral hind hoof print). Adjustments in stride length are the result of relatively large changes in tracking length and small changes in lateral length (Clayton 1995).

Although dressage horses are required to maintain a regular, four-beat rhythm in the walk, not all horses achieve this. Many dressage horses show lateral couplets, which produces a lateral or pacing rhythm, in one or more types of walk. Diagonal couplets occur less frequently (Clayton 1995). A tendency to walk with lateral couplets has also been noted in some gaited horse breeds, such as Tennessee Walking Horses (Nicodemus and Holt 2003).

	Collected Walk	Medium Walk	Extended Walk
Speed (m/min)	82	103	108
Stride Length (m)	1.57	1.87	1.93
Stride Rate (strides/min)	52	55	56

Table 14.1: Velocity, stride length, and stride rate for the different types of walk of dressage horses (Clayton 1995).

Running Walk

The running walk is a symmetrical, four-beat, stepping gait with a lateral sequence of limb placements. It is performed at speeds of 15 to 30 km/h, with a pronounced head nod and a large amount of over-tracking The running walk should have a regular rhythm, which is often the case (Nicodemus and Holt 2003), but, like the flat foot walk, it is sometimes performed with lateral couplets (Nicodemus and Clayton 2003). The limb-support sequence includes periods of unipedal support by a hind limb.

LIMB-SUPPORT SEQUENCE – RUNNING WALK

TEMPO: 88 strides/min

3 : 2 : 1 : 2 : 3 : 2 : 1 : 2

RH-RF-LH : RF-LH : LH : LH-LF : LH-LF-RH : LF-RH : RH : RH-RF

Rack

The rack is a symmetrical, four-beat, stepping gait with a lateral sequence of limb placements. The temporal characteristics are similar to the running walk, but the rhythm tends to be more regular (Nicodemus and Clayton 2003). A stylistic difference is that the racking horse shows minimal head movement, which is in contrast to the rhythmic head nod of the walking horse.

LIMB-SUPPORT SEQUENCE – RACK

TEMPO: 73 strides/min

3 : 2 : 1 : 2 : 3 : 2 : 1 : 2

RH-RF-LH : RF-LH : LH : LH-LF : LH-LF-RH : LF-RH : RH : RH-RF

Fox Trot

The fox trot is the gait of the Missouri Fox Trotter. It is a symmetrical, four-beat, stepping gait with a lateral sequence of limb placements. The rhythm is irregular with the footfalls occurring in diagonal couplets. One study measured an interval of 35 percent stride between hind and lateral front footfalls and 15 percent between front and diagonal hind footfalls (Clayton and Bradbury 1995). The periods of diagonal support are longer than those of lateral support.

LIMB-SUPPORT SEQUENCE – FOX TROT

TEMPO: 95 strides/min

3 : 2 : 3 : 2 : 3 : 2 : 3 : 2

RH-RF-LH : RF-LH : RF-LH-LF : LH-LF : LH-LF-RH : LF-RH : LF-RH-RF : RH-RF

Tölt

The tölt is one of the gaits of the Icelandic Horse. It is a symmetrical, four-beat gait with a lateral sequence of footfalls. Ideally, it should have a regular rhythm. The tölt is performed at a range of speeds, and the rhythm and limb-support sequences vary with speed. At slow speeds, there is a regular rhythm, with equal periods of lateral and bipedal support and periods of tripedal support (Nicodemus and Clayton 2003). In some horses, periods of bipedal support alternate with periods of unipedal support even when tölting slowly (Zips et al. 2001). At faster speeds, the rhythm changes, usually to lateral couplets or, occasionally, to diagonal couplets. In some horses, aerial phases replace the bipedal support phases (Zips et al. 2001).

LIMB-SUPPORT SEQUENCE – TÖLT (SLOW SPEED)

TEMPO: 105 strides/min

3 : 2 : 3 : 2 : 3 : 2 : 3 : 2

RH-RF-LH : RF-LH : RF-LH-LF : LH-LF : LH-LF-RH : LF-RH : LF-RH-RF : RH-RF

Paso Largo

The paso largo, which can be performed at speeds in excess of 30 km/h, is the fastest gait of the Paso Fino. It is a symmetrical, four-beat, stepping gait with a lateral sequence of limb placements. Although this gait is usually described as being performed with lateral couplets, a study of the temporal characteristics of the Paso Fino gaits indicated that most horses perform the paso largo with diagonal couplets (Nicodemus and Clayton 2003).

LIMB-SUPPORT SEQUENCE – PASO LARGO

TEMPO: 130 strides/min

3 : 2 : 1 : 2 : 3 : 2 : 1 : 2

RH-RF-LH : RF-LH : LH : LH-LF : LH-LF-RH : LF-RH : RH : RH-RF

Paso Corto

The paso corto is a gait of the Paso Fino performed at a medium speed, similar to that of the trot. It is a symmetrical, four-beat, stepping gait with a lateral sequence of limb placements. The rhythm of the paso corto has diagonal couplets (Nicodemus and Clayton 2003).

LIMB-SUPPORT SEQUENCE – PASO CORTO

TEMPO: 124 strides/min

3 : 2 : 1 : 2 : 3 : 2 : 1 : 2

RH-RF-LH : RF-LH : LH : LH-LF : LH-LF-RH : LF-RH : RH : RH-RF

Classic Fino

The classic fino is the hallmark gait of the Paso Fino. It is performed at slower speed than the paso corto and paso largo but at such a fast tempo that the rapidly occurring footfalls sound like the roll of a drum. The classic fino is a symmetrical, four-beat, stepping gait with a lateral sequence of limb placements. Unlike the other Paso Fino gaits, which have diagonal couplets, the classic fino has a regular four-beat rhythm (Nicodemus and Clayton 2003). The limb movements are difficult to see because they occur so rapidly: at a tempo of 166 strides/min, footfalls occur with a frequency of 664 beats/min or 11 beats/s. In competition, the classic fino is performed on a board that allows the judge to hear the regularity of the rhythm.

LIMB-SUPPORT SEQUENCE – CLASSIC FINO

TEMPO: 166 strides/min

3 : 2 : 3 : 2 : 3 : 2 : 3 : 2

RH-RF-LH : RF-LH : RF-LH-LF : LH-LF : LH-LF-RH : LF-RH : LF-RH-RF : RH-RF

Paso Llano

The paso llano is the slower gait of the Peruvian Paso. It is a symmetrical, four-beat, stepping gait with a lateral sequence of limb placements and is performed with a regular rhythm (Nicodemus and Clayton 2003). The paso llano is executed with a distinctive action of the front limbs, called termino, in which the front limbs roll outward as they swing forward. Termino is part of the natural action of the breed and should not be confused with winging or paddling, which are regarded as undesirable deviations in other breeds.

LIMB-SUPPORT SEQUENCE – PASO LLANO

TEMPO: 95 strides/min

3 : 2 : 3 : 2 : 3 : 2 : 3 : 2

RH-RF-LH : RF-LH : RF-LH-LF : LH-LF : LH-LF-RH : LF-RH : LF-RH-RF : RH-RF

Sobreandando

The sobreandando is the faster gait of the Peruvian Paso. It is a symmetrical, four-beat, stepping gait with a lateral sequence of limb placements. The rhythm is characterized by lateral couplets (Nicodemus and Clayton 2003). Like the paso llano, the sobreandando is performed with termino.

LIMB-SUPPORT SEQUENCE – SOBREANDANDO

TEMPO: 97 strides/min

3 : 2 : 3 : 2 : 3 : 2 : 3 : 2

RH-RF-LH : RF-LH : RF-LH-LF : LH-LF : LH-LF-RH : LF-RH : LF-RH-RF : RH-RF

Marcha Picada

The marcha picada is a gait of the Mangalarga Marchador Horse. It is a symmetrical, four-beat, stepping gait with a lateral sequence of limb placements, and is performed with a regular rhythm (Nicodemus and Clayton 2003).

LIMB-SUPPORT SEQUENCE – MARCHA PICADA

TEMPO: 65 strides/min

3 : 2 : 3 : 2 : 3 : 2 : 3 : 2

RH-RF-LH : RF-LH : RF-LH-LF : LH-LF : LH-LF-RH : LF-RH : LF-RH-RF : RH-RF

Marcha Batida

The marcha batida is a gait of the Mangalarga Marchador Horse. It is a symmetrical, four-beat, stepping gait with a lateral sequence of limb placements. Although the rhythm is usually described as resembling a broken pace, a study of the temporal characteristics revealed distinct diagonal couplets. This gait is unusual in that it shows periods of quadripedal support (Nicodemus and Clayton 2003).

LIMB-SUPPORT SEQUENCE – MARCHA BATIDA

TEMPO: 99 strides/min

4 : 3 : 2 : 3 : 4 : 3 : 2 : 3

LF-RH-RF-LH : RH-RF-LH : RF-LH : RF-LH-LF : RF-LH-LF-RH : LH-LF-RH : LF-RH : LF-RH-RF

Rein Back

The rein back is a symmetrical, four-beat, stepping gait in which the diagonal limb pairs move more-or-less synchronously and the horse progresses in a backward direction. The footfall sequence of the rein back is variable within and between horses. If the front and hind limbs move synchronously, the rein back has a two-beat rhythm. As with the trot, however, movements of the front and hind limbs may be slightly dissociated. The front footfall may precede that of the hind limb, or the hind footfall may precede that of the front limb, giving the rein back a four-beat rhythm. The same horse may show different limb placement sequences in successive rein backs. In the limb-support sequence shown below, the front limb contacts the ground before the diagonal hind limb, but the diagonal limb pair lift off synchronously.

LIMB-SUPPORT SEQUENCE – REIN BACK

TEMPO: 50 strides/min

4 : 2 : 3 : 4 : 2 : 3

LF-RH-RF-LH : RF-LH : RF-LH-LF : RF-LH-LF-RH : LF-RH : LF-RH-RF

Trot

The trot is a symmetrical, two-beat, leaping gait in which the diagonal limb pairs move more or less synchronously and the diagonal support phases are separated by aerial phases. The LF-RH (left diagonal) limbs move together and the RF-LH (right diagonal) limbs move together. Short periods of diagonal dissociation are common in the trot both at contact and lift-off (Clayton 1994a). In sport horses it is preferable for contact of the hind limb to precede the front limb, which is called positive diagonal dissociation or positive diagonal advanced placement (Holmström et al. 1994).

LIMB-SUPPORT SEQUENCE – TROT (NO DISSOCIATION)

TEMPO: 79 strides/min

2 : 0 : 2 : 0

LH-RF : AIRBORNE : RH-LF : AIRBORNE

LIMB-SUPPORT SEQUENCES – TROT (DIAGONAL DISSOCIATION)

TEMPO: 79 strides/min

1 : 2 : 1 : 0 : 1 : 2 : 1 : 0

LH : LH-RF : RF : AIRBORNE : RH : RH-LF : LF : AIRBORNE

OR

RF : LH-RF : LH : AIRBORNE : LF : RH-LF : RH : AIRBORNE

Dressage horses perform four types of trot: collected, working, medium, and extended. Changes in speed between the different types of trot are achieved primarily by changing stride length with only small changes in stride rate (table 14.2). Stride length is adjusted by changing the tracking distance, with the medium and extended trots showing considerable over-tracking.

Standardbreds trotting at racing speed show diagonal dissociation but, in contrast to sport horses, the front limb usually contacts and leaves the ground before the diagonal hind limb (figure 14.6). The magnitude of the dissociation increases with speed (Drevemo et al. 1980b). After the front limb contacts the ground, the hind limb continues moving forward until it makes ground contact. The longer the temporal dissociation, the further forward the hind limb is at contact, which results in a shorter diagonal length. Therefore, longer negative diagonal dissociation is associated with shorter diagonal length. Over-tracking, the distance by which the hind hoof steps ahead of the ipsilateral (same side) front hoof, makes a major contribution to stride length in the racing trot. Over-tracking reflects the distance covered during the aerial phase, and the most effective way to increase over-tracking is to prolong the aerial time. This is achieved by pushing off with a higher vertical velocity, so the horse stays airborne longer, allowing it to cover more ground in a horizontal direction.

	Collected Trot	Working Trot	Medium Trot	Extended Trot
Speed (m/min)	192	213	271	299
Stride Length (m)	2.5	2.7	3.3	3.6
Stride Rate (strides/min)	77	79	82	83

Table 14.2: Speed, stride length, and stride rate for the different types of trot in dressage horses (Clayton 1994a).

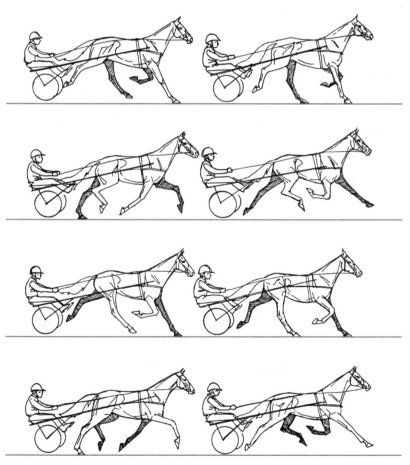

Figure 14.6: Gait pattern at the racing trot.

In horses trotting at racing speed, the gait is sometimes disrupted by an irregularity in hind limb rhythm, in which the horse appears to be trotting with the front limbs and galloping with the hind limbs. This distinctive coordination pattern is called the aubin (Barrey 2000).

The trot is the preferred gait for lameness detection and evaluation because the inherent symmetry of the gait facilitates the detection of asymmetric movement patterns. The presence of an aerial phase results in higher ground reaction forces than at the walk, which exaggerates the signs in supporting-limb lameness.

Jog Trot

The jog trot, as performed by western pleasure horses, is a symmetrical, two-beat, stepping gait. It is performed at a slow speed, with a smooth trajectory of body motion and a high degree of collection. At the very slow speeds performed in the show ring, movements of the diagonal limb pairs are dissociated with the front footfall preceding that of the diagonal hind limb. Consequently, the jog trot has a four-beat rhythm with a lateral sequence of footfalls (Nicodemus and Clayton 2001). It is an intermediate gait between walk and trot that preserves the lateral footfall-placement sequence of the walk, with the footfalls occurring as diagonal couplets.

LIMB-SUPPORT SEQUENCE – JOG TROT

TEMPO: 63 strides/min

3 : 2 : 3 : 4 : 3 : 2 : 3 : 4

RH-RF-LH : RF-LH : RF-LH-LF : RF-LH-LF-RH : LH-LF-RH : LF-RH : LF-RH-RF : LF-RH-RF-LH

Passage

Passage is a symmetrical, leaping gait of dressage horses in which the diagonal limb pairs move more or less synchronously, but with positive diagonal dissociation at ground contact (figure 14.7). The hind limb contacts the ground before the diagonal front limb as a consequence of the elevation of the forehand (Clayton 1997). The diagonal supports are separated by aerial phases. During the swing phase, the limbs pause momentarily in their most elevated position (figure 14.7), which gives the gait a regal appearance.

Passage is distinguished from the trot by having a slower tempo (55 strides/min), longer diagonal dissociation, and a momentary pause in the forward motion of the limbs during the swing phase.

Figure 14.7: Passage showing positive diagonal dissociation (left) and limbs hovering in their most elevated position in the swing phase (right).

LIMB-SUPPORT SEQUENCE – PASSAGE

TEMPO: 55 strides/min

1 : 2 : 1 : 0 : 1 : 2 : 1 : 0

LH : LH-RF : RF : AIRBORNE : RH : RH-LF : LF : AIRBORNE

Passage requires considerable muscular strength, and if the horse has asymmetrical muscular development between the left and right sides of the body, it may give rise to an irregular rhythm or uneven or unlevel steps.

Piaffe

Piaffe is a symmetrical, stepping gait of dressage horses in which the diagonal limb pairs move more or less synchronously with minimal, if any, forward progression. A characteristic feature of piaffe is that the limbs pause momentarily in their most elevated position during the swing phase. The tempo of piaffe is the same as passage (average 55 strides/min), but piaffe is performed with a shorter stride length. One of the distinguishing features of piaffe is the absence of an aerial phase. Some horses leap from one front limb to the other or from one hind limb to the other, but this is achieved by dissociation of the diagonal synchrony, so there is always at least one hoof in contact with the ground.

The movements of the diagonal limbs are often dissociated with either the front or hind limb making contact and lift-off earlier. The hind limb is more likely to precede the front limb in a better quality piaffe (Clayton 1997). Thus, positive diagonal dissociation appears to be a desirable feature in piaffe. Since the temporal variables for piaffe vary greatly between horses, there are a large number of possible limb-support sequences in different horses (Clayton 1997).

Pace

The pace is a symmetrical, two-beat, leaping gait. The lateral pairs of limbs move more or less synchronously, and the lateral support phases are separated by aerial phases.

LIMB-SUPPORT SEQUENCE – PACE (NO DISSOCIATION)

TEMPO: 80 strides/min

2 : 0 : 2 : 0

LH-LF : AIRBORNE : RH-RF : AIRBORNE

In the racing pace, the footfalls of the lateral limbs are dissociated with contact of the hind limb preceding the front limb on the same side (figure 14.8). Lateral dissociation increases with speed and, at racing speed, the pace is effectively a four-beat gait (Wilson et al. 1988b).

LIMB-SUPPORT SEQUENCES – PACE (LATERAL DISSOCIATION)

TEMPO: 130 strides/min

1 : 2 : 1 : 0 : 1 : 2 : 1 : 0

LH : LH-LF : LF : AIRBORNE : RH : RH-RF : RF : AIRBORNE

Pacing Standardbreds wear hobbles to ensure that the lateral pairs of limbs move synchronously and the horses stay gaited.

Stepping Pace

The stepping pace is a symmetrical, four-beat, leaping gait with a lateral sequence of limb placements. It is distinguished from the pace by an obvious dissociation of the lateral limb pairs even at slow speed; the hind limb contacts the ground before the lateral front limb, so the footfalls occur as lateral couplets. Aerial phases intervene between lateral stance phases.

LIMB-SUPPORT SEQUENCES – STEPPING PACE

TEMPO: 80 strides/min

1 : 2 : 1 : 0 : 1 : 2 : 1 : 0

LH : LH-LF : LF : AIRBORNE : RH : RH-RF : RF : AIRBORNE

182

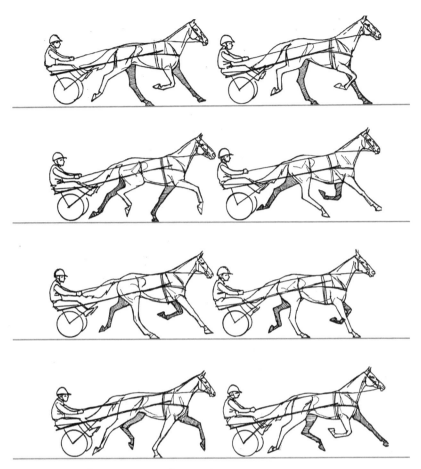

Figure 14.8: Gait pattern at the racing pace.

Gallop

In horses, the gallop is an asymmetrical, four-beat, leaping gait, with a transverse sequence of footfalls, and usually one aerial phase in each stride. A transverse sequence of footfalls implies that the limb placement sequence crosses (transverses) the body axis, moving alternately from left to right limbs (figure 14.9). The footfall sequence is LH, RH, LF, RF for the right-lead gallop and RH, LH, RF, LF for the left-lead gallop. An aerial phase follows lift-off of the leading front limb. Both the front and hind limb pairs are placed as couplets, and the leading limbs are on the same side for the front and hind limb pairs.

Some animals gallop using a rotary sequence of limb placements in which the order of footfalls follows a circular (rotary) pattern, either LH, RH, RF, LF on the left lead or RH, LH, LF, RF on the right lead. In the rotary sequence, the leading

183

limbs are on opposite sides of the body for the front and hind limb pairs, with the front limb lead being used to indicate the overall lead for the gait. A horse galloping with a rotary sequence is said to be disunited or on a crossed lead (figure 14.10). Horses often use a rotary sequence for a few strides during rapid acceleration before the horse settles into a transverse gallop or for one or more strides during a lead change. It may also be used in horses with lameness or back pain to avoid the transverse weight-bearing pattern. Gait diagrams for the transverse and rotary gallop are shown in figure 14.2.

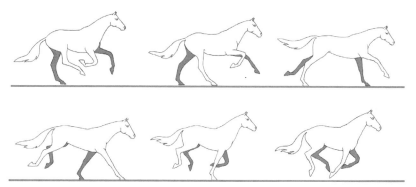

Figure 14.9: Outline drawings showing limb coordination pattern and placement sequence for the transverse gallop on the right lead. The left limbs are shaded.

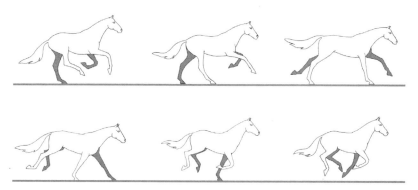

Figure 14.10: Outline drawings showing limb coordination pattern and placement sequence for the rotary gallop on the left lead. The left limbs are shaded.

In descriptions of the asymmetrical gaits it is convenient to refer to the trailing hind limb (TrH), leading hind limb (LdH), trailing front limb (TrF), and leading front limb (LdF), rather than describing the limb movements separately for the left and right leads. It is always possible to work out which limb (left or right) is being referred to from knowledge of the gallop type (transverse or rotary) and the leading front limb (left or right).

184

The limb support sequence in the gallop varies with speed. At slow speeds, each limb has a relatively long stance duration, and there are longer periods of overlap between the stance phases of different limbs. As speed increases, the stance durations of the individual limbs decrease, and there are corresponding reductions in overlap between limbs. Consequently, the number of limbs supporting the body throughout the stride is reduced.

LIMB-SUPPORT SEQUENCE - SLOW GALLOP

TEMPO: 115 strides/min

1 : 2 : 3 : 2 : 3 : 2 : 1 : 0

TrH : TrH-LdH : TrH-LdH-TrF : LdH-TrF : LdH-TrF-LdF : TrF-LdF : LdF : AIRBORNE

LIMB-SUPPORT SEQUENCE - FAST GALLOP

TEMPO: 140 strides/min

1 : 2 : 1 : 2 : 1 : 2 : 1 : 0

TrH : TrH-LdH : LdH : LdH-TrF : TrF : TrF-LdF : LdF : AIRBORNE

In small, lightweight animals that have a flexible vertebral column, such as dogs and cats, there are normally two aerial phases in each gallop stride (figure 14.11). A gathered aerial phase, which occurs after the leading front limb leaves the ground, is characterized by having the back flexed and the limbs gathered underneath the body. An extended aerial phase, which occurs after the leading hind limb leaves the ground, is characterized by having the back extended with the front and hind limbs widely separated. Galloping horses normally show

Figure 14.11: Gathered and extended aerial phases in the gallop stride of the cat (above) and equivalent stages of the stride in the horse (below).

only a flexed aerial phase, which is a consequence of the relatively inflexible nature of the equine thoracolumbar vertebral column. In a large, heavy quadruped like the horse, rigidity of the back is required to support the heavy viscera as propulsive forces are transmitted forward from the hind limbs.

When galloping at high speed, some horses have been reported to show a short, extended aerial phase between lift-off of the leading hind limb and contact of the trailing front limb, as in galloping dogs or cats. This has been referred to as double air time (Seder and Vickery 1993).

LIMB-SUPPORT SEQUENCE – GALLOP WITH DOUBLE AIR TIME

1 : 2 : 1 : 0 : 1 : 2 : 1 : 0

TrH : TrH-LdH : LdH : AIRBORNE: TrF : TrF-LdF : LdF : AIRBORNE

A small percentage of horses show a third, very short aerial phase between the two front limb stance phases when galloping close to maximal speed. This has been referred to as triple air time (Seder and Vickery 1993).

LIMB-SUPPORT SEQUENCE – GALLOP WITH TRIPLE AIR TIME

1 : 2 : 1 : 0 : 1 : 0 : 1 : 0

TrH : TrH-LdH : LdH : AIRBORNE: TrF : AIRBORNE : LdF : AIRBORNE

The frequency and duration of double and triple air times increase with speed.

Canter

The canter is an asymmetrical, three-beat, leaping gait with a transverse sequence of limb placements. An aerial phase follows lift-off of the leading front limb. The canter is a variation of the gallop in which the horse travels at a relatively slow speed with the leading hind and trailing front limbs moving more or less synchronously, though slow motion analysis has shown that there may be a short dissociation of the diagonal limb pair (Clayton 1994b). The footfall sequence for a right-lead canter is LH, RH-LF, RF. The footfall sequence for a left-lead canter is RH, LH-RF, LF.

LIMB-SUPPORT SEQUENCE – CANTER

TEMPO: 99 strides/min

1 : 3 : 2 : 3 : 1 : 0

TrH : TrH-LdH-TrF : LdH-TrF : LdF-TrF-LdF : LdF : AIRBORNE

	Collected Canter	Working Canter	Medium Canter	Extended Canter
Speed (m/min)	198	238	293	368
Stride Length (m)	2.0	2.4	2.9	3.5
Stride Rate (strides/min)	99	99	101	105

Table 14.3: Speed, stride length, and stride rate for the different types of canter in dressage horses (Clayton 1994b).

Four types of canter are performed in dressage competitions: collected, working, medium, and extended (table 14.3). These vary in speed, with the differences being achieved by changing stride length, while maintaining an almost constant stride rate (Clayton 1994b). Adjustments in stride length result mainly from changing the TrH placement relative to the LdF; in collected canter, the TrH contacts the ground about 60 cm behind the previous placement of the LdF, whereas in extended canter, the TrH contacts the ground about 40 cm ahead of the LdF.

Gait Adaptations for Racing

Survival of the equine species depended on the ability to accelerate rapidly and outrun predators over short distances, so horses evolved as sprinters. Modern racing sports encompass a spectrum of distances ranging from sprinting to endurance races. Successful racing performance over different distances requires specific types of conformation, movement, and training. Regardless of the length of a race, the goal is to complete the required distance in the shortest time, in other words, at the fastest average speed.

$$Speed = Stride\ Length \times Stride\ Rate$$

Stride Length

Stride length is a linear measurement of the distance covered by the center of mass during a complete stride. It is approximated by measuring the distance between successive hoof prints of the same hoof (chapter 3) or by summation of the distances between the individual hoof placements during a stride (figure 14.12). Extension of the stride implies that the horse reaches further between successive limb contacts. In the leaping gaits, most of the increase in stride length is achieved as a result of prolongation of the aerial phase(s).

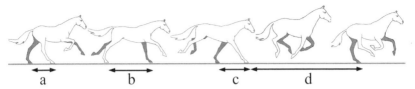

Figure 14.12: Stride length is the distance between successive placements of the same limb, which is the sum of the distances between placements of the individual limbs (a + b + c + d).

Stride Rate

Stride rate is the number of strides per minute. It is measured by counting the number of strides taken during a certain period of time and multiplying by the appropriate number to convert to strides/min.

Stride Rate = strides/minute

Stride Rate = strides/30 seconds x 2

Stride Rate = strides/15 seconds x 4

Stride Rate = strides/10 seconds x 6

Stride rate depends on stance duration and swing duration. In racehorses, high stride rates are achieved primarily by shortening stance duration, while swing duration shows relatively little change across a range of speeds. Consequently, as speed increases, the percentage of stride occupied by the stance phase decreases, and the percentage of stride occupied by the swing phase increases. This rule applies not only to the racing gaits, it is generally true across the entire range of gaits (table 14.4). For each limb, stance percentage is typically 55-70 percent at walk, 40-50 percent at trot, and <40 percent at gallop.

Gait	Stride ms	Stance Duration ms	% stride	Swing Duration ms	% stride
Walk	1080	725	67	355	33
Trot	750	350	47	400	53
Canter	600	280	47	320	53
Gallop	440	100	23	340	77

Table 14.4: Duration of stride, stance, and swing phases for a front limb in the walk, trot, canter, and gallop.

Impulse is the summation of the forces exerted over a period of time. As speed increases, the ability to maintain the impulse, in the face of decreasing stance duration, implies that the limbs must push more forcefully against the ground. The ability to generate large ground reaction forces is one of the main determinants of speed and is more important than the ability to move the limbs rapidly during the swing phase. Racehorses must, therefore, develop sufficient muscular strength to generate high forces over a short period of time.

Stride rate and stride length are adjusted to balance the requirements for acceleration, sprinting at maximal speed, maintaining submaximal speed, and energetic efficiency. For example, acceleration is maximized using short, quick strides, but these high stride rates burn a lot of energy. Therefore, a high stride rate is required for acceleration, but is inefficient for maintenance of speed over a distance. After accelerating to the required speed, energy stores are preserved by lengthening the stride and reducing stride rate.

Sprint racing calls for rapid acceleration and maintenance of a high maximal speed over a short distance, which is favored by a high stride rate, whereas races over longer distances require the ability to maintain submaximal speed over a longer distance, which is achieved using a longer stride length and slower stride rate.

Endurance racing does not call for maximal speed, but rather the ability to maintain a moderate speed for a long period of time, while minimizing energy expenditure. A variety of gaits and speeds are used during a race to delay the onset of fatigue by preserving glycogen stores, delaying lactate accumulation, and avoiding hyperthermia.

Successful endurance horses generally have a small body mass, which reduces the cost of transportation, and the locomotor muscles are not excessively bulky, which facilitates heat dissipation. The locomotor muscles are specialized for oxidative (aerobic) metabolism, so the muscle fibers tend to be of small diameter to facilitate diffusion of oxygen and energy substrates from the blood vessels. This is in contrast to the more bulky glycolytic (anaerobic) muscle fibers of horses involved in competitions that require speed or strength, rather than endurance.

Locomotor mechanisms for reducing energy expenditure are generally those of the cursorial life-style. These include having the large muscles located in the upper part of the limb close to its point of rotation and folding the limbs to facilitate protraction in the swing phase, both of which reduce the moment of inertia (chapter 8). Limb movements that are markedly outside of the sagittal plane, such as severe winging or paddling, tend to be inefficient, but may be acceptable, if not too severe. The addition of shoes and other equipment to the distal limbs increases the dynamic load and moves the moment of inertia away from the axis of rotation. The further down the limb the weight is added, the greater its effect. In other words, the addition of a steel shoe to the hoof increases energy expenditure much more than carrying the same amount of weight in a saddle pad. Heavy shoes add to the energy expended in every stride, a factor that is particularly significant in horses competing over long distances, in which thousands of strides are taken in the course of a race.

Gait Quality in Sport Horses

Unlike racing, in which the outcome is determined on an objective basis, many aspects of sport horses performance are judged subjectively, so aesthetics of movement are the prime consideration. In assessing quality of movement, judges and trainers tend to focus on the swing phase, since this is when the expressiveness or extravagance of the horse's movement is apparent. Differences in movement patterns between individual horses are most obvious in late swing around the time of maximal protraction and the start of retraction. It is during the stance phase, however, that large forces are applied to the musculoskeletal system. Consequently, deviations in the limb axis when it is bearing weight during stance are more likely to limit performance or predispose to lameness than faults in the swing phase.

Studies correlating subjective impressions of a judge with kinematics measured by gait analysis have shown that a long stride length and slow stride rate are highly desirable in warmblood sport horses (Back et al. 1994; Holmström et al. 1994). In warmblood dressage horses, average stride durations are around 55 strides/min for the walk, 80 strides/min for the trot, and 100 strides/min for the canter (Clayton 1994a; Clayton 1994b; Clayton 1995).

The components of stride duration are the stance and swing phases. It is preferred for sport horses to have short stance and long swing durations, which are associated with more cadence in the trot and more lift in the canter. The ability to shorten stance duration implies that horses must develop sufficient strength to generate higher ground reaction forces and impulses over a shorter stance time. Prolongation of the stance phase gives the strides the appearance of being earthbound.

Limb length is a determinant of stride length: longer limbs are associated with longer, more ground-covering strides. This is because the body mass travels further forward over the grounded hoof during stance, combined with the fact that longer limb bones offer greater leverage. Other factors that influence stride length include suppleness in the proximal limb, particularly the shoulder, elbow, and hip, which allows the limbs to rotate through a wider arc. A small increase in range of motion of the proximal limb is magnified into a considerably larger increase in motion of the hoof (figure 14.13).

The height of the flight arc of the hoof during the swing phase varies greatly between horses. At the position of maximal protraction, the front limb is more elevated in good movers due to greater flexion of the elbow joint (figure 14.14).

190

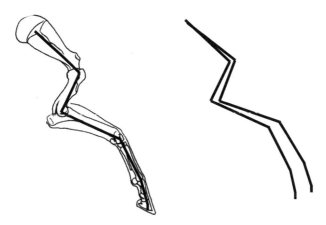

Figure 14.13: Skeleton of front limb at position of maximal protraction with superimposed stick figure (left), and stick figures showing the effect of a 5° change in protraction angle of the scapula on hoof position (right).

Elbow flexion is usually combined with a little flexion of the carpus, fetlock, and coffin joints, in contrast to the extended carpus and the upward flip of the toe that are sometimes seen in poor movers, especially in the extended trot (figure 14.14). The Iberian breeds tend to show more flexion of the elbow and carpus during the swing phase of the stride than warmbloods (Galisteo et al. 1997). Within the Iberian breeds, the amount of flexion may increase as the horse matures (Cano et al. 1999; Cano et al. 2001).

Figure 14.14: Kinematics of the front limb at full protraction in a good mover (left) and a poor mover (right). The good mover shows elevation of the withers, flexion of the elbow to raise the forearm, and a little flexion of the carpus and fetlock. The poor mover is down in the withers, has less elbow flexion, and has the carpal and fetlock joints extended, with the toe flipped up.

191

A more sloping conformation of the shoulder facilitates forward and upward movement of the front limb in late swing, and is, therefore, a favorable type of conformation (Holmström and Philipsson 1993). Since the height of the flight arc of the front hoof does not change much from trot to passage, the natural front limb movement at the trot may predict expressiveness in piaffe and passage (Holmström et al. 1995). However, training may bring significant changes in cadence and motion patterns.

The degree to which the hind limb is protracted is sometimes equated with engagement of the hindquarters. Some horses naturally place the hind limb further forward beneath the trunk but, contrary to the opinion of many trainers, hind limb protraction does not increase with collection. Horses do not step further underneath themselves in the collected gaits. What actually changes is that the hind limbs do not push out so far behind the horse. Therefore, it is important to observe limb position and angulation throughout stance, not just at contact.

After the limb reaches its position of maximal protraction in the swing phase, it is retracted prior to ground contact, which reduces hoof velocity relative to the ground at contact, especially in the front limb. Swing phase retraction time of the front limb is longer in good movers than in poor movers.

Good movers usually have positive diagonal dissociation at the trot (chapter 2), and the magnitude of the positive dissociation is correlated with gait quality (Holmström et al. 1994). Horses that have a longer dissociation tend to have more elevation of the withers relative to the croup, which is indicative of the horse moving in self carriage (figure 14.14).

How Locomotion Changes with Age

It would be advantageous if movement patterns were stable enough during growth and development to allow superior movement to be detected at a young age. It has been shown that Dutch Warmbloods have an inherent coordination pattern that is maintained from foal to adulthood (Back et al. 1995c). Stride duration and stance duration increase as the foals' limbs grow longer, but swing duration, protraction/retraction angles, and movements of the joints are consistent from foal age to adult. This has given rise to the concept of the *gait fingerprint* - a characteristic kinematic profile that doesn't change significantly with growth and aging.

Andalusian horses, which are noted for their extravagant front limb action during the swing phase, show increases in elbow and carpal flexion between 12 and 36 months of age, resulting in the characteristic front limb action of this breed (Cano et al. 2001). In addition, flexion of the shoulder and extension of the fetlock during the stance phase increase with age, which is thought to be a mechanism for absorbing the additional concussion associated with increasing

192

body weight. It appears that prediction of mature gait at an early age requires more caution in Andalusians than in Dutch Warmbloods.

Jumping technique also appears to be established early in life. By 6 months of age, foals without previous jumping experience showed similar sequence and timing of limb placements to older, more experienced jumping horses. As in mature jumpers, fence clearance by the hind limbs was greater than clearance by the front limbs in the foals. These findings suggest that jumping prospects may be selected on the basis of their jumping performance at a young age (Santamaría et al. 2002).

Changes in Gait Due to Training

Training promotes the development of suppleness, strength, and technical skills, which affect kinematics and kinetics. In young Thoroughbreds, a treadmill training program resulted in shorter front limb stance percentages and increased ranges of motion at the carpal and fetlock joints, causing a higher peak in the flight arc of the hoof (Corley et al. 1994). In Standardbreds, a prolonged (3-year) period of training was associated with increases in stride length, swing duration, and stride duration (Drevemo et al. 1980c).

In young Dutch Warmbloods, the initial 70-day training period was associated with a decrease in hind limb stance duration without any change in stride duration, indicating increased strength in the propulsive muscles (Back et al. 1995a). Ultimately, the ability to move with a shorter stance duration contributes to developing the cadence of the trot. The range of front limb motion decreases in the early stages of training under saddle, probably as a result of the horses beginning to use the front limbs to elevate the shoulders. In 3-year-old Andalusians, training resulted in the ability to protract the hind limb further, which increased the engagement of the hindquarters (Cano et al. 2000).

Long-term training is associated with changes in movement and ground reaction forces that accompany the development of collection and self-carriage. As collection increases, the forehand becomes more elevated relative to the hind quarters. This is due to small increases in flexion of the hind limb joints during weight bearing, together with elevation of the withers and shoulders produced by the action of the thoracic sling muscles, primarily the *serratus ventralis*. These muscles suspend the thorax between the front limbs, and when they contract the withers are raised relative to the horse's shoulders. In order for these muscles to be effective in maintaining the elevation of the forehand, the front limb must act as a strut in early stance, generating large vertical and braking forces that push upward and backward. The hind limbs also show an increase in vertical ground reaction force as self carriage improves, which is associated with increased weight-carrying by the hindquarters. At the same time, the hind limb longitudinal force becomes more propulsive.

193

GROUND REACTION FORCES

CHAPTER 15

Abbreviations used in this chapter:

CoM: Center of mass

GRF: Ground reaction force

GRF_{vert}: Ground reaction force, vertical component

GRF_{long}: Ground reaction force, longitudinal component

GRF_{trans}: Ground reaction force, transverse component

Locomotion occurs as a result of forces generated by the muscles and exerted through hoof contact with the ground. In accordance with Newton's laws of motion (chapter 7), the ground exerts a force against the hoof that is equal in magnitude and acts in the opposite direction; this is the ground reaction force or GRF. The effect of the GRF is to accelerate the horse's body in the direction in which it acts. Like other forces, the GRF is a vector. The direction of the GRF vector indicates the direction in which the force moves, or tends to move, the horse.

GRFs are measured using a force platform, which is a metallic plate supported by force sensors at the corners. Force platforms used for equine studies are usually embedded in the ground and covered by slip-resistant matting. When a horse steps on the platform, the GRF is recorded throughout the stance phase. If more than one hoof contacts the force platform simultaneously, the forces from the different hooves cannot be separated, and the output shows the summation of all the forces. In research studies, information is collected from trials in which data from a single hoof can be isolated.

For an individual horse moving at a consistent gait and speed, the GRF patterns vary little from stride to stride and are highly repeatable both in the short term (hour to hour), in the medium term (day to day), and in the long term, (year to year). In sound horses performing symmetrical gaits, the GRF patterns of the left and right sides are highly symmetrical, and differences in weight bearing between the left and right limbs may be indicative of lameness. In asymmetrical gaits, however, the trailing and leading limbs usually have different force profiles.

GRF Vector

Like other vectors, the GRF can be represented by an arrow; the length of the arrow is proportional to the magnitude of the force, and the direction of the arrow indicates the direction in which the force acts (figure 15.1). The three-dimensional GRF vector is usually resolved into vertical (GRF_{vert}), longitudinal (GRF_{long}), and transverse (GRF_{trans}) components, which facilitates interpretation of its effects. For details on vector resolution, see Appendix C.

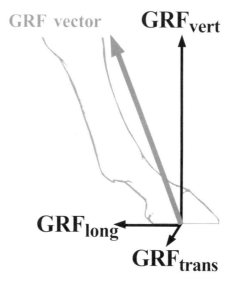

Figure 15.1: Three-dimensional ground reaction force vector (gray arrow) is resolved into three mutually perpendicular components acting in vertical (GRF_{vert}), longitudinal (GRF_{long}), and transverse (GRF_{trans}) directions.

GRF_{vert} counteracts the force of gravity that is pulling the horse downward, and it lifts the horse into the air in gaits that have an aerial phase or during jumping. GRF_{long} controls speed and movement in a forward-backward direction. GRF_{trans} produces turning or lateral movements.

The force-time graph in figure 15.2 shows the vertical, longitudinal, and transverse components of the GRF throughout the stance phase for the front limb of a horse trotting in hand. GRF_{vert} has the largest magnitude and is always positive. GRF_{long} has a negative (braking) phase, followed by a positive (propulsive) phase. Its magnitude is considerably smaller than that of the peak vertical force. GRF_{trans} has a very small magnitude when the horse travels in a straight line.

When a horse is viewed from the side, that is, in the sagittal plane, the observer sees a two-dimensional view of the kinematics and GRFs. In this view, the GRF

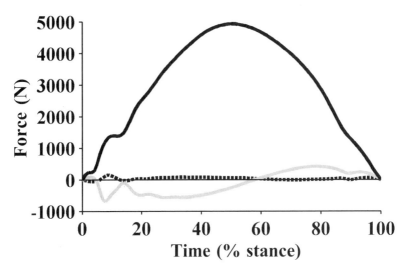

Figure 15.2: Force-time graph of the vertical (black line), longitudinal (gray line), and transverse (dashed line) components of front limb ground reaction force at trot.

vector represents the combined effects of the vertical and longitudinal forces. The magnitude and direction of the vector changes through the stance phase, such that its direction approximates the angle of the cannon bone. When the vector points toward the horse's tail in early stance, GRF_{long} has a decelerating or braking effect on forward motion. When the vector points toward the horse's head in the later part of stance, GRF_{long} provides forward propulsion. The vector is vertical when the longitudinal force is zero during the change from braking to propulsion.

Figure 15.3 shows a vector diagram, which is a series of sagittal plane GRF vectors plotted at intervals through the stance phase. The vectors are higher in the front limb than the hind limb, which indicates larger vertical forces. In the hind limb, the vector diagram leans to the right (toward the horse's head) indicating that the longitudinal force is predominantly propulsive.

Like other forces, the GRF is measured in newtons (N). Horses differ greatly in size and mass, which causes large differences in the magnitude of their GRFs (figure 15.4). Comparisons between horses of different sizes are facilitated by scaling the GRFs to body mass. A common way of doing this is to divide the force in newtons by the horse's body mass in kilograms. The resulting value, expressed in newtons per kilogram body mass (N/kg), is called the mass normalized GRF (figure 15.4). In evaluating force-time graphs, the reader should note whether the units of force are N (newtons), kN (kilonewtons), or N/kg (newtons/kg).

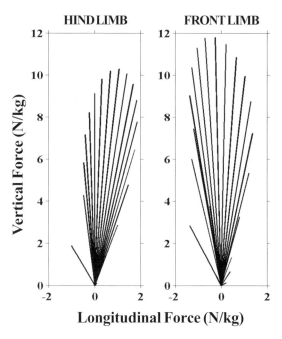

Figure 15.3:Vector diagrams for a hind limb (left) and front limb (right) of a horse trotting from left to right. The black lines represent the sagittal plane ground reaction force vectors shown at intervals of 5 per cent of stance duration from left to right of the diagrams.

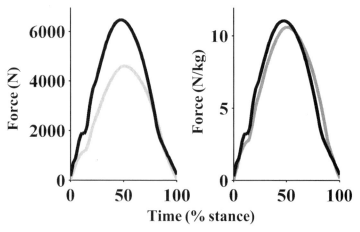

Figure 15.4: Force-time graphs of the vertical ground reaction force of a front limb for two horses of different sizes trotting at the same speed before (left) and after (right) normalization for body mass. Horse A (black line) has a mass of 600 kg and horse B (gray line) has a mass of 450 kg. Note the different units on the vertical axes of the two graphs.

Impulse

Impulse is the summation of the forces exerted over a period of time. Calculation of the impulse must take account of both the magnitude of the force and the time over which the force acts. For example, the impulse during an entire stance phase is represented by the area under the force-time curve (figures 15.6, 15.7, and 15.10).

The value of the impulse is calculated mathematically by integration of the force-time curve.

The SI units of measurement for impulse are those of force multiplied by time, as in newtons·seconds (N·s). Impulse is sometimes a more useful measurement than force data alone, since it takes account of both force magnitude and the time during which the force acts.

Vertical Component of the GRF (GRF$_{vert}$)

GRF$_{vert}$ has a positive value throughout the stance phase (figure 15.5). It acts to overcome the effect of gravity, which constantly pulls the horse's body downward, and to project the horse upward into an aerial phase in the leaping gaits or during jumping. The area under the vertical force-time curve is the vertical impulse (figure 15.5).

In symmetrical gaits, GRF$_{vert}$ is almost identical in the left and right limbs, but in asymmetrical gaits (canter, gallop) the trailing and leading limbs may have different GRF$_{vert}$ profiles. The peak value of GRF$_{vert}$ is usually higher in the

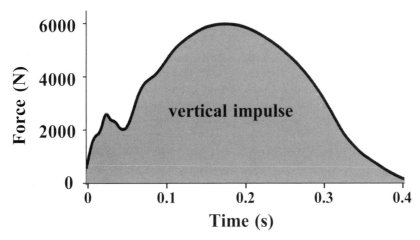

Figure 15.5: Vertical force-time graph for a front limb at the trot. The shaded area represents the vertical impulse.

front limbs than the hind limbs, because the horse's center of mass (CoM) is closer to the front limbs. On average, the front limbs carry about 58 percent of the horse's weight, compared with only 42 percent carried by the hind limbs. This difference in weight bearing is reflected by the higher vertical forces and impulses in the front limbs during locomotion (figure 15.3).

As speed increases, stance duration decreases. In order to maintain the vertical impulse, the amplitude of GRF_{vert} must increase to compensate for the decrease in stance duration (figure 15.6). Vertical impulse is approximately the same for the two curves in figure 15.6, in spite of differences in stance duration and peak vertical force.

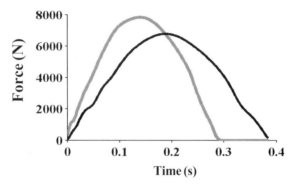

Figure 15.6: Vertical force-time graph for a slow trot (black line) and a fast trot (gray line) showing a higher force magnitude to compensate for the reduction in stance duration at the faster speed. Impulse is approximately the same for the two curves.

Longitudinal Component of the GRF (GRF_{long})

GRF_{long} acts in a horizontal direction along the longitudinal axis of the horse's body. Its action is to control forward and backward motion. When GRF_{long} is directed toward the horse's tail, it has a decelerative or braking effect that tends to slow the forward velocity or move the horse backward, as in a rein back. When GRF_{long} acts toward the horse's head, it is described as accelerative or propulsive because it tends to increase the forward velocity. During the stance phase, GRF_{long} initially has a braking effect, changing to a propulsive effect as the horse's body rolls over the grounded limb (figure 15.7).

Since the braking and propulsive forces act in opposite directions, they have different signs, negative and positive, respectively. The force platform is not sensitive to the horse's direction of travel; it simply records a positive force when the hoof pushes in one direction and a negative force when the hoof pushes in the opposite direction. Therefore, the longitudinal forces seen by the force platform are negative then positive when the horse runs in one

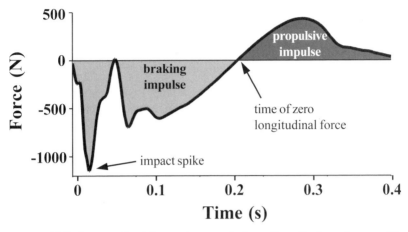

Figure 15.7: Longitudinal force-time graph for a front limb at the trot. The shaded areas represent the braking impulse (light shading) and the propulsive impulse (dark shading).

direction and positive then negative when the horse runs in the opposite direction. The direction of GRF_{long} is standardized during data processing by software that converts the longitudinal forces seen by the force platform to correspond with the directional planes of the horse's body. The convention used in this book is that braking forces are negative, propulsive forces are positive. The change from braking to propulsion occurs when the graph crosses the horizontal axis, which is the time of zero longitudinal force (figure 15.7).

The area between the braking part of GRF_{long} and the horizontal axis of the graph is the braking impulse, and the area between the propulsive part of GRF_{long} and the horizontal axis is the propulsive impulse (figure 15.7).

Example: For the graph shown in figure 15.7, the negative (braking) impulse is -160 N·s and the positive (propulsive) impulse is 79 N·s. The total longitudinal impulse of this limb over the entire stance phase is the algebraic sum of these two values:

$$\text{Total Impulse} = (-160 + 79) = -81 \text{ N·s}$$

The fact that the total longitudinal impulse is negative is indicative of a net braking effect that tends to reduce the forward velocity. For a horse trotting in hand, the total (net) longitudinal impulse is typically negative in the front limbs and positive in the hind limbs. The fact that the hind limbs provide forward propulsion in each stride fits well with the concept of the hind limbs being the horse's motor.

201

When a horse is moving at constant velocity on a horizontal surface, the net braking impulse of the front limbs is approximately equal in magnitude to the net propulsive impulse from the hind limbs. Because the effects are equal in magnitude and opposite in direction, they cancel each other out, so there is no net acceleration or deceleration. In other words, when speed is constant, the net braking impulse equals the net propulsive impulse.

In order to increase forward motion, the net propulsive impulse summed over all four limbs must be greater than the net braking impulse. The horse maximizes propulsion by leaning forward (figure 15.8), so the longitudinal GRFs of all limbs are directed forward.

Figure 15.8: The horse leans forward to maximize propulsion as shown by a draft horse pulling a heavy load (left) and a racehorse accelerating from a standing start (right).

A reduction in forward velocity occurs when the net braking impulse exceeds the net propulsive impulse summed over the four limbs. The horse maximizes the braking effect by leaning backward (figure 15.9), so the longitudinal GRFs of all limbs are directed backward.

Figure 15.9: The horse leans backward to maximize braking in the sliding stop (left) or to resist forward movement (right).

Transverse Component of the GRF (GRF_{trans})

GRF_{trans} acts from side to side across the horse's body. Its effect is to turn the horse or move it sideways. Interpretation of GRF_{trans} is based on its direction relative to the medial and lateral sides of the body. Since the force platform cannot differentiate the medial and lateral sides, software is used to make the necessary conversions. The convention used in this book is that medially directed transverse forces are negative, laterally directed transverse forces are positive. The medial and lateral impulses are the areas beneath the negative and positive parts of the curve, respectively (figure 15.10). GRF_{trans} for the left and right limbs are usually fairly similar in symmetrical gaits if the horse is traveling in a straight line.

During normal locomotion in a straight line, the transverse forces are much smaller than the vertical or longitudinal forces (figure 15.2). Larger transverse forces are recorded during turning, when GRF_{trans} is directed toward the inside of the turn (chapter 8).

When the horse performs lateral movements, in which the body moves forward and sideways, GRF_{trans} initially acts away from the direction of lateral movement then, as the horse's body rolls sideways over the grounded limb, GRF_{trans} acts toward the direction of lateral movement.

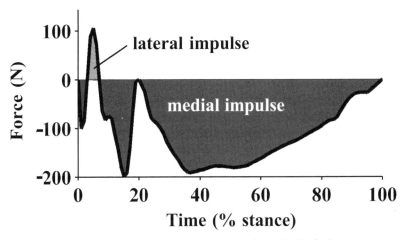

Figure 15.10: Transverse force-time graph for a front limb of a horse trotting in a straight line. Medially directed forces are negative, laterally directed forces are positive. The shaded areas represent the medial impulse (dark shading) and the lateral impulse (light shading). Note the scale on the vertical axis in comparison with figures 15.5 and 15.7.

Limb Loading During Stance

During each stance phase, GRFs are applied to the limbs in two distinct stages: the impact phase at the beginning of stance, followed by the loading phase that occupies the majority of stance. During the impact phase, which occurs immediately after the hoof contacts the ground, the hoof is rapidly decelerated, giving rise to a shock wave that travels up the limb. Through the remainder of the stance phase, the limb is loaded more gradually by the body weight. Since the behavior of the musculoskeletal tissues depends on the rate of loading, the tissues react differently to the rapid loading during impact compared with the more gradual loading in the middle part of stance. In general, the hard tissues of the bones and joints are more susceptible to injury during the impact phase, whereas the soft tissues, such as ligaments and tendons, may be more vulnerable in the middle of stance. An understanding of the characteristics of the impact and loading phases leads to a better appreciation of strategies for conditioning the musculoskeletal tissues and for preventing and treating musculoskeletal injuries.

Concussion during Impact

The hoof is moving forward and downward when it contacts the ground. It is rapidly brought to rest during the impact phase, which occupies the first 50 ms (1/20 s) after ground contact. As the hoof is decelerated, energy enters the locomotor system and travels up the limb. Even at relatively slow trotting speeds of around 4 m/s, the hoof experiences large impact accelerations of the order of 500 m/s^2 (Benoit et al. 1993).

The forces on the hoof during impact appear as impact spikes on the force-time graphs, particularly in the longitudinal component, which shows one or two large negative (braking) spikes in early stance (figure 15.7). The appearance of the impact loading, however, may be changed during data processing, and impact spikes that are readily visible in the raw data may be diminished or removed by filtering. Therefore, filtering should be performed with care when impact events are being studied.

Impact forces on the limbs are characterized by having high amplitude and rapid vibration frequency. Since these characteristics are potentially damaging to the bones and joints, the musculoskeletal system has several mechanisms for attenuating impact forces. Soft tissues inside the hoof, such as the laminae, digital cushion, and circulating blood, attenuate the impact vibrations (Lanovaz et al. 1998). Articular cartilage, which cushions the ends of the bones, and subchondral bone, which lies beneath the articular cartilage, play a role in shock absorption. Rapid rotation of some joints also helps to reduce concussion during the impact phase.

One of the characteristics of the musculoskeletal tissues is their ability to adapt to a moderate amount of regular exercise and the associated impact loading. During intense training, however, repetitive impact loading may exceed the safety threshold of the tissues leading to acute and chronic injuries to bones and joints, such as fractures and degenerative joint disease (osteoarthritis). Variations in the type and speed of exercise and the nature of the work surface lead to different injury patterns in different sports. Factors that exacerbate the damaging effects of impact shock include hard footing and high-speed exercise. Amelioration of impact shock throughout the training program can prolong a horse's athletic career.

Sclerosis of subchondral bone is an over-adaptation that occurs in response to excessive impact loading (Radin et al. 1973). The bones become harder, due to deposition of excessive amounts of minerals. In short bones and sesamoid bones, sclerosis may precede fractures that occur in well-defined patterns related to the stress lines (Pool 1992). In racehorses, for example, sclerosis of the front of the carpal bones predisposes to the development of slab fractures that occur at the boundary between the brittle, sclerotic bone and the underlying normal bone.

Frequent repetitions of high magnitude impact loading, which are associated with accumulating a large mileage at high speed, puts racehorses at risk of developing fatigue fractures. These are small cracks that can propagate through the bone. Catastrophic fractures of the long bones are almost always preceded by fatigue fractures (Stover et al. 1992).

Sport horses train at slower speeds than racehorses and experience lower impact shock. The damaging effects are relatively mild and may accumulate for many years before becoming apparent. The nature of the injuries is also different; sport horses experience fewer fractures than racehorses. Instead, the cumulative effects of impact loading over years of training and competition lead to degenerative joint disease, which is the primary reason for premature retirement of sport horses. It is important to realize that the damage is initiated long before the effects become obvious to the trainer or veterinarian.

Footing has a huge effect on impact, and the horse's athletic career can be prolonged by living and working on good surfaces. Stalls with hard floors should be covered with shock absorbent matting and/or adequately bedded. Tracks and arenas should be covered with an adequate depth of a suitable cushioning material; wood or rubber products are often added to sand or dirt to give the footing more resiliency and reduce concussion during impact. Surfaces with a higher content of water or organic material are generally associated with lower impact shock (Barrey et al. 1991).

The hoof is designed to attenuate impact shock, but the presence of shoes may affect this function. Steel shoes tend to increase impact shock, whereas certain types of shoes and pads may reduce it (Benoit et al. 1993).

205

Loading Phase

GRF_{vert} peaks in the middle part of the stance phase (figure 15.5). As the limb is loaded, the coffin and pastern joints flex and the fetlock joint extends under control of the digital flexor tendons and the suspensory ligament. These soft tissue structures experience their peak strain in the middle part of the stance phase. Strained flexor tendons (bowed tendons) and suspensory desmitis (pulled suspensory) are repetitive use injuries caused by frequent and excessive loading, usually during locomotion at high speed, during jumping, or when working with a high degree of either collection or extension.

The distal check ligament is maximally strained around the time of the initiation of breakover in late stance. Farriery techniques that facilitate breakover, such as shortening the toe, may reduce peak tension in the distal check ligament.

Ground Reaction Forces at Walk

The walk is a symmetrical gait, so the left and right limbs have similar GRF patterns and amplitudes (Merkens et al. 1986). Vertical GRFs for front and hind limbs of a horse moving at a slow walk and a fast walk are shown in figure 15.11. At a fast walk, there are two distinct peaks in the vertical force trace, one in early stance and one in late stance, separated by a dip in which a minimal value occurs (Khumsap et al. 2001; Khumsap et al. 2002). At a slow walk, the peaks are less well defined and may merge together as shown by the front limb in figure 15.11.

The relative heights of the two vertical force peaks differ in the front and hind limbs; the second peak is higher in the front limbs, whereas the first one is higher in the hind limbs. These differences have been ascribed to the position of the limbs relative to the horse's CoM; the front limbs are placed closer beneath the CoM in late stance, whereas the hind limbs are closer to the CoM in early stance. At a medium walk, the magnitudes of the early and late peaks represent 56 percent and 68 percent body weight, respectively, in the front limbs and 49 percent and 43 percent body weight, respectively, in the hind limbs (Ueda et al. 1981). The vertical impulses in the left and right limbs of sound horses are highly symmetrical (94-99 percent) (Merkens et al. 1986).

In each limb, GRF_{long} has an initial braking phase followed by a propulsive phase (figure 15.11). Limb coordination is such that, at any time, only one limb provides a large braking force and only one limb provides a large propulsive force (Merkens and Schamhardt 1988a). The time of zero longitudinal force tends to occur later at faster walking speeds (figure 15.11).

The left-right symmetry of the braking and propulsive impulses is high, in the range of 88-92 percent (Merkens et al. 1986). Summation of the braking and propulsive impulses over the four limbs is close to zero.

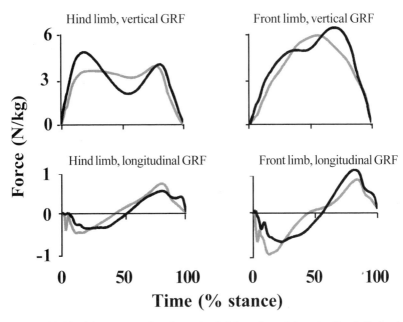

Figure 15.11: Mass normalized vertical (above) and longitudinal (below) ground reaction forces of a hind limb (left) and a front limb (right) of a horse walking at a slow velocity (1.0 m/s, gray lines) and a fast velocity (1.6 m/s, black lines). GRF: ground reaction force.

GRF_{trans} acts primarily in a medial (negative) direction at the walk. In the front limbs, the medial force has a single, wide peak, whereas in the hind limbs it has two small peaks that coincide with the peaks in GRF_{vert}. The left-right symmetry of the transverse impulse is around 80 percent, which is lower than for the vertical and longitudinal forces (Merkens et al. 1986). The low symmetry in this component may reflect conformational differences between left and right limbs or deviations from walking in a straight line over the force platform.

Ground Reaction Forces at Trot

Since the trot is a symmetrical gait, the left and right limbs show similar force patterns and amplitudes. After the impact phase, GRF_{vert} rises smoothly, peaking around the middle of stance, then decreasing to zero at lift-off (figure 15.12). The pattern is similar in all limbs, but the amplitude is higher in the front limbs than the hind limbs (Niki et al. 1982; Seeherman et al. 1987; Merkens et al. 1993a), which reflects the fact that the CoM lies closer to the front limbs. At a working trot, peak GRF_{vert} is approximately equal to body weight of the horse. As trotting speed increases, peak GRF_{vert} increases in the front limbs and sometimes, though not always, in the hind limbs. Higher vertical forces tend to be accompanied by increases in maximal fetlock joint extension.

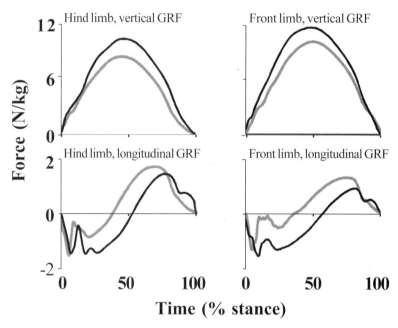

Figure 15.12: Mass normalized vertical (above) and longitudinal (below) ground reaction forces of a hind limb (left) and a front limb (right) of a horse trotting at a slow speed (3.5 m/s, gray lines) and a fast speed (5.0 m/s, black lines). GRF: ground reaction force.

At the trot, GRF_{long} has an initial braking phase followed by a propulsive phase in both front and hind limbs (figure 15.12). The front limbs usually have a higher peak braking force and a larger braking impulse than the hind limbs, whereas the hind limbs tend to have a higher peak propulsive force and a larger propulsive impulse than the front limbs. When a horse moves with more collection, there is a greater discrepancy between the longitudinal forces in the front and hind limbs, with an increase in braking impulse in the front limbs and an increase in propulsive impulse in the hind limbs.

GRF_{trans} is directed medially in all four limbs at the trot, and is small in magnitude.

Ground Reaction Forces at Canter

The canter or lope is an asymmetrical gait and the GRFs may be different for the trailing and leading limbs (figure 15.13). In fact, each of the four limbs has distinct functional responsibilities that are represented by characteristic vertical and longitudinal GRF profiles (Merkens et al. 1993b).

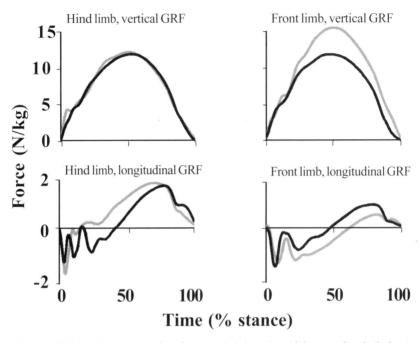

Figure 15.13: Mass normalized vertical (above) and longitudinal (below) ground reaction forces for the trailing (gray lines) and leading (black lines) hind limbs (left) and front limbs (right) of a cantering horse. GRF: ground reaction force.

In all limbs, GRF_{vert} rises to a single peak, the magnitude of which increases with speed. In working canter, peak GRF_{vert} is approximately equal to body weight in the hind limbs and the leading front limb, but is considerably higher in the trailing front limb.

GRF_{long} is almost entirely propulsive in the trailing hind limb, which acts to redirect the movement of the CoM in a forward direction at the end of the aerial phase. The leading hind and trailing front limbs (diagonal pair) have obvious braking and propulsive components (figure 15.13). Propulsion predominates in the leading hind limb, whereas braking predominates in the trailing front limb. The leading front limb has a small braking component and larger propulsive component. In the front limbs, the braking impulses increase with collection, which helps to maintain the elevation of the forehand throughout the stride.

GRF_{trans} is small at the canter and is highly variable between and within horses. It acts primarily in a medial direction in the hind limbs and trailing front limb, but tends to be directed laterally in the leading front limb (Merkens et al. 1993b).

Ground Reaction Forces during Jumping

The GRFs during the final stages of the approach and take-off determine the height and width jumped and the angular momentum of the horse's body during the aerial phase. Both front limbs have high peak vertical forces in the final approach stride (figure 15.14), especially the trailing front limb, which has a peak vertical force of around 180 percent body weight compared with 130 percent body weight for the leading front limb in a horse jumping a vertical fence 1.3 m high (Schamhardt et al. 1993). The front limbs exert large braking forces that decelerate forward movement. The trailing front limb provides a little forward propulsion just before leaving the ground, but the leading front limb is pulled off the ground just after it becomes vertical and before it is in a position to generate propulsion. The forces exerted by the front limbs act eccentrically around the CoM, resulting in an upward and backward rotation of the forehand (counterclockwise rotation in figure 15.15).

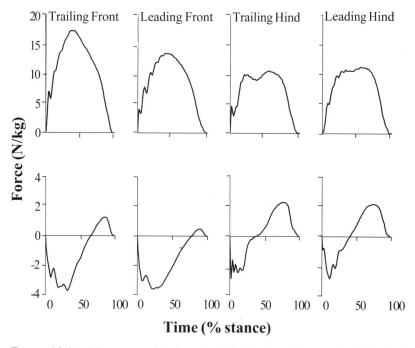

Figure 15.14: Mass normalized vertical (above) and longitudinal (below) ground reaction forces of a horse taking off to jump a vertical fence 1 m high. The graphs, from left to right, represent the trailing front limb and leading front limb during the final approach stride, and the trailing hind limb and leading hind limb at take off.

210

Figure 15.15: Jumping sequence showing the overall effect of the ground reaction forces (arrows) of the front and hind limbs at take off and landing.

The functions of the hind limbs at take-off are to impart vertical and horizontal velocity to the body and to reverse the direction of rotation of the horse's trunk. The vertical and longitudinal GRFs at take-off determine the path of the CoM, which must be raised high enough for all body parts to clear the fence.

The two hind limbs often show almost identical GRF profiles at take-off (figure 15.14) with the vertical force rising rapidly to a plateau that is maintained through most of stance. In figure 15.14, time is normalized to stance duration, so differences in stance durations are not apparent. In fact, stance durations of the hind limbs are prolonged during take off, which allows the generation of large vertical impulses.

The longitudinal force of the hind limbs at take-off initially brakes the forward velocity, but the force soon becomes propulsive, which provides the forward velocity needed to carry the horse across the width of the fence.

The hind limb forces at take-off act eccentrically around the CoM, which overcomes the backward rotation of the trunk and causes the horse's body to rotate forward during the aerial phase (clockwise in figure 15.15). It is important for the horse to generate an appropriate amount of angular momentum to take-off from the hind limbs and land safely on the front limbs: over-rotation carries the risk of somersaulting during landing, under-rotation may fail to lift the hind limbs high enough to clear the fence.

In contrast, the courbette, which is movement performed in high school dressage, consists of a series of jumps on the hind limbs without rotation of the horse's body. Forward rotation is avoided by having the hind limbs push off with the GRF vector acting through the CoM.

Peak vertical forces are higher at landing than at take-off due to the short duration of the stance phases, which allows less time to generate the necessary impulses. The first limb to contact the ground, the trailing front limb, has the highest peak GRF_{vert} (figure 15.16), and lands with an almost vertical orientation (figure 15.15) that is not conducive to generating a braking force. Therefore, GRF_{long} is almost entirely propulsive for the trailing front limb at landing. In contrast, the leading front limb contacts the ground with a more acute orientation (figure 15.15) and exerts primarily a braking force, followed by a small propulsive force (figure 15.16).

211

The fact that the trailing and leading front limbs are subjected to different forces during jumping may explain why some horses have a preferred lead for take-off and landing, and habitually switch to their preferred lead one or two strides before take-off or during the aerial phase. These horses usually have either a marked strength asymmetry between left and right sides that allows one limb to generate larger forces, or they have a mild injury that is painful when loaded with large forces.

The front limb forces during landing act eccentrically on the CoM to reverse the direction of rotation of the horse's trunk (figure 15.15). This allows the hindquarters to rotate forward beneath the body mass, so the hind hooves contact the ground under the horse's trunk.

During the first departure stride, the horse regains its balance and the hind limbs re-establish forward movement by generating large propulsive forces and impulses, especially the trailing hind limb (figure 15.16).

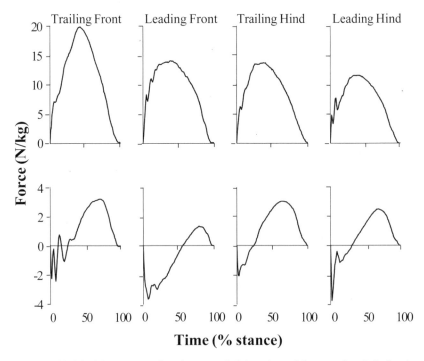

Figure 15.16: Mass normalized vertical (above) and longitudinal (below) ground reaction forces of a horse landing over a vertical fence 1 m high. The graphs from left to right represent the trailing front limb and leading front limb at landing, and the trailing hind limb and leading hind limb in the first departure stride.

When a horse jumps a fence less than 1.0 m high, it requires little, if any, elevation of the CoM to clear the fence. Consequently, the GRFs are not much larger than those of a normal canter stride. For example, in jumping a fence 0.8 m high, the combined vertical impulses of the front and hind limbs increase by only about 8 percent on the take-off side and 3 percent on the landing side, compared with a working canter stride. Over larger fences, the need to elevate the CoM increases progressively with the height of the fence, with a consequent increase in the vertical forces and impulses at take-off and landing. For example, when jumping a vertical fence 1.3 m high, peak GRF_{vert} is around 200 percent body weight in the trailing front limb and 150 percent body weight in the leading front limb (Schamhardt et al. 1993).

While horses that jump with good technique have vertical and longitudinal force profiles at take-off that resemble those for a normal canter stride, horses with poor jumping technique register considerably higher forces both at take-off and landing (Schamhardt et al. 1993). Poor jumpers tend to compensate for a weak propulsive impulse of the hind limbs at take-off by increasing the braking action of the front limbs in the preceding approach stride. As an example, the forces used by a horse with poor technique to clear a fence 0.8 m high are similar in magnitude to those used by a good jumper over a fence 1.3 m high. Consequently, horses that jump with poor technique might show earlier signs of wear and tear injuries than horses with good technique.

The landing forces are not equally distributed among the different tendinous structures that support the front limbs (Meershoek et al. 2002b). The superficial digital flexor tendon is relatively more loaded than the deep digital flexor tendon, especially over larger fences, which contributes to the higher incidence of injuries in the superficial, compared with the deep, digital flexor tendon in jumping horses.

Rider Effect on Ground Reaction Forces

The presence of a rider affects both kinematics (chapter 15) and GRFs, especially in the front limbs (Schamhardt et al. 1991; Clayton et al. 1999). At the walk, the front limbs show increases in peak GRF_{vert} and vertical impulse when the horse is ridden, whereas hind limb GRFs show minimal changes. An experienced rider has an effect equivalent to a sandbag of equal mass (Schamhardt et al. 1991).

When horses are ridden at sitting trot, peak GRF_{vert} increases in all limbs, with the effect being more obvious in the front limbs. The greatest increase in limb loading occurs between 50-70 percent stance, and causes the front fetlocks to be more extended at this time (Clayton et al. 1999). The presence of a rider has little effect on GRF_{long} at sitting trot (Clayton et al. 1999).

In posting trot, the rider's motion causes a left-right asymmetry in the GRFs, with higher vertical forces being recorded for the diagonal limb pair on which the rider sits (Schamhardt et al. 1991).

Ground Reaction Forces in Lameness

The effects of lameness on GRFs are most easily detected in gaits that have inherent symmetry, such as walk and trot, with the trot being the gait of choice for detecting gait asymmetries because the GRFs are higher than at the walk.

Lame horses redistribute the GRFs to unload the painful limb, which may result in left-right asymmetries in the GRFs and changes in force distribution between the front and hind limbs. Even in sound horses, however, GRF_{vert} is not always identical in the left and right limbs; horses may carry slightly more weight on one side, which is probably a reflection of sidedness.

At the walk, vertical and longitudinal braking forces are reduced in the lame front limb. The reduced GRF_{vert} is compensated mainly by an increase in the opposite front limb, with smaller increases in both hind limbs. The reduced braking force is compensated by the opposite front limb and lateral hind limb. Horses with hind limb lameness show decreases in vertical and longitudinal braking forces in the lame limb at the walk. The reduced GRF_{vert} is compensated mainly by the diagonal front limb and, to a lesser extent, by the lateral front limb. The reduced braking force is compensated by the opposite hind limb (Merkens and Schamhardt 1988b).

Vertical forces are higher in trot than walk due to the need to propel the horse into an aerial phase and absorb the concussion associated with landing. In

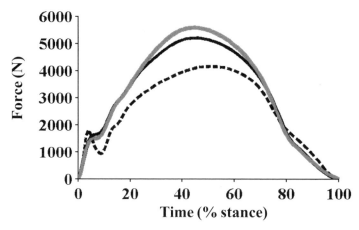

Figure 15.17: Effect of front limb lameness on vertical ground reaction force at trot. Forces for lame front limb (dashed line) and compensating front limb (gray line) are compared with the front limb of a sound horse (black line).

mild lameness, the horse moves with less elevation in the aerial phase, which is associated with smaller vertical forces. In fact, the first sign of a mild or subclinical lameness may be that the horse moves with less lift in the stride, which is perceived as a decline in the quality of movement. This is associated with lower vertical forces in all limbs, while maintaining left-right symmetry. However, there is a limit to the amount of unweighting that can be achieved by this mechanism, so it is effective only in mild lameness. In more severe cases, further unloading of the lame limb is accomplished by redistribution of load from the lame limb to the compensating limbs.

Front limb lameness is usually associated with reductions in vertical and longitudinal braking forces, which are redistributed mainly to the opposite front limb (figure 15.17) and, to a lesser extent, to the diagonal hind limb (Morris and Seeherman 1987; Clayton et al. 2000a). In association with the reduced vertical force, the affected front limb shows less fetlock extension in midstance than the opposite front limb, which has a small increase in fetlock extension.

Hind limb lameness at the trot is associated with reductions in the vertical and longitudinal braking GRFs and impulses in the lame limb. Often, the opposite hind limb shows a compensatory increase, but in other cases it is the diagonal front limb that shows the largest compensatory increase.

Force data of lame horses may be evaluated using symmetry indices that compare GRF variables in the left and right limbs (Merkens et al. 1988). Discrepancies result from changes in both the lame limb and the compensating limb, with the degree of asymmetry indicating the severity of lameness. Symmetry indices are useful for monitoring how lameness progresses over time.

Footing and Ground Reaction Forces

Generation of the GRF relies on having a stable surface to resist the pushing force from the hoof: the more resistance the surface offers, the greater the reaction to a specific pushing force. Horses are usually ridden on surfaces that have some 'give' to cushion the effect of concussion. However, these surfaces result in dissipation of a portion of the GRF. As a result, the horse receives less propulsion from the same amount of force generation. To put it another way, the horse must work harder to produce the same amount of propulsion on a soft surface compared with a firmer one.

When a horse moves on slippery ground, the surface is unable to resist the longitudinal GRF, so the hoof tends to slide forward in early stance as it exerts a braking force, and it tends to slide backward in late stance as it exerts a propulsive force. To compensate for the loss of security, the horse reduces its longitudinal forces by maintaining the GRF vector in a more vertical orientation. This is achieved using a limited range of protraction and retraction, which causes the steps to become short and stilted.

Normal Reaction Force

When a body is supported by a surface, the component of the GRF that acts perpendicular to the contact surface is called the normal reaction or normal force (F_{normal}). On a horizontal surface, the normal force is the same as the vertical component of the GRF. On a sloped surface, however, the normal force is calculated by resolving the GRF into components that act perpendicular (F_{normal}) and parallel ($F_{parallel}$) to the surface. In figure 15.18 the forces normal and parallel to the surface in the front limbs are:

$$F_{normal} = GRF \cos\theta$$

$$F_{parallel} = GRF \sin\theta$$

where F_{normal} is the component of the GRF acting perpendicular to the surface, $F_{parallel}$ is the component of the GRF acting parallel to the surface, and θ is the angle of elevation of the surface.

The value of the normal force is important in some instances, for example, when calculating friction (chapter 10).

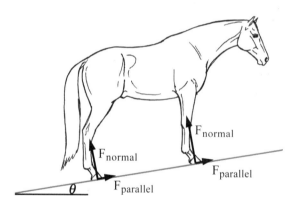

Figure 15.18: Ground reaction force components acting normal (F_{normal}) and parallel ($F_{parallel}$) to the surface for a horse standing on an incline at an angle θ to the horizontal.

Example: For a horse that weighs 500 N standing on a treadmill with an inclination (θ) of 10°, the normal component of the horse's weight (W) is:

$$F_{normal} = W \cos\theta = 500 * 0.9848 = 492.4 \text{ N}$$

LIMB MECHANICS

Abbreviations used in this chapter:

GRF: Ground reaction force

Locomotion is the act of moving from place to place: rotational movements of the limb segments are converted into translational motion of the horse's body. During locomotion, the horse is constantly being pulled downward under the influence of gravity, but successive hoof contacts "catch" the body before it falls too far. Contractions of the limb muscles generate ground reaction forces (GRF) to counteract the downward motion and provide forward propulsion. This chapter explores some of the structural and functional properties of the musculoskeletal system that facilitate cursorial locomotion.

Musculoskeletal Tissues

The musculoskeletal tissues includes bone, muscle, tendon, and ligament. The bony skeleton provides a rigid framework upon which the muscles, tendons, and ligaments exert forces that move or stabilize the joints. The lengths of the bones and the angles between them determine limb conformation, and affect leverage during locomotion. Rigidity of the skeleton is necessary for transmission of locomotor forces. If a long bone is fractured, skeletal rigidity is compromised, and the limb may be unable to bear weight or provide propulsion.

Bones articulate at the joints, with the joint above a bone segment being regarded as the fulcrum about which the bone rotates. Most joints allow a certain amount of mobility in specific directions. The amount and type of movement are limited by the shape of the bones and by tension in ligaments that stabilize the joints to prevent dislocations. The length and orientation of the ligamentous fibers is such that they become taut at critical positions in the movement cycle, where they restrict further motion of the joint. Excessive forces, especially if they are applied repeatedly, can tear the ligamentous fibers, resulting in desmitis (strained ligament).

217

Muscles are responsible for causing and controlling movements of the joints. When a muscle contracts, it generates a tensile force that tends to cause both translation and rotation of the bones at a joint (figure 16.1). Forces exerted by the ligaments overcome the tendency to translate, so muscular contraction creates a torque around the joint. The effect of the muscular force on a bone is similar, therefore, to the effect of pulling on a gate that is constrained to rotate around its hinges (chapter 8). As a result of the ligaments constraining the bones to rotate around the joints, muscles act as torque generators.

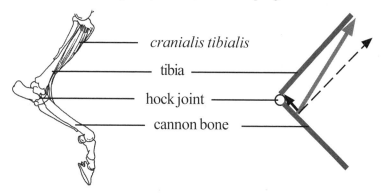

Figure 16.1: Anatomical location (left) and diagram showing the action (right) of the cranialis tibialis. *Muscular tension (heavy gray arrow) tends to cause both translation (black arrow) and rotation (dashed black arrow) of the cannon bone relative to the tibia.*

The attachment site of a muscle relative to a joint affects the amount and type of leverage it exerts and the amount of torque it generates. Many muscles act as third-class levers, but some of the more powerful locomotor muscles act as first-class levers (chapter 9).

Muscles attach to bones directly or via tendons that transmit muscular forces to the bone. One of the characteristics of the horse's limbs is the presence of long tendons that act elastically. Typically, the tendons are strained as the limb is loaded in early stance. As the tendons are strained, they store elastic energy. Later in stance, the limb is unloaded, allowing the tendons recoil and release their stored energy. The tendons' ability to store and release elastic energy at appropriate times in the locomotor cycle reduces the amount of energy that must be supplied by active muscular contractions.

Movement at the Joints

Rotational movements of the limb segments are converted into translations of the entire body, which move the horse from place to place. Gait analysis evaluates these movements and the associated forces. The analytic process is often simplified by confining the analysis to the sagittal plane, which is the view

218

Figure 16.2: Sagittal plane view of a trotting horse with superimposed stick figure. The limb segments are represented by lines, and the angles between adjacent lines represent the flexion and extension angles at the joints.

seen when watching the horse from the side (figure 16.2). This is a reasonable approximation because the predominant movement of most of the horse's joints is flexion and extension in a sagittal plane.

Flexion and extension of the proximal joints, primarily the hip in the hind limb and the elbow in the front limb, swings the entire limb back and forth along the longitudinal axis of the body. Flexion of the carpus and hock raises the hoof clear of the ground during swing. The fetlock, pastern and coffin joints assist in raising the limb in swing and also absorb concussion during the stance phase.

Transverse (sideways) movements of the limbs are wasteful in terms of energy expenditure. Horses evolved to move economically, and adaptations in the structure of the bones and joints restrict the amount of motion occurring outside of the sagittal plane. The shoulder and hip, however, are capable of relatively large amounts of abduction, in which the limb segments swing laterally away from the midline of the body, and adduction, in which the segments swing medially toward the midline of the body. These movements are viewed most easily when watching the horse from in front or behind (figure 16.3).

Some joints also show a small amount of rotation along the longitudinal axis of the limb. Internal rotation, also called pronation, causes the dorsum (front surface) of the limb to rotate inward; external rotation, also called supination, causes the dorsum of the limb to rotate outward. In horses, rotation of the front limb is restricted by fusion of the ulna with the radius, which fixes the limb in a pronated position. Other species have joints between these two bones that allow the digit to be pronated and supinated. Similarly, in the equine hind limb, pronation and supination are limited by fusion of the fibula with the tibia.

219

Figure 16.3: Frontal view of a horse showing adduction of the shoulder joints in the half pass.

Action of Muscles

Muscles can be classified according to their action at specific joints (chapter 8) as flexors or extensors, abductors or adductors, and internal or external rotators. Since most of the motion in the equine limbs involves flexion and extension in the sagittal plane, the majority of the muscles act as flexors or extensors. Often, there are several muscles with similar actions; these are called agonists. For example, the *biceps brachii* and the *brachialis* muscles both flex the elbow, so they are agonists or synergists (figure 16.4). Antagonistic muscles have opposite effects. For example, the *biceps brachii*, a flexor of the elbow, is antagonistic to the *triceps brachii*, an extensor of the elbow (figure 16.4). Antagonistic muscles may contract simultaneously to stabilize a joint. This is called cocontraction.

When a muscle crosses a single joint, it is said to be monoarticular, and its action can be deduced from the locations of its attachments. The *brachialis* (figure 16.4) is a monoarticular elbow flexor; it runs from the proximal part of the humerus across the front (flexor surface) of the elbow joint to the proximal part of the radius.

Some muscles cross more than one joint, when they are described as biarticular (crossing two joints) or multi-articular (crossing multiple joints). The *biceps brachii* is a biarticular muscle; it crosses the extensor side of the shoulder and the flexor side of the elbow (figure 16.4). The long head of the *triceps brachii* is also biarticular crossing the flexor side of the shoulder and the extensor side of the elbow (figure 16.4). Biarticular muscles coordinate the movements of different joints, and they transfer energy between the joints. Their action is regulated by tension in monoarticular muscles.

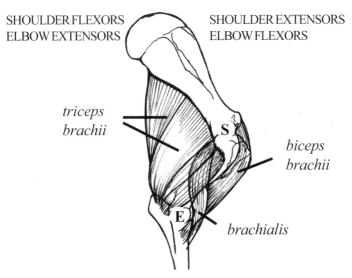

SHOULDER FLEXORS
ELBOW EXTENSORS

SHOULDER EXTENSORS
ELBOW FLEXORS

triceps brachii

biceps brachii

S

E

brachialis

Figure 16.4: Extensor and flexor muscles of the shoulder joint (S) and elbow joint (E), lateral view.

The outcome of a muscular contraction depends on the magnitude of the muscular force in relation to any opposing forces. As a muscle develops tension, the entire muscle may shorten (concentric muscular action), lengthen (eccentric muscular action), or maintain the same length (isometric muscular action). The change in muscle length determines the type of work done across the joint and the nature of the mechanical energy changes (chapter 13).

In a concentric muscular action, a muscle shortens as it generates tension, so its attachments points are pulled closer together. This occurs, for example, when a flexor muscle flexes a joint or an extensor muscle extends a joint. Concentric muscular actions generate mechanical energy and the muscles perform positive work (figure 16.5).

In an eccentric muscular action, a muscle lengthens as it generates tension in opposition to a larger force, which is causing movement of the joint (figure 16.5). Under these circumstances, the muscle controls the rate of movement. Eccentric action of a flexor muscle controls extension of a joint, eccentric action of an extensor muscle controls flexion of a joint. Mechanical energy is absorbed during an eccentric muscular action and the muscle performs negative work.

In an isometric muscular action, a muscle generates tension without any change in length. This type of action maintains the joint in a static position or resists movement in the presence of an opposing force. Since no movement occurs in an isometric muscular action, no mechanical work is done (figure 16.5).

Sometimes joints are stabilized by simultaneous activity in antagonistic muscles. This is called cocontraction. Cocontractions are prevalent when a

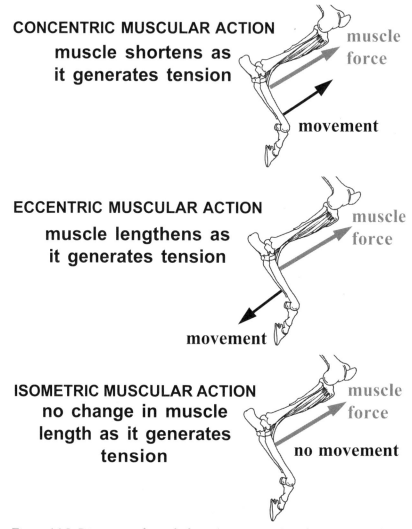

Figure 16.5: Directions of muscle force (gray arrows) and joint motion (black arrows) in concentric (above), eccentric (middle), and isometric (below) muscular actions of the tibialis cranialis *muscle.*

horse or rider is learning a new skill. In the early stages of practice, the muscles are poorly coordinated and the performance is jerky due to unnecessary muscular activations and cocontractions that increase energy expenditure. With practice, unnecessary cocontractions are reduced, and the movements become smooth and well coordinated. The end result is a fluid and graceful performance, in which contributions of different muscle groups are coordinated without conscious effort and without unnecessary cocontractions. Consequently, the expert performer expends less energy in performing the skill.

Energy Saving Tendons

A characteristic of the equine limbs is that some muscles have become tendinous throughout their length, so their effect is purely mechanical. This is an energy-saving strategy, since it reduces the need for active muscular contractions. Tendons that behave in this manner include the suspensory ligament, which has evolved from the *interosseus medius* muscle, and the digital flexor tendons acting through their check ligaments.

Reciprocal Apparatus

In the hind limb, the *peroneus tertius* and the superficial digital flexor tendon comprise the reciprocal apparatus (figure 16.6). The *peroneus tertius* crosses the extensor surface of the stifle and the flexor surface of the hock on the front of the limb. The superficial digital flexor tendon crosses the flexor surface of the stifle, the extensor surface of the hock, and the flexor surface of the fetlock

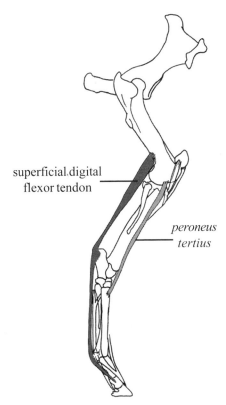

superficial digital
flexor tendon

*peroneus
tertius*

Figure 16.6: The reciprocal apparatus of the hind limb: the tendinous peroneus tertius *(light shading) and superficial digital flexor tendon (dark shading) coordinate flexion and extension of the stifle and hock joints.*

on the back of the limb (figure 16.6). The effect of the reciprocal apparatus is to synchronize movements of these joints, without requiring the expenditure of muscular energy. In the swing phase, as the hind limb swings forward, the reciprocal apparatus ensures that the stifle, hock, and fetlock flex synchronously. Later in the swing phase, the stifle and hock extend together as the limb prepares for ground contact. During the stance phase, movements of these joints generally occur in synchrony, though in late stance the GRF is sufficiently large to stretch the *peroneus tertius*, so the hock extends slightly more than the stifle. As the hoof lifts off and the GRF decreases, the *peroneus tertius* recoils, releasing stored elastic (strain) energy that is used to flex the hock in early swing.

Suspensory Apparatus

The suspensory apparatus acts as an elastic spring to support the fetlock joint. It consists of the suspensory ligament, proximal sesamoid bones, distal sesamoidean ligaments, and extensor branches of the suspensory ligament (figure 16.7). The suspensory ligament originates from the cannon bone, between the splint bones, and attaches to the proximal sesamoid bones just above the fetlock joint. It is continued by the distal sesamoidean ligaments that insert on the pastern bones. Since there is no muscular component to

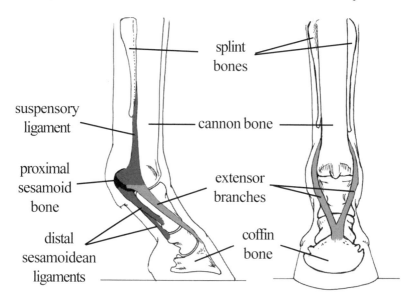

Figure 16.7: Suspensory apparatus of the front limb: lateral view (left) and dorsal view (right). The suspensory ligament attaches to the proximal sesamoid bones and is continued distally by the distal sesamoidean ligaments. The medial and lateral extensor branches join the extensor tendon (not shown) before attaching to the coffin bone.

adjust its length, tension in the suspensory apparatus is determined by limb orientation, primarily fetlock angle. As the fetlock extends, the suspensory ligament is stretched, reaching maximal strain in the middle of stance (Meershoek et al. 2002a). Excessive fetlock extension, which occurs during high-speed activities, such as racing, may cause disruption of the suspensory apparatus.

The extensor branches of the suspensory ligament arise at the level of the proximal sesamoid bones and pass forward around the medial and lateral sides of the pastern, before joining the extensor tendon and attaching to the front of the pastern and coffin bones (figure 16.7). They are taut in early stance to prevent the coffin and pastern joints from buckling forward (Jansen et al. 1993).

Digital Flexor Tendons

In the front limbs, the superficial digital flexor tendon and its proximal check (or accessory) ligament act mechanically to support the carpal, fetlock, and pastern joints. The proximal check ligament arises behind the radius and merges with the superficial digital flexor tendon, which inserts on the long and short pastern bones (figure 16.8). During stance, tension in the superficial digital flexor tendon controls extension of the carpus and fetlock, and helps to prevent the pastern joint from buckling forward. This tendon, and the muscle associated with it, stiffen the limb and damp limb oscillations in early stance (Wilson et al. 2001;

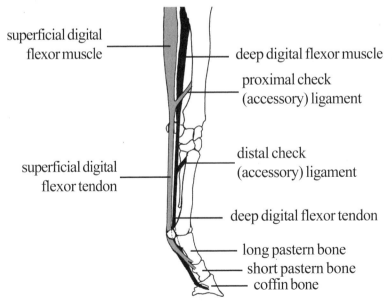

superficial digital flexor muscle

deep digital flexor muscle

proximal check (accessory) ligament

superficial digital flexor tendon

distal check (accessory) ligament

deep digital flexor tendon

long pastern bone

short pastern bone

coffin bone

Figure 16.8: Digital flexor muscles and tendons of the front limb. Medial view of the location and attachments of the deep digital flexor and its distal check ligament (dark shading) and the superficial digital flexor and its proximal check ligament (light shading).

Meershoek et al. 2002a). The tendon is maximally stretched in the first half of stance (Meershoek et al. 2002a), and is liable to be injured when the fetlock joint undergoes excessive extension. After being strained during the stance phase, the superficial digital flexor tendon recoils in early swing to flex the carpal and fetlock joints. In the hind limb, the superficial digital flexor is entirely tendinous. It forms part of the reciprocal apparatus (figure 16.6), and has a strong attachment to the point of the hock.

The deep digital flexor tendon and its distal check ligament support the fetlock, pastern, and coffin joints. In the front limb, the distal check ligament arises behind the carpal joint and cannon bone, just above the suspensory ligament. It blends into the deep digital flexor tendon, then runs over the flexor aspect of the fetlock, pastern, and coffin joints before inserting on the underside of the coffin bone (figure 16.8). In the hind limb, the distal check ligament is poorly developed. The deep digital flexor tendon is maximally strained in the middle part of stance. The tendon and its associated deep digital flexor muscle contribute to the propulsive force in the second half of stance (Meershoek et al. 2002a). Maximal strain of the distal check ligament occurs just before the start of breakover, when it acts through the deep digital flexor tendon to flex the coffin joint and raise the heel.

Cursorial Adaptations

All animals have the same types of musculoskeletal tissues, but the way these tissues are organized and arranged varies between species. Factors that influence musculoskeletal organization include the type of locomotion for which the species is adapted, such as running, swimming, or jumping, and the need for special locomotor qualities, such as speed, stability, or maneuverability. The horse is described as a cursorial (running) species, which implies that the limbs have undergone evolutionary adaptations designed to enhance speed.

Adaptations in limb structure that favor a cursorial life-style in horses include adoption of the unguligrade stance, elongation of the distal limb segments, reduction in the number of digits, restriction of limb movements to the sagittal plane, and concentration of muscle mass in the upper part of the limbs. As a result of these adaptations, the modern day horse is taller than its ancestors and has longer limbs relative to its height.

Unguligrade Stance

One of the most obvious evolutionary changes in the equine limbs is the adoption of the unguligrade stance (figure 16.9), which means the horse is, effectively, standing on tip toe, and bearing weight on the nail, which has been strengthened to form the hoof wall. Indeed, the term unguligrade is derived from the Latin word *unguis* meaning nail.

226

Human beings use a plantigrade stance, in which the entire plantar surface of the foot, from the ankle (tarsus) to the toes, is in contact with the ground (figure 16.9). If the horse were to stand like this, the limb would be flat on the ground from the hock distally in the hind limb, and from the carpus distally in the front limb. Cats and dogs have a digitigrade stance that is intermediate between plantigrade and unguligrade. In the digitigrade stance, the metacarpal and metatarsal bones are elevated from the ground (figure 16.9), and weight is borne by the three phalanges, which are cushioned by digital pads. In horses and other ungulates, the cannon bone and all three phalanges are elevated from the ground, and the digital pad has been enveloped by the hoof to form the digital cushion, located between the bones of the hoof and the frog.

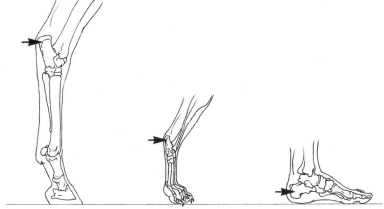

Figure 16.9: Unguligrade stance of the horse (left), compared with digitigrade stance of dog (center), and plantigrade stance of human (right). Arrow indicates calcanean process.

Elongation of the Limbs

Limb bones that are raised from the ground contribute to the length of the limb. In horses, this includes all the bones below the carpus and hock. These bones, especially the cannon bones, have become greatly elongated, so they make a considerable contribution to total limb length.

Reduction of the Moment of Inertia

The amount of energy used to swing the limbs back and forth depends on their resistance to rotation due to inertia. The moment of inertia depends on the mass of the limb and the distribution of that mass relative to its point of rotation (chapter 8). By locating heavy tissues, such as the large, powerful locomotor muscles, close to the point of rotation in the proximal limb, the moment of inertia of the entire limb is reduced.

227

The largest muscles in the front limb are concentrated around the shoulder and elbow, with smaller muscles surrounding the forearm (figure 16.10). Below the carpus, there is virtually no muscle tissue; instead, long tendons transmit tensile forces from these muscles to the distal limb segments. Tendons are much lighter in weight than muscles and, as a result, the front cannon, pastern, and hoof segments account for less than 1 percent of the horse's weight (table 16.1).

The largest muscles in the hind limbs are around the hip and stifle, with less bulky muscles surrounding the gaskin. Below the hock, long, lightweight tendons transmit the muscular forces to the digit. As in the front limb, the hind cannon, pastern, and hoof segments account for less than 1 percent of body mass (table 16.1).

Another weight-saving mechanism in the distal limb is the reduction in the number of digits. During the course of evolution, the three front toes and four hind toes that were present in the prehistoric ancestors of the horse have been reduced to a single functional digit in each limb. The third digit persists, flanked by the medial and lateral splint bones (figure 16.7), which are remnants of the second and fourth digits. The single-toed equine digit is even lighter in weight than the two-toed digit of cloven-hoofed species, such as cattle.

The rotation point of the limb affects the effective limb length. The front limbs rotate around a point on the scapula that is about one third of the distance from the withers toward the point of the shoulder (figure 16.11). The point of rotation

Front Limb Segments	Percent Body Mass	Hind Limb Segments	Percent Body Mass
Shoulder	2.1		
Arm	1.6	Thigh	3.5
Forearm	1.2	Gaskin	1.6
Front Cannon	0.3	Hind Cannon	0.3
Front Pastern	0.1	Hind Pastern	0.2
Front Hoof	0.2	Hind Hoof	0.2
TOTAL	5.5	TOTAL	5.8

Table 16.1: Mass of front and hind limb segments as a percentage of total body mass (Buchner et al. 1997). The thigh was removed at the hip joint, and the pelvis was considered part of the trunk.

228

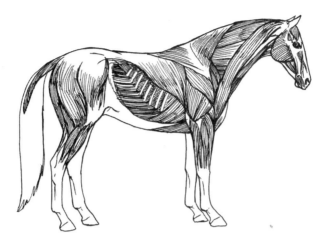

Figure 16.10: Distribution of the horse's muscle mass. The largest muscles are concentrated around the neck, trunk, and proximal limbs. Smaller muscles surround the forearm and gaskin. The distal limbs, below the knees and hocks, are devoid of muscles.

of the hind limbs depends on the type of gait. In symmetrical gaits, such as walk, trot, pace, tölt, and foxtrot, the left and right hind limbs swing out of phase with each other and the pivot point is the hip joint (figure 16.11). In asymmetrical gaits such as canter and gallop, the two hind limbs swing forward almost in unison, and their point of rotation moves to the lumbosacral joint (figure 16.11). The lumbosacral joint, between the last lumbar vertebra and the sacrum, is the only vertebral joint from the withers to the pelvis that shows a significant amount of flexion and extension. When the limbs rotate around the lumbosacral joint, the pelvis swings back and forth with the hind limbs, which has the effect of lengthening the entire hind limb and, thus, increasing stride length. This is one of the reasons why the gallop is a faster racing gait than the pace or trot.

Figure 16.11: Points of rotation for the front and hind limbs are shown by asterisks. The front limbs rotate around the proximal scapula. The hind limbs rotate around the hip joint in a symmetrical gait (left) and around the lumbosacral joint in an asymmetrical gait (right).

During the swing phase, the moment of inertia of the limbs is further reduced by flexion of the joints, which lifts the hoof clear of the ground and brings the distal segments closer to their axis of rotation (figure 16.12). At faster speeds, there is more joint flexion and hoof elevation, which facilitates limb protraction by further reducing the moment of inertia (figure 16.13).

Figure 16.12: Limb shortening during the swing phase. A line connecting the point of rotation on the scapula with the coffin joint is longer during stance (left) than during swing (right).

Since the hoof is located so far from the point of rotation of the limb, its mass has a large effect on inertia. Typically, hoof mass is less than 1 kg in a 500 kg horse, which represents only 0.2 percent of body mass. Addition of a steel shoe, with a mass of about 0.5 kg, has a significant effect on limb dynamics (Balch et al. 1996; Willemen et al. 1998; Lanovaz and Clayton 2001; Singleton et al. 2003). The increase in moment of inertia due to heavy shoes requires more energy to protract and retract the limb in the swing phase (Singleton et al. 2003), which is a disadvantage in racing and other sports that rely on economy of movement. This is why lightweight aluminum plates are favored for racing. On the other hand, heavy shoes may be used to increase animation of the swing phase in horses competing in sports that are not reliant on economy of movement, such as dressage horses, fine harness horses, and gaited horses.

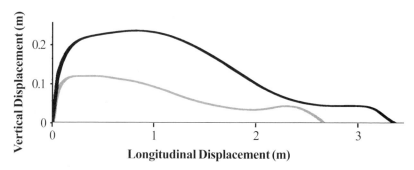

Figure 16.13: Flight arc of the front hoof during the swing phase at a slow trot (gray line) and fast trot (black line). Note that the scales are different on the vertical and horizontal axes.

230

The higher flight arc of the hoof with heavy shoes is due to greater activity in the elbow flexor muscles (Singleton et al. 2003). This is the basis for adding weights to the hooves or distal limbs as a strength training method for improving animation or expressiveness of front limb movements. It should be noted, however, that when a horse wears heavy shoes, the fetlock and coffin joints are more extended at ground contact. This may increase the risk of injury, particularly in the extended gaits, when there is some loss of control of hoof placement. Therefore, heavy shoes should be used with caution.

Limbs as Levers

The limbs comprise a series of rigid bones connected by joints and moved by muscles. In mechanical terms, the bones act as levers and the muscles act as torque (force) generators. The use of the limbs as levers implies that a force is applied at one location to overcome a resistance that acts at a different location (chapter 9). Muscular forces overcome resistance to limb movement that is primarily due to the GRF in the stance phase and to the mass of the limb (inertial force) in the swing phase.

The relative positions of the force (muscle or tendon attachment), the fulcrum (center of rotation of the joint), and the resistance determine the effect of a lever (chapter 9). The relative lengths of the force arm and the resistance arm indicate whether a limb lever is designed to overcome a large resistance or to increase the speed or distance of movement of the distal limb.

The majority of limb muscles act as third-class levers, which are characterized by having the force and resistance acting on the same side of the fulcrum, with the force arm shorter than the resistance arm. The effect of the leverage is to increase the range or speed of motion, which is effective for protracting the limb through a wide arc during the swing phase, when resistance to movement is small. These muscles often pass close to the joint, however, which tends to give them a short force arm. The presence of sesamoid bones between a muscle or its tendon and a joint increases the length of the force arm and the torque generated by the muscle. For example, the navicular bone increases the force arm of the deep digital flexor tendon at the coffin joint. As the tendon winds around the navicular bone, its direction of pull also changes (figure 16.14).

Breakover of the hoof in terminal stance is an example of the effect of a third-class lever. The hoof rotates around the coffin joint, which acts as the fulcrum (figure 16.14). Breakover is initiated by tension in the distal check ligament and the deep digital flexor tendon, which inserts on the underside of the coffin bone, close to the coffin joint. Resistance to coffin joint flexion is provided by the GRF acting through the solar surface of the hoof in front of the coffin joint.

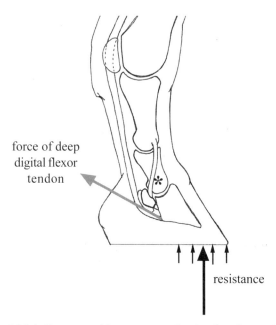

force of deep
digital flexor
tendon

resistance

Figure 16.14: Forces and leverage involved in breakover. The ground exerts a force against the front of the hoof (small black arrows) that resists flexion of the coffin joint around its center of rotation (*). The summation of the resistive forces is represented by the heavy black arrow. Breakover begins when the force in the deep digital flexor tendon (gray arrow) overcomes the resistance offered by the ground.

Since the force of the deep digital flexor tendon is applied closer to the coffin joint than the resistance, it is classified as a third-class lever. Breakover begins when the torque of the flexor tendon, which increases in late stance, exceeds the torque of the GRF, which is decreasing in late stance. Breakover may be delayed by a number of factors, such as increasing the magnitude of the resistance (harder surface), lengthening the resistance arm (longer toe), or reducing the force exerted by the deep digital flexor tendon (raised heel).

The effects of a change in hoof shape are not always intuitively obvious. If hoof angle is increased by elevating the heels, it might be assumed that breakover will be facilitated and occur earlier in stance. In fact, breakover is delayed because raising the heels reduces tension in the deep digital flexor tendon and, consequently, it takes longer for the tendon force to increase sufficiently to overcome the GRF (Clayton et al. 2000b). Although the onset of breakover is delayed by raising the heels, the initiation of breakover is associated with less force in the deep digital flexor tendon and distal check ligament than with a lower heel.

Joints that require large torques to drive the movements of the limbs and the body during the stance phase often feature bony protrusions called tuberosities, that project above the center of joint rotation. Examples of tuberosities include the olecranon (point of the elbow), the greater trochanter of the femur, and the calcanean tuberosity (point of the hock). Muscles that attach to these tuberosities act as first-class levers. Since the tuberosities increase the length of the force arm, the muscles that attach to them generate high torques. The *triceps brachii*, which attaches to the olecranon process, produces an extensor torque at the elbow that extends the joint and retracts the front limb during stance. The *gluteus medius*, which attaches to the greater trochanter, extends the hip joint, retracts the hind limb, and propels the body forward in the stance phase. The *gastrocnemius* and hamstring muscles attach to the calcanean tuberosity, where they produce large extensor torques to drive the horse forward during the stance phase.

The leverage afforded by the long limb bones of the horse favors rotation of the hoof through a wide arc at a rapid speed. The drawback to this arrangement is that elongation of the limb lengthens the resistance arm, so more force is needed to overcome the resistance of the GRF. Provided the muscles generate sufficient power to overcome this resistance, a combination of long levers and high torques is optimal for locomotor speed.

Limbs as Springs

Elasticity describes the ability of an object to rebound after being pushed, pulled, or twisted out of shape (chapter 11). In the horse's limbs, tendons contain elastic tissue that stretches when a tensile force is applied and recoils when tension is released. The stretching process stores mechanical energy, which is released during recoil to provide propulsion. This spring-like function is characteristic of tendon and ligament behavior in the leaping gaits. Elastic energy is stored as the limb is loaded, then released when the limb is unloaded.

Elastic energy storage and release are associated with a joint power curve in which a burst of negative power and energy absorption (storage) is followed immediately by a similar burst of positive power and energy generation (release) (figure 16.15). The stored elastic energy must be released immediately, or some is lost. The horse's limbs make extensive use of elastic recoil. For example, the flexor tendons and suspensory ligament store elastic energy as the fetlock joint extends in early stance, then release it as the fetlock flexes later in stance and in early swing (Clayton et al. 2000b). The fact that the areas under the negative and positive parts of the power curve for the fetlock have almost equal areas, and there is no delay between them, is characteristic of elastic recoil (figure 16.15).

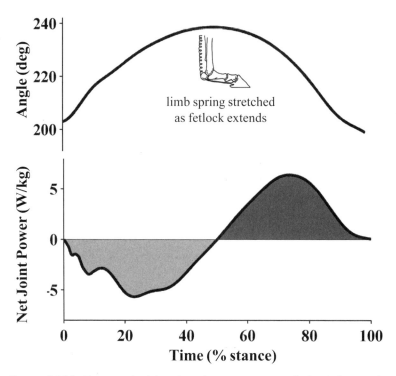

Figure 16.15: Joint angle (above) and net joint power (below) during elastic energy storage and release at the fetlock joint in the stance phase of trot. The amount of energy stored (lightly shaded area) is approximately equal to the amount of energy released (darkly shaded area).

Although the fetlock is an important contributor to the spring-like function of the limbs, it is not the only site of elastic energy storage and release. Strong tendons and ligaments abound throughout the horse's limbs, including the tendon of the *biceps brachii*, which acts across the shoulder and elbow joints in the front limb. It is stretched in late stance, then recoils in early swing to catapult the front limb forward (Wilson et al. 2002). Similarly, the *peroneus tertius*, which crosses the stifle and hock joints, is stretched in late stance then recoils in early swing to flex the hock and protract the distal hind limb (figure 16.6).

Energy Exchanges During Locomotion

Locomotion is an expensive activity in terms of energetic cost. Economies in energy expenditure are achieved by transferring energy between limb segments. According to gait, horses may use an inverted pendulum and/or elastic spring mechanism to conserve mechanical energy (Cavagna et al. 1977).

Inverted Pendulum Mechanism

In the walk, the joints do not need to absorb a lot of concussion, so there is limited joint rotation and limb compression during weight acceptance. The body mass pivots up and over the grounded hoof, and the limb behaves like an inverted pendulum (figure 16.16); the body is lowest at the moments when the hoof makes contact and lift-off, and rotates over the grounded hoof in an arc that reaches its highest point in midstance. As the body rises, its gravitational potential energy (energy due to height) increases. At the same time, velocity decreases, with a consequent reduction in kinetic energy (energy due to movement). As the body descends in the second half of stance, its gravitational potential energy declines, but at the same time there is a rise in kinetic energy due to an increase in velocity. The oscillations in potential and kinetic energy are out of phase with each other: as one increases the other decreases, which allows an efficient exchange between the two forms of mechanical energy.

Spring Mechanism

Leaping gaits have higher vertical forces than stepping gaits due to the presence of an aerial phase. Higher impact forces are associated with landing from an aerial phase, and some of the resulting concussion is absorbed by rotation of the joints, which has the effect of compressing the limb during stance. Consequently, the body is high at contact (high potential energy), sinks in the middle of stance (low potential energy), then rises again prior to lift-off (high potential energy). Kinetic energy is lowest in midstance due to the velocity being reduced. Thus, changes in potential energy and kinetic energy are in phase in the leaping gaits (figure 16.17), which precludes exchanges between these two types of energy.

Energy saving in the leaping gaits is achieved through the spring-like action of elastic structures, such as the flexor tendons and suspensory ligament. As the body sinks during the first half of stance, these structures are stretched, storing elastic energy. Limb compression and elastic energy storage are maximal around the middle of stance, after which the stored elastic energy is released in the form of gravitational potential energy and kinetic energy as the body rises into the next aerial phase. This mechanism of energy storage and release offers considerable savings in the amount of mechanical (and metabolic) energy used by the system.

In asymmetrical leaping gaits, such as the gallop, an additional energy-saving mechanism involves flexion and extension of the trunk as the hind limbs are protracted and retracted. These cyclic trunk movements allow some additional energy exchanges between potential energy and kinetic energy. Therefore, the gallop makes use of both mechanisms to reduce energy expenditure.

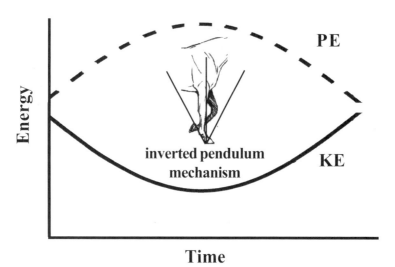

Figure 16.16: Inverted pendulum mechanism in the walk. Changes in gravitational potential energy (PE) and kinetic energy (KE) are out of phase allowing an exchange between the two forms of mechanical energy.

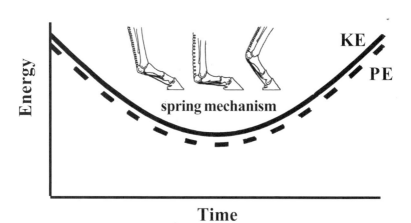

Figure 16.17: Limb spring mechanism in a leaping gait. Changes in gravitational potential energy (PE) and kinetic energy (KE) are in phase. Mechanical energy is conserved by storage and release of elastic energy.

Lameness Mechanics

Lameness has traditionally been classified as supporting limb, swinging limb or mixed according to the part of the stride in which the effects of lameness are most apparent. Gait deficits are obvious primarily in the stance phase in a supporting limb lameness, in the swing phase in a swinging limb lameness, and in both stance and swing phases in a mixed lameness. Gait analysis shows that almost all lamenesses produce changes during both stance and swing, with those in the stance phase predominating in most cases.

The trot is the gait of choice for evaluating lameness because it is a symmetrical gait, which facilitates detection of left-right asymmetries, and the forces on the limbs are higher than at the walk, which tends to exaggerate the effects of supporting limb lameness. Evaluation on a firm surface may also make lameness more obvious, due to the higher impact forces and the inability of the toe to dig into the surface during push off.

The effects of lameness on the stride characteristics vary with the affected limb and the site of lameness within that limb. The absence of an aerial phase following the lame diagonal stance phase is a fairly consistent alteration. It avoids the need for the lame limb to exert high vertical forces to lift the body mass into the air. Instead, the weight is transferred smoothly to the compensating diagonal, which performs the task of elevating the body before the next contact of the lame diagonal (Buchner et al. 1996b).

In horses with moderate to severe lameness, the trunk is higher above the ground during the lame diagonal stance compared with the compensating diagonal stance (figure 16.18). The limbs of the compensating diagonal raise the body, so the trunk is highest at the start of the lame diagonal stance phase.

Figure 16.18: Kinematics of a right front limb lameness. The head is raised and the body is higher during stance of the lame front limb (left) than the compensating front limb (right). After midstance on the compensating diagonal, the head, neck, and body are raised prior to the next contact of the lame diagonal. The left limbs are shaded.

237

It sinks gradually during the lame diagonal stance phase, and continues to sink as weight is transferred from the lame to the compensating diagonal without the intervention of an aerial phase. After midstance on the compensating diagonal, the trunk is again raised in preparation for the next stance phase of the lame diagonal (Buchner et al. 1996b).

In a predominantly supporting limb lameness, the horse carries less weight on the lame limb; peak vertical force on that limb is reduced, and stance duration may increase to maintain the necessary impulse. Redistributions of the vertical GRF are reflected by changes in coffin joint flexion and fetlock joint extension at midstance. Reductions in peak coffin joint flexion and fetlock joint extension in the lame limb are among the most consistent and sensitive kinematic indicators of lameness (figure 16.18). There may be compensatory increases in these joint angles in one or more of the other limbs. During the stance phase of a lame front limb, the CoM is shifted slightly rearward (about 1 cm) and sideways toward the compensating front limb (Buchner et al. 2001).

The behavior of the more proximal joints in response to lameness is less consistent than that of the distal joints. In foot lameness, increased flexion of the shoulder in the front limb or the hock in the hind limb have been reported to act as load-damping mechanisms (Buchner et al. 1996a). By contrast, hock lameness is associated with reduced hock flexion (Khumsap et al. 2003).

The range of protraction and retraction of the limb as a whole may change when the horse is lame. In front limb lameness, retraction of both fore limbs tends to be reduced, whereas in hind limb lameness, protraction of both hind limbs tends to be reduced. This is thought to reflect the fact that the front limb is closer to the horse's center of mass during retraction, whereas the hind limb is closer to the center of mass during protraction.

The head, withers, and tuber sacrale normally show a sinusoidal pattern in their vertical displacement during trotting. A change in the head movement pattern is the best indicator of a front limb lameness, with the head being highest early in the stance phase of the lame front limb, sinking until midstance of the compensating front limb, then being raised prior to the start of the next stance phase of the lame limb.

The best indicator of hind limb lameness is the vertical excursion of the haunches. The haunches rise just before ground contact of the lame limb, then sink during the stance phase of the lame hind limb and early stance of the compensating hind limb. These movements can be seen by watching the horse from the front, from behind, or from the side. In hind limb lameness, the head and neck may be lowered during the lame diagonal stance phase. This is sometimes described as a *false lameness*, since it can be confused with an ipsilateral front limb lameness.

238

BIBLIOGRAPHY

Back W, Barneveld A, Bruin G, Schamhardt HC, Hartman W. (1994) Kinematic detection of superior gait quality in young trotting warmbloods. *Veterinary Quarterly* 16, Supplement 2, S91-96.

Back W, Hartman W, Schamhardt HC, Bruin G, Barneveld A. (1995a) Kinematic response to a 70 day training period in trotting Warmbloods. *Equine Veterinary Journal Supplement* 18, 127-135.

Back W, Schamhardt HC, Hartman W, Barneveld A. (1995b) Repetitive loading and oscillations in the distal fore and hind limb as predisposing factors for equine lameness. *American Journal of Veterinary Research* 56, 1522-1528.

Back W, Schamhardt HC, Hartman F, Bruin G, Barneveld A. (1995c) Predictive value of foal kinematics for the locomotor performance of adult horses. *Research in Veterinary Science* 59, 64-69.

Balch OK, Clayton HM, Lanovaz JL. (1996) Weight- and length-induced changes in limb kinematics in trotting horses. *Proceedings of the American Association of Equine Practitioners* 42, 218-219.

Barrey E. (2000) Interlimb coordination. In: *Equine Locomotion*. Eds Back W, Clayton H, WB Saunders, London. pp 80-81.

Barrey E, Landjerit B, Wolter R. (1991) Shock and vibration during the hoof impact on different track surfaces. In: *Equine Exercise Physiology* 3. Eds Persson SGB, Lindholm A, Jeffcott LB, ICEEP Publications, Davis, California. pp 97-106.

Benoit P, Barrey E, Regnault JC, Brochet JL. (1993) Comparison of the damping effect of different shoeing by the measurement of hoof acceleration. *Acta Anatomica* 146, 109-113.

Buchner HHF, Obermüller S, Scheidl M. (2001) Body centre of mass movement in the lame horse. *Equine Veterinary Journal Supplement* 33, 122-127.

Buchner HHF, Savelberg HHCM, Schamhardt HC, Barneveld A. (1996a) Limb movement adaptation in horses with experimentally induced fore- or hindlimb lameness. *Equine Veterinary Journal* 28, 63-70.

239

Buchner HHF, Savelberg HHCM, Schamhardt HC, Barneveld A. (1996b). Head and trunk movement adaptations in horses with experimentally induced fore- or hindlimb lameness. *Equine Veterinary Journal* 28, 71-76.

Buchner HHF, Savelberg HHCM, Schamhardt HC, Barneveld A. (1997) Inertial properties of Dutch warmblood horses. *Journal of Biomechanics*, 30, 653-658.

Cano MR, Miró F, Vivo J, Galisteo AM. (1999) Comparative biokinematic study of young and adult Andalusian horses at the trot. *Journal of the Veterinary Medical Association* 46, 91-101.

Cano MR, Miró F, Diz AM, Agüera E, Galisteo AM. (2000) Influence of training on the biokinematics in trotting Andalusian horses. *Veterinary Research Communications* 24, 477-489.

Cano MR, Miró F, Monterde JG, Diz A et al. (2001) Changes due to age in the kinematics of trotting Andalusian foals. *Equine Veterinary Journal Supplement* 33, 116-121.

Cavagna GA, Heglund NC, Taylor CR. (1977) Mechanical work in terrestrial locomotion: two basic mechanisms for minimizing energy expenditure. *American Journal of Physiology* 233, R243-R261.

Clayton HM. (1991a) *Conditioning sport horses*. Sport Horse Publications, Mason, Michigan.

Clayton HM. (1991b) Gait evaluation: making the most of your home video system. *Proceedings of the American Association of Equine Practitioners* 36, 447-455.

Clayton HM. (1994a) Comparison of the stride kinematics of the collected, working, medium and extended trot in horses. *Equine Veterinary Journal* 26, 230-234.

Clayton HM. (1994b) Comparison of the collected, working, medium and extended canters. *Equine Veterinary Journal Supplement* 17, 16-19.

Clayton HM. (1995) Comparison of the stride kinematics of the collected, medium, and extended walks in horses. *American Journal of Veterinary Research* 56, 849-852.

Clayton HM. (1996) Instrumentation and techniques in locomotion and lameness. In: *Veterinary Clinics of North America: Equine Practice* 12, 337-350.

Clayton HM. (1997) Classification of collected trot, passage and piaffe using stance phase temporal variables. *Equine Veterinary Journal Supplement* 2, 54-57.

Clayton HM, Barlow DA. (1989) The effect of fence height and width on the limb placements of show jumping horses. *Journal of Equine Veterinary Science* 9, 179-185.

Clayton HM, Barlow DA. (1991) Stride characteristics of four Grand Prix jumping horses. *Equine Exercise Physiology* 3. Eds Persson SGB, Lindholm A, Jeffcott LB, ICEEP Publications, Davis, California. pp 151-157.

Clayton HM, Bradbury JW. (1995) Temporal characteristics of the fox trot: a symmetrical equine gait. *Applied Animal Behaviour Science* 42, 153-159.

Clayton HM, Colborne RG, Burns TE. (1995) Kinematic analysis of successful and unsuccessful attempts to clear a water jump. *Equine Veterinary Journal Supplement* 18, 166-169.

Clayton HM, Colborne GR, Lanovaz J, Burns TE. (1996) Linear kinematics of water jumping in Olympic show jumpers. *Pferdeheilkunde* 12, 657-660.

Clayton HM, Lanovaz JL, Schamhardt HC, van Wessum R. (1999) Rider mass effects on ground reaction forces and fetlock kinematics at the trot. *Equine Veterinary Journal Supplement* 30, 218-221.

Clayton HM, Schamhardt HC, Lanovaz JL, Colborne GR, Willemen MA. (2000a) Net joint moments and joint powers in horses with superficial digital flexor tendinitis. *American Journal of Veterinary Research* 61, 197-201.

Clayton HM, Willemen MA, Lanovaz JL, Schamhardt HC. (2000b) Effects of a heel wedge in horses with superficial digital flexor tendinitis. V*eterinary Comparative Orthopedics and Traumatology* 13, 1-8.

Colborne GR, Clayton HM, Lanovaz JL. (1995) Factors that influence vertical velocity during take off over a water jump. *Equine Veterinary Journal Supplement* 18, 138-140.

Corley JM, Goodship AE. (1994) Treadmill training induced changes to some kinematic variables measured at the canter of Thoroughbred fillies. *Equine Veterinary Journal Supplement* 17, 20-24.

Dalin G, Drevemo S, Fredricson I, Jonsson K, Nilsson G. (1973) Ergonomic aspects of locomotor asymmetry in Standardbred horses trotting through turns. *Acta Veterinaria Scandinavica Supplement* 44, 111-137.

Deuel NR, Lawrence LM. (1986) Gallop velocity and limb contact variables of Quarter Horses. *Journal of Equine Veterinary Science* 6, 143-147.

Deuel NR, Park J-J. (1990) The gait patterns of Olympic dressage horses. *International Journal of Sport Biomechanics* 6, 198-226.

Deuel NR, Park J-J. (1991) Kinematic analysis of jumping sequences of Olympic show jumping horses. *Equine Exercise Physiology* 3, Eds Persson SGB, Lindholm A, Jeffcott LB, ICEEP Publications, Davis, California. pp158-166.

Deuel NR, Park J-J. (1993) Gallop kinematics of Olympic three-day event horses. *Acta Anatomica* 146, 168-174.

Drevemo S, Dalin G, Fredricson I, Hjertén G. (1980a) Equine locomotion: 1. The analysis of linear and temporal stride characteristics of trotting Standardbreds. *Equine Veterinary Journal* 12, 60-65.

Drevemo S, Fredricson I, Dalin G, Bjorne K. (1980b) Equine locomotion: 2. The analysis of coordination between limbs of trotting Standardbreds. *Equine Veterinary Journal* 12, 66-70.

Drevemo S, Fredricson I, Dalin G, Bjorne K. (1980c) Equine locomotion: 3. The reproducibility of gait in Standardbred trotters. *Equine Veterinary Journal* 12, 71-73.

Fredricson I, Dalin G, Drevemo S, Hjertén G, Alm LO. (1975a) A biotechnical approach to the geometric design of racetracks. *Equine Veterinary Journal* 7, 91-96.

Fredricson I, Dalin G, Drevemo S, Hjertén G, Nilsson G. (1975b) Ergonomic aspects of poor racetrack design. *Equine Veterinary Journal* 7, 63-65.

Galisteo AM, Vivo J, Cano MR, Morales JM et al. (1997) Differences between breeds (Dutch Warmblood vs Andalusian Purebred) in forelimb kinematics. *Journal of Equine Science* 8, 43-47.

Hildebrand M. (1965) Symmetrical gaits of horses. *Science* 150, 701-708.

Hodgson DR, Rose RJ. (1994) *The Athletic Horse*. W.B. Saunders Company, London.

Holmström M, Philipsson J. (1993) Relationships between conformation, performance and health in 4-year-old Swedish warmblood riding horses. *Livestock Production Science* 33, 293-312.

Holmström M, Fredricson I, Drevemo S. (1994) Biokinematic differences between riding horses judged as good and poor at the trot. *Equine Veterinary Journal* 17, 51-56.

Holmström M, Fredricson I, Drevemo S. (1995) Biokinematic effects of collection on the trotting gaits in the elite dressage horse. *Equine Veterinary Journal* 27, 281-287.

Jansen MO, van Buiten A, van den Bogert AJ, Schamhardt HC. (1993) Strain of the musculus interosseus medius and its rami extensorii in the horse, deduced from in vivo kinematics. *Acta Anatomica* 147, 118-124.

Khumsap S, Clayton HM, Lanovaz JL. (2001) Effect of walking velocity on ground reaction force variables in the hind limb of clinically normal horses. *American Journal of Veterinary Research* 62, 901-906.

Khumsap S, Clayton HM, Lanovaz JL, Bouchey M. (2002) Effect of walking velocity on forelimb kinematics and kinetics. *Equine Veterinary Journal Supplement* 34, 325-329.

Khumsap S, Lanovaz JL, Rosenstein DL, Byron C, Clayton HM. (2003) Effect of unilateral synovitis of distal intertarsal and tarsometatarsal joints on sagittal plane kinematics and kinetics of trotting horses. *American Journal of Veterinary Research* 64, 1491-1495.

Lanovaz JL, Clayton HM. (2001) Sensitivity of equine fore limb swing phase inverse dynamics solutions to errors in inertial parameters. *Equine Veterinary Journal, Supplement* 33, 27-31.

Lanovaz JL, Clayton HM, Watson LG. (1998) *In vitro* attenuation of impact shock in equine digits. *Equine Veterinary Journal Supplement* 26, 96-102.

Leach DH, Ormrod K. (1984) The technique of jumping a steeplechase fence by competing event-horses. *Applied Animal Behaviour Science* 12, 15-24.

Leach DH, Ormrod K, Clayton HM. (1984) A standardised terminology for the description and analysis of equine locomotion. *Equine Veterinary Journal* 16, 522-528.

Marlin D, Nankervis K. (2002) *Equine exercise physiology*. Blackwell Science Inc., Oxford, UK.

Meershoek LS, Lanovaz JL, Schamhardt HC, Clayton HM. (2002a) Calculated forelimb flexor tendon forces in horses with experimentally induced superficial flexor tendinitis and the influence of heel wedges. *American Journal of Veterinary Research* 63, 432-437.

Meershoek LS, Roepstorff L, Schamhardt HC, Johnston C, Bobbert MF. (2002b) Joint moments in the distal forelimbs of jumping horses during landing. *Equine Veterinary Journal Supplement* 33, 410-415.

Merkens HW, Schamhardt HC. (1988a) Distribution of ground reaction forces of the concurrently loaded limbs of the Dutch Warmblood horse at the normal walk. *Equine Veterinary Journal* 20, 209-213.

Merkens HW, Schamhardt HC. (1988b) Evaluation of equine locomotion during different degrees of experimentally induced lameness. II. Distribution of ground reaction force patterns on the concurrently loaded limbs. *Equine Veterinary Journal Supplement* 6, 107-112.

243

Merkens HW, Schamhardt HC, Hartman W, Kersjes AW. (1988) The use of H(orse) INDEX: A method of analysing the ground reaction force patterns of lame and normal gaited horses at the walk. *Equine Veterinary Journal* 20, 29-36.

Merkens HW, Schamhardt HC, Hartman W, Kersjes AW. (1986) Ground reaction force patterns of Dutch Warmblood horses at normal walk. *Equine Veterinary Journal* 18, 207-214.

Merkens HW, Schamhardt HC, Osch GJVM, van den Bogert AJ. (1993a) Ground reaction force patterns of Dutch Warmblood horses at normal trot. *Equine Veterinary Journal* 25, 134-137.

Merkens HW, Schamhardt HC, Osch GJVM, Hartman W. (1993b) Ground reaction force patterns of Dutch Warmbloods at the canter. *American Journal of Veterinary Research* 54, 670-674.

Morris EA, Seeherman HJ. (1987) Redistribution of ground reaction forces in experimentally induced carpal lameness. *Equine Exercise Physiology* 2. Eds Gillespie JR, Robinson NE, ICEEP Publications, Davis, California. pp 553-563.

Nicodemus MC, Clayton HM. (2001) Temporal variables of the 4-beat stepping jog and lope. *Proceedings of the Equine Nutrition and Physiology Symposium* 17, 248-253.

Nicodemus MC, Clayton HM. (2003) Temporal variables of four-beat, stepping gaits of gaited horses. *Applied Animal Behaviour Science* 80, 133-142.

Nicodemus MC, Holt KM. (2003) Temporal variables of the 3-gaited plantation shod Tennessee Walking Horse. *Proceedings of the Equine Nutrition and Physiology Symposium* 18, 207-212.

Niki Y, Ueda Y, Yoshida K, Masumitsu H. (1982) A force plate study in equine biomechanics 2. The vertical and fore-aft components of floor reaction forces and motion of equine limbs at walk and trot. *Bulletin of the Equine Research Institute* 19, 1-17.

Pool RR. (1992) Third carpal bone injuries. *Equine Veterinary Data* 16, 279.

Radin EL, Parker HG, Pugh JW, Steinberg RS et al. (1973) Response of joints to impact loading - III Relationship between trabecular microfractures and cartilage degeneration. *Journal of Biomechanics* 6, 51-57.

Ratzlaff MH, Shindell RM, White KK. (1985) The interrelationships of stride length and stride times to velocities of galloping horses. *Journal of Equine Veterinary Science* 5, 279-283.

Santamaría S, Back W, van Weeren PR, Knaap J, Barneveld A. (2002) Jumping characteristics of naïve foals: lead changes and description of temporal and linear parameters. *Equine Veterinary Journal Supplement* 34, 302-307.

Schamhardt HC, Merkens HW, van Osch GJVM. (1991) Ground reaction force analysis of horses ridden at the walk and trot. *Equine Exercise Physiology* 3. Eds Persson SGB, Lindholm A, Jeffcott LB, ICEEP Publications, Davis, California. pp120-127.

Schamhardt HC, Merkens HW, Vogel V, Willekens C. (1993) External loads on the limbs of jumping horses at take-off and landing. *American Journal of Veterinary Research* 54, 675-680.

Seder JA, Vickery CE. (1993) Double and triple fully airborne phases in the gaits of racing speed Thoroughbreds. *Proceedings of the Association for Equine Sports Medicine* 12, 65-75.

Seeherman HJ, Morris EA, Fackelman GE. (1987) Computerized force plate determination of equine weight-bearing profiles. *Equine Exercise Physiology* 2. Eds Gillespie JR, Robinson NE, ICEEP Publications, Davis, California. pp 536-552.

Singleton WH, Clayton HM, Lanovaz JL, Prades M. (2003) Effects of shoeing on forelimb swing phase kinetics of trotting horses. *Veterinary Comparative Orthopedics and Traumatology* 16, 16-20.

Sloet van Oldruitenborgh-Oosterbaan MM, Barneveld A, Schamhardt HC. (1995) Effects of weight and riding on workload and locomotion during treadmill exercise. *Equine Veterinary Journal Supplement* 18, 413-417.

Sprigings E, Leach D. (1986) Standardised technique for determining the center of gravity of body and limb segments of horses. *Equine Veterinary Journal* 18, 43-49.

Stover SM, Johnson BJ, Daft BM, Read DH, et al. (1992) An association between complete and incomplete stress fractures of the humerus in racehorses. *Equine Veterinary Journal* 24, 260-263.

Ueda Y, Niki Y, Yoshida K, Masumitsu H. (1981) Force plate study of equine biomechanics. Floor reaction force of normal walking and trotting horses. *Bulletin of the Equine Research Institute* 18, 28-41.

van den Bogert AJ. (1989) *Computer simulation of locomotion in the horse.* PhD Thesis, University of Utrecht.

Vorstenbosch MATM, Buchner HHF, Savelberg HHCM, Schamhardt HC, Barneveld A. (1997) Modeling study of compensatory head movements in lame horses. *American Journal of Veterinary Research* 58, 713-718.

Willemen MA. (1997) *Horseshoeing, a Biomechanical Analysis.* PhD Thesis, University of Utrecht.

Wilson AM, McGuigan MP, Su A, van den Bogert AJ. (2001) Horses damp the spring in their step. *Nature* 414, 895-899.

Wilson AM, Watson JC, Lichtwark GA. (2002) A catapult action for rapid limb protraction. *Nature* 414, 895-899.

Wilson BD, Neal RJ, Howard A, Groenendyk S. (1988a) The gait of pacers 1: kinematics of the racing stride. *Equine Veterinary Journal* 20, 341-346.

Wilson BD, Neal RJ, Howard A, Groenendyk S. (1988b) The gait of pacers 2: factors influencing pacing speed. *Equine Veterinary Journal* 20, 347-351.

Yamanobe A, Hiraga A, Kubo K. (1992) Relationships between stride frequency, stride length, step length and velocity with asymmetric gaits in the Thoroughbred horse. *Japanese Journal of Equine Science* 3, 143-148.

Zips S, Peham C, Scheidl M, Licka T, Girtler D. (2001) Motion pattern of toelt of Icelandic horses at different speeds. *Equine Veterinary Journal Supplement* 33, 109-111.

SI Units of Measurement

APPENDIX A

Measurement	Unit	Abbreviation
Time	hour	h
	minute	min
	second	s
Distance	kilometer	km
Displacement	meter	m
	centimeter	cm
Speed	kilometer/hour	km/h
Velocity	meter/minute	m/min
	centimeter/second	cm/s
Acceleration	kilometer/hour/hour	km/h^2
	meter/minute/minute	m/min^2
	centimeter/second/second	cm/s^2
Angular Distance	revolution	rev
Angular	radian	rad
Displacement	degree	deg or $^\circ$
Mass	kilogram	kg
Force	newton	N
Torque	newton·meter	N·m
Impulse	newton·second	N·s
Pressure	newton/centimeter/centimeter	N/cm^2
Momentum	kilogram·meter/second	kg·m/s
Moment of Inertia	kilogram·meter·meter	$kg·m^2$
Angular Momentum	kilogram·meter·meter/second	$kg·m^2/s$
Work	newton·meter	N·m
Energy	joule	J
Power	watt	W

INDEX OF SYMBOLS

a	linear acceleration	KE_{rot}	rotational kinetic energy
d	displacement	KE_{trans}	translational kinetic energy
g	gravitational acceleration	I	moment of inertia
h	height	P	power
k	constant	PE	potential energy
l	distance (length)	R	resistance
m	mass	T	torque
r	radius	W	work
s	speed	α	angular acceleration
t	time	ϕ	angular distance
v	velocity	μ	coefficient of friction
E	energy	π	radians in a circle
F	force	θ	angular displacement
H	angular momentum	σ	angular speed
KE	kinetic energy	ω	angular velocity

A bar over an abbreviation indicates an average value over a period of time:

$\bar{v}$: average velocity

Subscripts indicate times at which variables are measured or the direction in which they act:

$_f$: final; $_i$: initial; $_{hz}$: horizontal; $_{vert}$: vertical

249

Dealing with Vectors

A vector quantity is described not only in terms of its
magnitude, but also by the direction in which it acts.

Examples of vector quantities include displacement, velocity, acceleration, and force.

Calculation of the Resultant Vector from Two Components

The resultant of two vectors can be determined graphically using a vector diagram (rectangle or parallelogram) or it can be calculated mathematically using formulae that apply the principles of trigonometry. Solution of the formulae may require looking up the values of the sine (sin), cosine (cos), tangent (tan), or arctangent (arctan) of an angle in a table of trigonometric functions. The formulae that are applied depend on whether the component vectors are perpendicular to each other or at some other angle.

Perpendicular Components

Example: A polo ball is hit with a velocity of 30 m/s in a direction parallel to the long side of the field. A crosswind, blowing across the field perpendicular to the direction in which the ball is traveling, imparts a velocity of 5 m/s to the ball.

Graphical Solution

The graphical solution for determining the final velocity of the ball is shown in figure C.1. The velocity imparted by the mallet (30 m/s) is represented by vector A, and the velocity imparted by the wind (5 m/s) is represented by vector B. A rectangle is constructed with the lengths of its sides proportional to the magnitudes of vectors A and B. The diagonal line drawn from the corner between the origins of vectors A and B represents the magnitude and direction of the resultant vector, which can be measured using a ruler and a protractor.

251

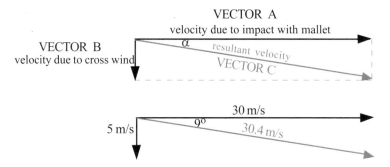

Figure C.1: Summation of vectors acting perpendicular to each other. Black arrows representing the component vectors A and B form adjacent sides of a rectangle. The resultant is the diagonal line shown by the gray arrow (vector C).

Mathematical Solution

When the angle between two component vectors (*A* and *B*) is 90° as in figure C.1, the magnitude of their resultant (C) is found using Pythagoras Theorem:

$$C^2 = A^2 + B^2$$
$$C = \sqrt{A^2 + B^2}$$
$$C = \sqrt{30^2 + 5^2} = \sqrt{900 + 25} = \sqrt{925} = 30.4 \text{ m/s}$$

To calculate the angle α between the resultant and vector *A*, the following formula is used:

$$\tan \alpha = \frac{B}{A}$$
$$\alpha = \arctan \left[\frac{B}{A} \right] = \arctan \left[\frac{5}{30} \right] = \arctan 0.167 = 9°$$

Non-perpendicular Components

Example: A ball is hit with a velocity of 30 m/s in a direction parallel with the direction of the field and a crosswind, acting at 45° to the direction in which the ball is travelling, imparts a velocity of 5 m/s to the ball.

Graphical Solution

A parallelogram of vectors is constructed in which the velocity imparted by the mallet is represented by vector A, and the velocity imparted by the wind is represented by vector B (figure C.2). A parallelogram is constructed with the lengths of the sides of the parallelogram are proportional to the magnitude and indicative of the orientation of vectors A and B. The diagonal originating in the corner between vectors A and B, shown as vector C, indicates the magnitude and direction of the ball's final velocity, which can be measured with a ruler and protractor.

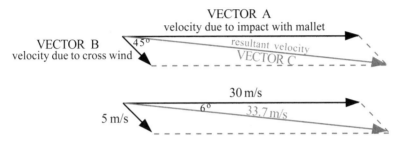

Figure C.2: Graphical method of summation of two vectors (black arrows A and B) acting at an angle of 45° to each other. The vectors form adjacent sides of a parallelogram. The magnitude and direction of the resultant velocity are indicated by the diagonal (gray arrow C).

Mathematical Solution

Mathematical summation of two, non-perpendicular vectors is achieved by constructing a triangle (figure C.3) in which the lengths of the adjacent sides are known but the length of the third side is not known. In figure C.3, side A (30 m/s) and side B (5 m/s) are known, but the length of side C is not known. The angles opposite sides A, B, and C are designated a, b, and c, respectively. Angle c is 135° (180° - 45°).

Length C is calculated using the cosine rule:

$$C^2 = A^2 + B^2 - 2AB \cos b$$
$$C = \sqrt{A^2 + B^2 - 2AB \cos b}$$
$$= \sqrt{30^2 + 5^2 - (2 * 30 * \cos 135)}$$
$$= \sqrt{30^2 + 5^2 - (2 * 30 * (-\sin 45)}$$
$$= \sqrt{900 + 25 - (2 * 30 * (-0.707)}$$
$$= \sqrt{900 + 25 - 212.1}$$
$$= 33.7 \text{ m/s}$$

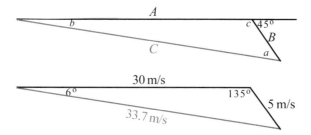

Figure C.3: Trigonometric summation of two vectors (A and B) acting at an angle of 45°. The vectors form adjacent sides of a triangle (above). The resultant velocity (C) is the third side of the triangle.

To calculate angle *b*:

$$\frac{A}{\sin a} = \frac{B}{\sin b} = \frac{C}{\sin c}$$

$$\sin b = \frac{B \sin c}{C}$$

$$= \frac{5 * 0.707}{33.7}$$

$$= 0.105$$

$$b = 6°$$

Summation of a Series of Vectors

Sometimes it is necessary to calculate the resultant of a series of vectors. If a graphical method is used, the vector arrows are joined end-to-end, with the base of each new arrow being joined to the tip of the previous one.

Example: A ball is hit four times as it progresses from one end of a polo field to the other. Figure C.4 shows the successive displacements as a series of arrows, each of which has a length proportional to the magnitude of the ball's displacement and a direction indicative of the direction of the displacement. Vectors can be 'added together' in this manner. The total displacement is measured by the length and direction of an arrow joining the start of the first arrow with the tip of the last arrow in the series.

The final displacement of the ball could also be solved mathematically. One way to do this is to determine the components of each displacement acting along and across the field (i.e. calculate the perpendicular components), then sum the displacements in each (perpendicular) direction. Finally the magnitude and direction of the overall displacement are calculated as the resultant of the two perpendicular components using Pythagoras Theorem.

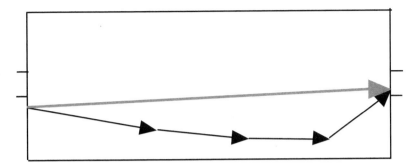

Figure C.4: Total displacement of a polo ball (gray arrow) that was hit four times (black arrows) as it moved from one end of the polo field to the other.

Calculation of Vector Components from the Resultant

Sometimes, the resultant vector is known and components acting in specific directions are required. For example, it is a common practice to resolve a displacement, velocity, acceleration, or force vector into into vertical and horizontal components. This is achieved by constructing a rectangle or parallelogram of vectors or by calculating the vector components mathematically.

For vector A acting at an angle of α to the horizontal (figure C.5), the vertical and horizontal components (A_{vert} and A_{hz}) are:

$$A_{vert} = A \sin\alpha$$
$$A_{hz} = A \cos\alpha$$

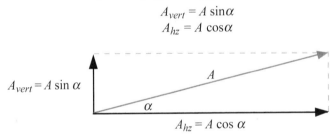

Figure C.5: Resolution of a vector (gray arrow A) into components acting perpendicular to each other. Black arrows representing the horizontal (A_{hz}) and vertical (A_{vert}) components form adjacent sides of a rectangle with the resultant as the diagonal.

Example: during kinematic analysis of a jumping horse, the instantaneous velocity at take off (v) can be measured from video footage. If the take off velocity (v) is 8 m/s and it is oriented at an angle (α) of 25° to the horizontal, the vertical (v_{vert}) and horizontal (v_{hz}) components of the take off velocity can be calculated:

$$v_{vert} = v * \sin\alpha = 8 * \sin 25 = 8 * 0.423 = 3.384 \text{ m/s}$$
$$v_{hz} = v * \cos\alpha = 8 * \cos 25 = 8 * 0.906 = 7.248 \text{ m/s}$$

INDEX

A

abduction 1, 15-16, 219
acceleration 1, 44-49, 73, 79-80, 189, 202
acoustic energy 157
adduction 1, 15-16, 219
advanced completion 1
advanced placement 1
aerial phase 1, 22, 26, 29, 48, 49, 61-68, 84, 102, 104, 152, 163, 167, 170, 178, 180, 185, 187, 200, 214-215, 235, 237-238
aerial time 49, 66-68
age 192-193
agonist 99, 220
Andalusian horse 192-193
angle of elevation 62-68, 115
angle of impact 125
angle of incidence 125-126
angle of reflection 125-126
angle-time diagram 52
angular acceleration 57
angular displacement 1, 51-55
angular distance 1, 51-55
angular kinematics 51-60
angular kinetics 93-106
angular momentum 6, 100-104, 211
angular speed 1, 55-56, 59-60
angular vector 57
angular velocity 1, 55-56, 59-60, 100-104, 152

antagonist 99, 158, 220-222
approach 210
articular cartilage 204
ascent time 66
asymmetrical gait 4, 163-167, 170, 183, 195, 200, 228, 235
aubin 180
average acceleration 48
average angular acceleration 57
average angular speed 55-56, 60
average angular velocity 55-56
average speed 40-43, 59
average velocity 40-43

B

balance 130, 138-144, 172
ball 65, 80, 119, 122, 124, 125, 130, 137
banking 105-106
bareback rider 58
barrel racing 41-42, 84-85, 144
base of support 1, 136-144
beat 22
biarticular muscle 220
biceps brachii 99, 154, 220-221, 234
biomechanics 1, 9, 145
bipedal support 171-172
bit 98
body 1
body mass 189
body segments 135

257

ORDER FORM

Send mail orders to:

Sport Horse Publications
3145 Sandhill Road
Mason, MI 48854-9425

Quantity discounts are available on orders of 5 or more copies of the same title.

For information, contact Sport Horse Publications at the above address or at (517) 333-3833 (phone or fax).

....

Please send me:

.... copies of *The Dynamic Horse* @ $50 .... $_____

.... copies of *Conditioning Sport Horses* @ $40 ..... $_____

.... copies of *Activate Your Horse's Core* @ $50..... $_____

Shipping per book: North America $5, elsewhere $10.. $_____

TOTAL $_____

Write your name and full postal address clearly in block letters:

....

....

....

....